全国职业技能英语系列教材

FINANCIAL ENGLISH

金融英语

主　编　赵惠娟　唐树良

编　者　赵向阁　熊晓轶　陈　宇

审　订　张长建　陈建杰

北京大学出版社
PEKING UNIVERSITY PRESS

图书在版编目(CIP)数据

金融英语 / 赵惠娟,唐树良主编. —北京:北京大学出版社,2008.8
(全国职业技能英语系列教材)
ISBN 978-7-301-13831-1

Ⅰ. 金… Ⅱ. ①赵…②唐… Ⅲ. 金融－英语－职业教育－教材 Ⅳ. H31

中国版本图书馆 CIP 数据核字(2008)第 067925 号

书　　　　名:	金融英语
著作责任者:	赵惠娟　唐树良　主编
组 稿 编 辑:	张建民
责 任 编 辑:	叶　丹
标 准 书 号:	ISBN 978-7-301-13831-1/H·1994
出 版 发 行:	北京大学出版社
地　　　　址:	北京市海淀区成府路 205 号　100871
网　　　　址:	http://www.pup.cn
电　　　　话:	邮购部 62752015　发行部 62750672　编辑部 62754382　出版部 62754962
电 子 信 箱:	zbing@pup.pku.edu.cn
印 刷 者:	涿州市星河印刷有限公司
经 销 者:	新华书店
	787 毫米×1092 毫米　16 开本　15 印张　374 千字
	2008 年 8 月第 1 版　2019 年 8 月第 7 次印刷
定　　　　价:	38.00 元(配有光盘)

未经许可,不得以任何方式复制或抄袭本书之部分或全部内容。
版权所有,侵权必究
举报电话:(010)62752024　电子信箱:fd@pup.pku.edu.cn

全国职业技能英语系列教材

编委会

顾问

胡壮麟（北京大学）　　　　刘黛琳（中央广播电视大学）

总主编

丁国声（河北外国语职业学院）

编委会名单（以姓氏笔画为序）

丁小莉（山东商业职业学院）
王乃彦（天津对外经济贸易职业学院）
牛　健（中央广播电视大学）
伍忠杰（电子科技大学）
李相敏（河北外国语职业学院）
李恩亮（江苏海事职业技术学院）
张　冰（北京大学出版社）
张九明（开封大学）
张春生（衡水职业技术学院）
陆松岩（江苏城市职业学院）
陈玉华（成都航空职业学院）
林晓琴（重庆电力高等专科学校）
赵　倩（重庆机电职业技术学院）
赵　鹏（北京联合大学）
赵爱萍（浙江水利水电专科学校）
赵翠华（承德民族师范高等专科学校）
胡海青（南京交通职业技术学院）
贾　方（辽宁装备制造职业技术学院）
黄宗英（北京联合大学）
崔秀敏（承德石油高等专科学校）
蒋　磊（河南商业高等专科学校）
程　亚（江西景德镇陶瓷学院）
黎富玉（成都航空职业学院）
潘月洲（南京工业职业技术学院）
Martin Fielko (Cornelsen Press GmbH & Co. KG)

总　序

我国高职高专教育的春天来到了。随着国家对高职高专教育重视程度的加深，职业技能教材体系的建设成为了当务之急。高职高专过去沿用和压缩大学本科教材的时代一去不复返了。

语言学家 Harmer 指出："如果我们希望学生学到的语言是在真实生活中能够使用的语言，那么在教材编写中接受技能和产出技能的培养也应该像在生活中那样有机地结合在一起。"

教改的关键在教师，教师的关键在教材，教材的关键在理念。我们依据《高职高专教育英语课程教学基本要求》的精神和编者做了大量调查，秉承"实用为主，够用为度，学以致用，触类旁通"的原则，历经两年艰辛，为高职高专学生编写了这套专业技能课和实训课的英语教材。

本套教材的内容贴近工作岗位，突出岗位情景英语，是一套职场英语教材，具有很强的实用性、仿真性、职业性，其特色体现在以下几个方面：

1. 开放性

   本套教材在坚持编写理念、原则及体例的前提下，不断增加新的行业或岗位技能英语分册作为教材的延续。

2. 国际性

   本套教材以国内自编为主，以国外引进为辅，取长补短，浑然一体。目前已从德国引进了某些行业的技能英语教材，还将从德国或他国引进优秀教材经过本土化后奉献给广大师生。

3. 职业性

   本套教材是由高职院校教师与行业专家针对具体工作岗位、情景过程共同设计编写。同时注重与行业资格证书相结合。

4. 任务性

   基于完成某岗位工作任务而需要的英语知识和技能是本套教材的由来与初衷。因此，各分册均以任务型练习为主。

5. **实用性**

　　本教材注重基础词汇的复习和专业词汇的补充。适合于在校最后一学期的英语教学，着重培养和训练学生初步具有与其日后职业生涯所必需的英语交际能力。

　　本教材在编写过程中，参考和引用了国内外作者的相关资料，得到了北京大学出版社外语编辑部的倾力奉献，在此，一并向他们表示敬意和感谢。由于本套教材是一种创新和尝试，书中瑕疵必定不少，敬请指正。

丁国声

教育部高职高专英语类专业教学指导委员会委员

河北省高校外语教学研究会副会长

河北外国语职业学院院长

2008 年 6 月

编 写 说 明

随着全球经济一体化进程的加快以及中国入世以后金融竞争的加剧，涉外金融业务随之增加，迫切需要金融服务尽快与国际接轨，这就对金融一线从业人员的对外语言能力提出了更高的要求。为了提高金融对外服务水平，提升一线人员的综合素质，树立国际化一流金融机构的良好形象，我们特编写了《金融英语》一书。

本书以金融业的三大支撑即银行、保险、证券为线索搭建结构框架：其中银行业务是主导，主要涉及商业银行日常办理的存款、贷款、外汇、银行卡、中间业务、汇兑以及信用证等业务；然后介绍了保险业和证券业的主要业务；最后是银行业务中涉及的应用文体写作。附录中收录了世界货币名称、国内外主要银行机构、各国中央银行和国际金融机构名称。

全书共分十单元，每一单元都包括背景知识介绍、业务对话、练习和补充阅读等部分。其中背景知识与全国金融专业英语证书考试大纲要求的知识点一致，主要介绍业务的性质、特点、作用和工作流程，有助于学生在应用之前掌握基础的专业词汇和基本的专业知识；业务对话根据具体工作流程设计，着重体现金融从业人员的专业服务素质，对于重点的专业词汇给予必要的中文注释，并且配备相应的专业词汇英汉互译练习、单词与解释的匹配练习、单项选择；任务型练习包括根据听力材料填空以及完成句子、根据实务情景培养听力理解能力、根据所给信息结合实务组成句子、根据划线部分完成对话、根据所给的具体信息练习对话和根据情景模拟对话，难度依次递增；补充阅读中包括了与业务相关的更广层面、更深层次的信息资料，有利于扩充学生的专业词汇量，拓宽学生的专业视野。

参与本书编写的人员均来自金融英语教学的第一线，有较为深厚的理论功底和丰富的教学实践经验。另外，我们还邀请曾先后在中国人民银行、工商银行和交通银行工作的金融专家张长建先生和中国农业银行总行个人业务部陈建杰副处长对专业术语以及业务情景、任务设计等方面进行了审稿把关。

本书重在突出实用性，与金融实务紧密结合，旨在培养学生运用英语处理基本金融业务的能力，可操作性强。适合高等专科学校、高等职业技术学院的金融专业学生培养职业技能，也适合金融机构一线人员提升业务素质。

CONTENTS

Unit 1	Deposits	1
Unit 2	Loans	16
Unit 3	Foreign Exchange	33
Unit 4	Bank Cards	49
Unit 5	Intermediary Services	64
Unit 6	Remittance	79
Unit 7	Letter of Credit	94
Unit 8	Insurance	110
Unit 9	Securities	128
Unit 10	Banking Business Letters	145

Vocabulary 163

Tapescripts 167

Keys 199

Appendix 215

References 230

Unit 1 Deposits

AIMS

- Opening an account
- Handling withdrawals
- Checking account balance
- Reporting a loss of a passbook
- Closing the account

Information bank

Deposit taking is an important business for a bank. There are many kinds of deposit accounts, for example, demand deposits, time (fixed) deposits, call deposits, offshore deposits, foreign currency deposits. Bank customers can open any type of accounts by their preference.

Demand deposits are deposits that are subject to depositors' withdrawals at any time. Demand deposits facilitate those who only want to deposit funds for a short period of time. Due to this feature, banks pay little or even no interest to demand deposits in developed countries. Time deposits are not subject to depositors' withdrawals at any time but have different fixed maturities. That means, the deposits are payable after a special period varying from months to years. The depositors are paid different interest rates depending on the length of deposit.

A request for opening an account for organizations must be accompanied by an application form, a specimen signature. Identity card is needed for individuals. If a fixed deposit is established, the bank shall issue to the depositor a fixed deposit certificate in his name while if a demand deposit is opened, the depositor will get a passbook or bankcard by his choice.

Where there are deposits, there are also withdrawals. When a withdrawal is made before maturity because of a special need, the interest on the account drawn shall be paid at the rate for current deposit on the date of withdrawal, while the remaining amount shall continue to bear interest at the rate allowed at the time deposit. When an advanced withdrawal is made, the depositor must show the bank staff the relevant identification and documents needed.

The depositor has a right to check his bank balances. When he doesn't need the bank account, the depositor can ask for closing. Once his passbook, bankcard or certificate of deposit is lost or stolen, he can give banks a stop payment order, reporting a loss.

Procedures for Account Opening

1. A passbook may be got and a debit card may be applied for at the same time at bank if a deposit slip is filled in and a certain amount of cash (RMB 1 yuan at least) is deposited.

2. At the time of account opening, the client may choose the method of withdrawal by the password or by the passbook. If the method of withdrawal password is chosen, the client shall put on the spot a six-digit password into the said savings account. The password is put in through the password device on the counter and is unknown to any other person including the clerk of the bank. The password is the key with which to withdraw and must be kept in mind firmly and not leaked to others.

Vocabulary Assistant

passbook 存折   debit card 借记卡   deposit slip 存单
password 密码   on the spot 当场   six-digit 六位数
counter 柜台

1 Retell the procedures for account opening in your own words.

Step 1:

Step 2:

Step 3:

2 Select the answer that correctly completes the sentences.

1. Current account means a demand account, which is called a _____ in the West.
   A. fixed account   B. time account   C. checking account

2. A fixed deposit takes the form of a _____ issued in the name of the depositor.
   A. deposit certificate   B. bank card   C. deposit certificate and a card

3. There is no _____ on the current account.
   A. interest   B. maturity   C. passbook

4. Early withdrawals from a time deposit account are often subject to _____.
   A. interest penalty   B. interest bonus   C. no interest
5. _____ is not required for opening an account for deposits.
   A. A passbook   B. An application form   C. A specimen signature
6. _____ records a depositor account, which shows his or her deposit, withdrawals and interest payment by the bank.
   A. A passbook   B. A deposit receipt   C. A withdrawal slip
7. In order to withdraw deposit, the bank requires your _____.
   A. slip with signature   B. name   C. balance

Conversation 1: Opening an Account

Clerk: Good morning, Sir! What can I do for you?

Customer: Good morning! I'd like to open an account, but I don't know what account it should be. Could you give me some advice?

Clerk: Of course. Generally speaking, if you want to make deposits and withdrawals at any time and you don't care about the interest, you may choose a current account. But if you don't need your money for a comparatively long time and you want a higher rate, you may choose the fixed account.

Customer: Oh, I see. How can I withdraw my money from a current account?

Clerk: The current account takes the form of a deposit book as well as a bank card. You may withdraw money at any time with the card from ATMs or over the counter.

Customer: Thanks for your help. I'd rather open a current account.

Clerk: Ok, please fill in this application form.

Customer: Here are the form and the money.

Clerk: Thank you. Please show me your passport.

Customer: Here you are.

Clerk: Good. Everything is done. Here is your deposit book and passport.

Customer: Thank you very much.

Clerk: It's my pleasure.

Vocabulary Assistant

deposit 存款   withdrawal 取款   current account 活期账户
fixed account 定期账户   deposit book 存折
ATM 自动提款机   passport 护照

Conversation 2: Handling Withdrawals

Clerk: Can I help you, Madam?
Customer: Yes, please. I have a fixed time deposit here. But it will mature two months from now. I need the money for an emergency. Can I get it right now?
Clerk: Yes. You may withdraw your money, but you can't receive the stated interest. You can only get interest on a current account instead.
Customer: What about the remaining if I don't withdraw all my funds?
Clerk: The account remaining shall continue to bear interest at the rate of the fixed time deposit.
Customer: I see. I want to draw RMB 6,000 yuan.
Clerk: OK. Your balance is RMB 4,000 yuan. And how would you like your money?
Customer: Well, please give me three thousand in hundreds and the rest in fifty, will you?
Clerk: Certainly. Here is your money and the interest you've earned. Please check it.
Customer: Thank you very much. Well, Could you tell me the rate of a current deposit?
Clerk: The detailed information is posted on the bulletin board over there in the lobby.
Customer: OK. I'll have a look at it. Thanks.

Vocabulary Assistant
a fixed time deposit 定期存款
mature 到期

3 Translate the phrases into English.

1. 定期存款
2. 活期存款
3. 存折
4. 银行卡
5. 存款单
6. 挂失
7. 单利
8. 复利
9. 查询余额
10. 外币账户

4 Match the following terms with their respective explanations.

balance	a deposit account
deposit	the fixed time deposit becomes due
fixed account	difference between two columns of an account
current account	any type of bank account that earns more than a deposit account
	any type of account that earns interest
saving account	checking account
	bank account from which money can be drawn without previous notice
mature	sum paid into an account

5 Listening exercises

Spot Dictation: In this section you'll hear two short paragraphs. There are some words or phrases missing in each paragraph. Each paragraph will be read three times. For the first time you just listen and for the second time, you'll have a break of 20 seconds. During the break, you can write down the missing words or phrases. The third time is for you to check your writing. Now let's begin.

1

Secondly, there are time deposits which always ___(1)___ interest. The name time deposit arises because, ___(2)___, these deposits may not usually be ___(3)___ without notice. The notice will be agreed between the bank and the ___(4)___ when the deposit is first opened. However, there is one ___(5)___ of time deposits called ___(6)___ savings accounts where ___(7)___ withdrawals may be made ___(8)___.

2

Some countries ___(1)___ bank deposits but do not assess deposit premiums until a bank has failed. This is the ___(2)___ in Turkey where only after a bank has failed are other banks asked to furnish the funds to pay depositors of the failed bank. In addition, ___(3)___, which makes it difficult for someone to ___(4)___ the business of banking. Thus, Turkish banks ___(5)___ to operate more safely since no fund for depositor payoffs ___(6)___ until after a bank failure. The ___(7)___ made at that time may be very high, ___(8)___.

UNIT 1 DEPOSITS

■ **Complete Sentences:** In this part you will hear 6 sentences. Each sentence will be read twice. For the first time you just listen and for the second time, you'll have a break of 10 seconds following each sentence. During the break, try to complete the sentences according to what you have just heard. Please watch your spelling.

1. Time is the duration over which _____.
2. Making payments by writing cheques against cheque account deposits is popular, _____.
3. But the cheque itself is not "money"; it is only _____ which is considered to be "money".
4. The balance standing to a customer's credit on current account is _____ and _____.
5. There are three main types of bank deposits: _____, _____ and _____.
6. Certificates of deposit are large deposits, _____ and _____.

■ Conversation 3: Checking Account Balance

Clerk: Is there anything I can do for you, sir?
Customer: Yes, please. I sold some shares last week through a bank and I think the money should have been credited to my savings account. Could you update my passbook for me please?
Clerk: Certainly. Here is your updated passbook, sir.
Customer: Thanks. Oh, the money is there already. And I have a current account in Pound Sterling. I'd like to know how much the balance is.
Clerk: Yes, sir. Have you got the passport?
Customer: Yes. Here you are.
Clerk: Thank you. And do you know the number?
Customer: Sorry, I'm afraid I forgot it.
Clerk: One moment, then, please. I'll check it for you.... The number of your account is 64986 and you have a credit balance of £282.
Customer: Thanks. Could you send me my statement at the end of the month?
Clerk: Certainly.
Customer: Thank you very much.
Clerk: You're welcome.

Vocabulary Assistant
shares 股份   credited 记入贷方

Loss Reporting Procedures

If a certificate of deposit, a bank passbook or a seal of a client is lost or stolen, or the password is forgotten, loss reporting may be handled at the bank according to the following procedures:

The client shall immediately handle written loss reporting procedures at the original depository bank. In reporting loss, the client shall present personal credentials (I.D. card, residence permit, passport, etc.) and also provide related deposit contents such as account, account holder's name, time of account opening, amount, type of currency and maturity. The loss reporting procedures may be handled after the bank certifies and finds them correct, and the bank is to confirm that payment has not been made before handling the procedure. If the client is unable to be present at the bank in handling loss reporting, he or she may authorize another person to handle on his / her behalf and at the same time the credentials of the agent shall be presented. Loss reporting of password may not be handled on agency.

In handling loss reporting procedures, the client shall fill in the application for loss reporting, with one extra copy of the application kept by the client, and shall apply for a new certificate of deposit through handling redepositing or cashing procedures at the depository bank seven days later by presenting the application and his or her credentials.

If for objective reason the client is unable to handle loss reporting at the bank in time or by himself or herself, he or she may first request for interim loss reporting orally, by mail or by telephone, and then handle the formal loss reporting procedures at the depository bank within five days. Otherwise, the loss reporting will be invalid.

For a current account passbook opened with a savings outlet connected with the computer network, interim loss reporting procedures may be handled at any savings outlet. But the formal written loss reporting procedures shall be handled at the depository bank.

Vocabulary Assistant

loss reporting 挂失	depository bank 开户行
I.D. card 身份证	residence permit 居住许可证（户口本等）
interim 临时的	savings outlet 储蓄营业厅

6 Retell the procedures for loss reporting in your own words.

Step 1:

Step 2:

Step 3:

Conversation 4: Reporting a Loss of a Passbook

Clerk: May I help you, Madam?

Customer: Yes, please. I'm afraid I've lost my savings passbook. Could you check for me whether my money is still here?

Clerk: Certainly. Please let me have your name, address and your account number if you remember it.

Customer: My name is John Green. My address is No.1602, Taihua Mansion, Changping Avenue. But I can't recall my account number.

Clerk: Don't worry, Mr. Green. Let me try to check it for you. One moment, please. Yes, Mr. Green. I have your account number here. The balance is RMB 8,000 yuan.

Customer: Thank Goodness. My funds are still available. Thank you very much.

Clerk: It's my pleasure. Please fill out this lost passbook affidavit and list the code word you used when you first opened your account.

Vocabulary Assistant
lost passbook affidavit 书面挂失单

7 Select elements from columns A, B and C to make at least five sentences. Be sure that the sentences you form make sense.

A	B	C
(1) The teller	(1) wanted to	(1) write a check
(2) A depositor	(2) tried to	(2) open a checking account
(3) The bank	(3) forgot to	(3) endorse his paycheck
		(4) handle cash for the depositors
		(5) store the customer's check on microfilm

8 Complete the following conversations.

1. A: Good morning, Miss. _____(1)_____?
   B: Could you tell me where _____(2)_____ an account?
   A: Right here. I'll _____(3)_____ for you.
   B: Thanks a lot.
   A: _____(4)_____.

2. A: Good morning, sir. _____(1)_____?
   B: Yes. I'd like to open a demand account.
   A: _____(2)_____?
   B: RMB 2000 yuan, please.
   A: All right. Please fill in _____(3)_____.

3. A: May I open an account with your bank?
   B: _____(1)_____. What kind of accounts do you like to open?
   A: Well, I'm not sure.
   B: Do you often deposit money and draw money?
   A: Yes.
   B: Then you may open a _____(2)_____, which is also called a _____(3)_____.
   A: Can I _____(4)_____ from the account whenever I need it?
   B: Yes, of course.

4. A: Hello, Miss. I need to _____(1)_____ from my time deposit for three years.
   B: OK. Your certificate, please. I'm sorry, sir. _____(2)_____. It's only two days before maturity.
   A: Yes, I know. It's a pity. I'm going abroad on urgent business in the afternoon this Sunday. I'm afraid you won't be here at that time.
   B: Oh, I understand, sir. We have 24 hours service every day. Will you come again on Sunday morning? I'll help you _____(3)_____ as quickly as possible. Then you won't lose interest.
   A: It's very kind to tell me. I'll do that. Thank you.
   B: It's our duty to _____(4)_____ and serve them warm-heartedly.

5. A: Excuse me, I want to _____(1)_____ in your bank.

B: Yes. Do you _____(2)_____ with us?

A: No, I haven't. It's the first time I've come to deposit money here. And I want to deposit at least for one year.

B: Oh, you want a _____(3)_____. Then please fill in _____(4)_____ with your name, address, identity card and deposit time.

6. A: Hello. What can I do for you?

B: Yes, may I establish a foreign currency deposit account with your bank?

A: Of course. _____(1)_____?

B: It's US Dollars.

A: All right. _____(2)_____?

B: Fixed is better. I want to open an account for one year. What is the interest rate?

A: Two point five two percent for one year.

B: Can I _____(3)_____ if I have an urgent need?

A: No problem, but the rate will be calculated at _____(4)_____ instead.

B: Thank you. Please handle it for me.

Conversation 5: Closing an Account

Clerk: May I help you, Sir?

Customer: Yes. I want to close my personal checking account, because I'm leaving for my home country.

Clerk: OK. Do you want to withdraw all the money in your account?

Customer: Actually, could you please transfer the entire balance to an account in the name of Mrs. Agenes White, who is my wife.

Clerk: Of course. Please show me your account number, passport and your wife's passport, too.

Customer: Here you are.

Clerk: Thanks. Just a moment, please. I'm now doing the transfer for you.

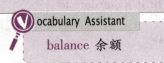

Vocabulary Assistant

balance 余额

9 Listening exercises

Listen to the following sentences and choose the best answer to each of the sentence you have just heard. Each of the sentences will be only read once.

1. A. The account number is 30798410.   B. The account number is 30789410.
   C. The account number is 30798401.   D. The account number is 30798140.

2. A. USD 3,674,596.09   B. USD 3,674,593.01
   C. USD 3,674,596.01   D. USD 3,374,593.09

3. A. Refuse to pay the check.
   B. Accept the check and wait for the customer to appear.
   C. Tie up the balance of the account of the customer.
   D. Tell the police to find the customer.

4. A. There is something wrong with your passport.
   B. There is nothing wrong with your passport.
   C. I have to know who you are.
   D. I have to check your passport.

5. A. I haven't opened a check account yet.
   B. I haven opened a check account.
   C. I have to open a check account.
   D. I did not know I could open a check account.

6. A. You have to deposit your money once a month.
   B. You can use your money at any time you need it.
   C. Your money is immediately run out
   D. Your money can immediately make more money.

7. A. The right number is 173-722.   B. The right number is 173-227.
   C. The right number is 137-272.   D. The right number is 173-272.

8. A. What? I have a telephone number of my own.
   B. My telephone number has no problem. You can call me.
   C. Yes, my phone is wrong.
   D. Yes. It's 383-8245.

UNIT 1 DEPOSITS

9. A. Mr. Martin wishes his colleague had opened the same account.
    B. Mr. Martin hasn't opened the same kind of account as his colleague did.
    C. Mr. Martin has opened the same account as his colleague's.
    D. Mr. Martin and his colleague opened the same account.

10. A. The bank makes profits only from its own money.
    B. The bank makes profits from not only the deposits but also its own money.
    C. The bank has a special obligation to make profits.
    D. The bank makes profits by having special obligations to depositors.

■ **Listen to the following conversation from a woman and a man, after each conversation there will be a question. Find out the correct answer to the question you have heard. Each conversation will be read once.**

1. A. 3%. B. 5%. C. 11%. D. None.

2. A. 2,000 francs. B. 20,000 francs. C. 472 francs. D. 427.20 francs.

3. A. Between three o'clock and six o'clock. B. Before six o'clock.
   C. Before three o'clock. D. After three o'clock.

4. A. 9 a.m.. B. 12 noon. C. 3 p.m.. D. 6 p.m..

5. A. Mr. Jones. B. Mr. Yamaha.
   C. British Embassy. D. The man.

6. A. That she needs $200 to open an account.
   B. That savings accounts earn low interest.
   C. That she should not open an account.
   D. That $2,000 will earn reasonable interest.

7. A. 4%. B. 4.5%. C. 5%. D. 5.5%.

8. A. She likes it very much. B. She likes it in hundred notes.
   C. She likes it to be only hundred francs. D. She likes it for it is her only money.

9. A. Six months. B. Twelve months. C. One month. D. A half month.

10. A. The amount. B. The address.
    C. The name. D. The account number.

Listen to the short passage and choose the best answer to the question you have heard after each of the passage. You will hear the passage only once.

Passage One

1. A. It allows you to use a cheque book.
   B. It earns interest for you.
   C. The bank will charge you for this account.
   D. No charges will be paid if it remains in credit.

2. A. 11%.   B. 3%.   C. 7%.   D. It fluctuates.

3. A. A safe and convenient way of handling money.
   B. People are paid in cash.
   C. Your salary goes straight into your account.
   D. Your money is paid straight into your account from other's.

Passage Two

1. A. A safe and convenient way.   B. One of the most important services.
   C. An important service.   D. One more important service.

2. A. It will refund the customer.   B. It will find it back to the customer.
   C. It will find the lost cheque for him.   D. It will be refunded by the customer.

3. A. To anyone who applies for it.
   B. To those who fill out a form.
   C. To those who tell about their salaries and other income.
   D. To those who are with good credit.

10 Make conversations with the information given below, taking into account the logical relationship of the content.

1. A clerk helps a new customer with formalities of a demand account.

Clerk	Customer
Greetings	Have no idea about
Fill a form	No pen
On the rack of the desk	Finished filling
Miss out	Make it up
Deposit	RMB 3,000 yuan
A deposit slip and ID	Thanks for

2. A clerk helps an Australian businessman to open a foreign currency deposit account.

Clerk	Businessman
Open an account?	Yes. 10,000 Australian dollar.
Sorry. Not on the list.	
Change...	What foreign currencies?
Six, which one?	Pound Sterling
Deposit term?	Need money regularly

3. Mr. John Black has to close his account because he is leaving for his home country.

Mr. John Black	Bank teller
Go home / close an account	What account?
Savings deposit account	Account number?
Forgot / Bank book	Identity card?
Passport	Find out
Interest?	Bulletin Board / Finished
US dollars?	Window 3

11 Make conversations according to the cases given below.

Case 1
A customer comes to Beijing Branch of the Industrial and Commercial Bank of China. He enquires about the types of accounts offered by the bank. Make a conversation between the bank officer and the customer.

Case 2
Mr. Green has maintained a three-year time deposit in Renminbi with China Construction Bank. He needs some money for an emergency. Make a conversation between the bank officer and Mr. Green.

Case 3
Miss White lost her bank card, so she came to Guangzhou Branch of the Agricultural Bank of China to report a loss and check whether her money was still available. Make a conversation between the bank officer and Miss White.

Case 4
Mr. Johnson is leaving China. He wants to close his savings account with Shanghai Branch of the Bank of China. Make a conversation between the bank officer and Mr. Johnson.

Supplementary Reading: A Cheque

A cheque is a written instruction to the bank to pay money to someone. This is a very valuable service because people do not have to carry large amounts of cash with them when they go shopping. Cheque books must at all times be kept safely, and as necessary under lock and key so that they are not available to unauthorized persons.

On opening of an account, a check book will be issued to the account holder. Cheques should be drawn in the local currency. The amount should be stated clearly in words and figures in the space provided on the cheques. When a signed cheque or a cheque book is lost or stolen, the account holder must immediately report such loss in writing to the bank. All checks must be written in non-erasable in Chinese and be signed in conformity with the specimen signature registered with the bank.

The account holder should exercise care when drawing cheques and agree that he / she will not draw cheques by any means in any manners which may enable a cheque to be altered or may facilitate fraud or forgery. When issuing checks, the amount, both in words and figures, should be as close to each other and to the left-hand margin as possible so as to leave no space for insertions. The word "only" should be added after the amount is stated in words. Only Arabic numerals should be used for figures.

Applications for a new cheque book may be made by presenting the duly completed and signed cheque book application form contained therein to the bank or by any other means accepted by the bank. Upon the receipt of a new cheque book, the account holder should verify the cheques serial numbers, account number and the name of the account holder printed thereon as well as the number of cheques before use. Any irregularities should be promptly reported to the bank.

When writing a cheque, the account holder should pay attention to the restrictions on the transferability of the cheques. For example, an open or uncrossed cheque refers to the cheque which is written on a plain bank form, implying that the cheque can be exchanged for cash at the drawer's bank account on which it is drawn. However, a crossed cheque refers to two parallel lines drawn across the face of the cheque. This implies that the cheque can only be paid into the bank account of the payee.

Unit 2 Loans

AIMS

- Applying for a loan
- Offering a foreign exchange loan
- Getting a mortgage loan
- Overdraft

Information bank

With a personal loan, a bank customer agrees to borrow a fixed sum, say $1,200, and also agrees a repayment schedule which might, for example, involve repaying $100 a month over the next year. Some personal loans are made for as long as 10 years. Interest is charged at a fixed rate that is agreed in advance. The rate on a personal loan is linked to the base rate at the time when the loan is made, but it is always higher than the base rate. The addition is measured in terms of basis points. For example, if the addition in the case of one borrower is 800 basis points, then that borrower will pay a rate that is 8% above base rate, each basis point adding 0.01%. Then the number of basis points on a loan may depend a little on the length of the loan and on the amount borrowed, but it will depend chiefly on the credit-worthiness of the borrower. The stated interest rates on personal loans often look deceptively low because they may not be the actual interest rates. This arises because the stated rates are sometimes expressed by working out the interest payments as a percentage of the initial loan, which would be $120 in the example given here, even though the average amount borrowed over the period of the loan is considerably lower.

Introduction to a Loan

1. A mortgage is a loan that is made for a long period to help someone buy or improve a home. Bank mortgages are made at floating rates and closely resemble building society mortgages, most of which are made specially for buying or improving homes. Building society mortgages are usually made on a long-term basis, often up to 25 years, but many of them are paid off within that time as people rarely stay in one home so long.

Of course, when people move, they may want a new mortgage to help purchase their new home. Mortgages are typically made on a floating rate basis. Some mortgages are made on the understanding that borrowers will pay them off steadily over the period of the loan, while others are made on the understanding that the borrowers will pay them off at the end in a single installment.

2. Lending to commercial customers is more complex than lending to personal customers. This is because business customers are involved in a much wider range of activities. Commercial lending refers to lending services to sole proprietors (sole traders), partnerships, private limited companies and public limited companies. As the term implies, commercial lending services offered by banks provide financial assistance to the business and commercial sectors. In Hong Kong, the most popular is trade financing in the import-export sector, followed by building and construction, wholesale and retail business, and of course, the manufacturing and production sectors. Depending on the size of the operation, the need for financing in the commercial sector may range form a few thousand dollars to billions of dollars.

Vocabulary Assistant

building society mortgage 房屋互助协会抵押贷款
on a long-term basis 长期地
on a floating rate basis 按浮动利率
in a single installment 一次性付清
commercial lending services 商业贷款服务
wholesale and retail business 批发和零售业务

UNIT 2 LOANS

1 Select the answer that correctly completes the sentences.

1. The interest rates that banks charge on overdrafts are always well above their base rate, and the interest rate is called _____.

    A. a floating rate   B. a fixed rate

    C. a base rate   D. a fluctuating rate

2. _____ is a loan that is made for a long period to help someone buy or improve a home.

    A. An overdraft   B. A personal loan

    C. A card loan   D. A mortgage

Conversation 1: Applying for a Loan

Li Feng: Hi! Mr. Smith. Haven't seen you for a long time!

Mr. James: Exactly. I've been very busy recently. This is my friend Mr. Cannon. He wants to arrange for a loan.

Li Feng: Glad to meet you, Mr. Cannon!

Mr. Cannon: Glad to meet you.

Li Feng: What can I do for you?

Mr. Cannon: I'm from a joint venture. We manufacture baby cats. We exported some of our products last month, but the money has not been repaid. Now we are anxious for a sum of money.

Li Feng: I see. What do you think of a short term loan? About six months or so.

Mr. Cannon: That's exactly what we need now.

Li Feng: By the way, are you our client?

Mr. Cannon: No. I'm not.

Li Feng: I'm sorry. According to our policy, our loans only go to our clients. Well, I have an idea. Mr. Smith is a regular old client. If he agrees to act as your guarantor, everything will be OK.

Mr. Cannon: That's what we think about.

Li Feng: Oh. Good. Let's have a further discussion now.

Mr. Cannon: OK.

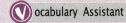

Vocabulary Assistant

arrange for a loan 申请贷款
guarantor 担保人

Conversation 2: Offering a Foreign Exchange Loan (1)

Liu Mei: Morning. This is ICBC Zhejiang Branch International Business Department Foreign Currency Loan Division. Can I help you?

Tom: Yes. I'm Tom from the Mobile Phone Company Ltd of joint-venture. Could you supply a foreign currency loan to us?

Liu Mei: We can. What currency of loan do you want?

Tom: US Dollars. Would you please explain the terms and interest rate respectively?

Liu Mei: We have short-term, mid-term and long-term loans, fixed or floating rate loans, loans with security or without. For you, we'd adopt a floating rate foreign currency loan with security. The interest will be calculated at the floating rate.

Tom: That sounds good.

Liu Mei: Do you have an account with us?

Tom: Yes, we want a loan of US $500,000 first.

Liu Mei: No problem. Please come tomorrow presenting your application and some documents that are required.

Tom: Thank you. See you tomorrow.

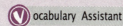ocabulary Assistant

terms 期限	interest rate 利息率
floating rate 浮动利率	fixed rate 固定利率
loans with security 抵押贷款	loans without security 无抵押贷款

Conversation 3: Offering a Foreign Exchange Loan (2)

Li Ming: Good morning.

Jim: Good morning. I really need your help.

Li Ming: What can I do for you?

Jim: Our plant is short of funds in foreign exchange. Could you supply a foreign currency loan to us?

Li Ming: According to the regulations, we must first make an investigation of your credit standing, the operational state of the enterprise, the possibility of repayment and so on.

Jim: You are right. Here are some information and documents and detailed report about our factory.

Li Ming: What currency of loan do you want?

Jim: Japanese yen. What about the interest rate?

Li Ming: We'd adopt a floating rate loan for you. The interest will be calculated at the floating rate. How much do you want to loan?

Jim: 30,000,000 Japanese Yen for 12 months.

Li Ming: Generally speaking, there should be no problem. Anyway, I have to check your documents. Please fill out this loan application.

Jim: Thank you very much.

Vocabulary Assistant

loan application 贷款申请书

2 Translate the phrases into English.

1. 长期贷款
2. 期限
3. 贷款申请书
4. 资信状况
5. 还款
6. 经营情况
7. 利息率
8. 担保人
9. 浮动利率贷款
10. 规定, 条例

3 Substitution drills and try to translate each sentence into Chinese.

1. How much do you want _____?
   A. to borrow   B. to loan   C. to get
2. Can you supply _____ to us?
   A. a foreign loan   B. a mortgage loan C. a housing loan
3. Do you have a detailed report or some information about your _____?
   A. financial status   B. mortgage loan   C. housing loan
4. Please present _____.
   A. a loan application B. financial reports C. documents
5. Do you have any _____?
   A. property   B. stocks
   C. other business   D. investments

4 Fill in the blanks with the proper words or phrases given below.

capability	service	real	submit
business	cash flow	sources of income	
repay	principal	repayment capability	

  The borrower must be able to __(1)__ the debt, i.e., he must be able to pay interest and __(2)__ when due. The banker will examine, in general, the possible __(3)__ of the borrower and, in particular, determine whether there will be sufficient __(4)__ over the term of the loan to service the debt. In order to make the loan application successful, a customer is normally required to __(5)__ detailed financial statements that will substantiate his __(6)__ to generate adequate funds to __(7)__ the loan. The statements submitted by the customer are an income statement, balance sheet and projected growth of the __(8)__. The banker will then review and analyze the __(9)__ financial position of the borrower so far as __(10)__ is concerned.

| commitment | financial | strong | sure |
| repayment | capital | competition | loan |

  "Capital" refers to the "cushion of assets" for __(1)__ of the bank's advances in the event of the borrower experiencing __(2)__ difficulties. The banker should make __(3)__ that the borrower has sufficient __(4)__ to operate his business effectively and to meet keen __(5)__ in order to maintain his ability to make __(6)__ repayment. A __(7)__ capital base will demonstrate the customer's ability to repay his loans. It also indicates the customer's __(8)__ to sustaining production capability in securing future.

Conversation 4: Getting a Mortgage Loan

Customer: Excuse me, but how can I get to the loan department?

Li Feng: Here it is. What can I do for you?

Customer: I'd like to arrange for a loan, but I don't know what I shall go about.

Li Feng: What kind of loan do you plan to apply for?

Customer: I have no idea yet. I've found a house that I'd like to buy, but I'm short of money, so...

Li Feng: Oh, I see. What do you think of housing loan? As to this loan, we offer two kinds of services: one is mortgage and the other is installment. Which do you prefer?

Customer: What conditions should I have if I'd like to apply for installment.

Li Feng: Steady income is the most important condition.

Customer: And mortgage?

Li Feng: You have to possess something, such as old houses or other valuable things.

Customer: Well, I think the latter is what I want. By the way, can I rent the old house if it is used as collateral?

Li Feng: Why not? What we need is only your house.

Customer: Where shall I come in if I apply for a mortgage loan.

Li Feng: Do you have an account in our bank?

Customer: I've been banking here since we established our business eight years ago.

Li Feng: Thank you. In the case, you enjoy privilege. For further procedure, I'll ask Mr. Wang to help you. He is our loan officer.

Customer: Thank you.

Li Feng: You are welcome.

Vocabulary Assistant

housing loan 住房信贷　　　mortgage 抵押款
installment 分期付款,按揭贷款　　collateral 抵押品
loan officer 信贷员

Term Explanation for Loans

Collateral

"Collateral" refers to security provided by a borrower to offset the apparent weaknesses of a loan. These weakness include inadequate capital, and certain risks and uncertainty arising from market conditions. It should be noted that collateral may make a loan safe, but it will not necessarily make it sound. Therefore, collateral should be considered as a protection rather than as a source of repayment. Collateral can never make a bad loan good, but it can turn a good loan into a better one. Collateral should be the last item to be considered in a loan approval.

Character of the Borrower

"Character" refers to the borrower's determination to repay the loan; it can be assessed by examining his track record. A bank can obtain information from credit card companies and other financial institutions. The banker should ask himself these questions: is the borrower reliable in making repayment according to schedule? If he is a new customer, are there any bank records showing his account? Is the borrower exaggerating his business conditions? These questions involve judgment on character and reliability.

Capacity

The word "capacity" indicates the person's ability, financial circumstances, and legal capacity to borrow. The main principle in assessing a borrower's capacity is visible in the following questions: for a limited company to borrow, does it have the legal authority given under the memorandum and articles of association to borrow? How much can it borrow? And will it be able to repay?

Capital

"Capital" refers to the "cushion of assets" for repayment of the bank's advances in the event of the borrower experiencing financial difficulties. The banker should make sure that the borrower has sufficient capital to operate his business effectively and to meet keen competition in order to maintain his ability to make loan repayment. A strong capital base will demonstrate the customer's ability to repay his loans. It also indicates the customer's commitment to sustaining production capability in securing future.

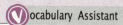ocabulary Assistant

collateral 担保品
character of the borrower 借款人的还款决心
legal authority 法律授权
inadequate capital 资本不足
capacity 还款能力
cushion of assets 资产的缓冲

Pricing of Loans

The bank has to calculate its own costs of providing loans to customers. Most banks usually set a rate (interest rate) at some percentage (commonly known as "margin") over the prime rate. The "margin", in fact, indicates the possible credit risk that the loans may bear. Therefore, the rate quoted for a loan depends on various factors: size of the loan, financial strength of the borrower and nature of security offered by the customer. Hence, the higher the possible risk involved, the higher the margin over the prime rate to be charged to the loan. When one can borrow at prime, it implies that the loan is seen to carry the minimum risk.

Vocabulary Assistant

pricing of the loans 贷款的定价   margin 差额
nature of security 抵押品的性质

5 In this part you will hear 6 sentences. Each sentence will be read twice. For the first time you just listen and for the second time, you'll have a break of 10 seconds following each sentence. During the break, try to complete the sentences according to what you have just heard. Please watch your spelling.

1. *Character of the Borrower*
   ◇ "Character" refers to the borrower's ___(1)___ to repay the loan; it can be ___(2)___ by examining his track record. A bank can obtain information from credit card companies and other financial institutions.

2. *Capacity*
   ◇ The word "capacity" indicates the person's ability, ___(3)___, and legal capacity to borrow.

3. *Collateral*
   ◇ "Collateral" refers to ___(4)___ provided by a borrower to ___(5)___ the apparent weaknesses of a loan.
   ◇ These weakness include ___(6)___ capital, and certain risks and ___(7)___ arising from market conditions.

4. *Pricing of Loans*
   ◇ The bank has to ___(8)___ its own costs of providing loans to customers.
   ◇ Most banks usually set an interest rate at some ___(9)___ which is commonly known as "___(10)___" over the prime rate.

6 **The loan officers may use the following sentences when they remind their customers repaying the loan. Practice these sentences.**

1. I'm afraid you have to pay thirty percent of the price.
2. Do you mind if I say you can delay no longer?
3. I don't think there is any possibility.
4. Excuse me, but it's our regulation.
5. I'm sorry, but we have to do it according to our policy.

Conversation 5: Overdraft

Han Lin: I'm terribly sorry about this, but is it possible for us to get an overdraft at your bank? You know, I am very much in need of this money.

Liu Li: Well, er, in your case, I see no reason why not. What's your proposition?

Han Lin: I've got $400 in my account, so I need another $200.

Liu Li: All right. What sort of period could you repay us in?

Han Lin: My annual allowance is coming in two months. Is it OK to repay the amount in three months' time?

Liu Li: Yes, for such a sum of money we would expect repayment within 12 months, so that's quite all right.

Han Lin: Terrific. Is there any interest on this money?

Liu Li: Yes. We'll charge 5 percent interest on it.

Han Lin: That's OK.

Liu Li: Now please fill in this form, and sign your name at the bottom.

Han Lin: All right. Here we go.

Liu Li: Thank you. Now in what denominations would you like the money?

Han Lin: Six one hundreds, please.

Liu Li: OK, that's one hundred, two hundred, three hundred, four hundred, five hundred and six hundred dollars.

Han Lin: Thanks a lot. Have a good day.

Liu Li: You too. Next.

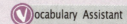

proposition 建议,想法   allowance 津贴
denomination 票面

7 Complete each statement of the following with the best ONE from the four choices given.

1. _____ refers to the borrower's determination to repay the loan; it can be assessed by examining his track record.
   A. "Character"   B. "Capital"   C. "Capacity"   D. "Collateral"

2. When one can borrow at a prime rate, it implies that the loan is considered to carry _____.
   A. the maximum risk   B. different types of risk
   C. the minimum risk   D. no risk

3. The word "capacity" indicates the person's ability, financial circumstances, and _____.
   A. his repayment determination   B. legal capacity to borrow
   C. integrity   D. experience in operation

4. "Capital" refers to _____ for repayment of the bank's advances in the event of the borrower experiencing financial difficulties.
   A. working capital   B. realization of the assets into cash
   C. financial assets   D. fixed assets

5. Whether the customer is able to make the repayment of a loan depends largely on the _____ produced by the business.
   A. quality of the products   B. quantity of the products
   C. protection of the products   D. profitability of the products

8 Complete the following conversations.

1. Customer: I'd like to apply for a loan.
   Clerk: _____(1)_____?
   Customer: Two thousand yuan.
   Clerk: Please fill in the application form.
   Customer: _____(2)_____?
   Clerk: The interest rate is five percent.
   Customer: _____(3)_____?
   Clerk: Yes. Your payment will be 196.67 yuan each month.

2. Clerk: This is the Credit Loan Department. _____(1)_____?
   Customer: I am from Mobile Phone Corporation, which is an enterprise with a foreign venture. Can we borrow some dollars?
   Clerk: Yes, you can, after we _____(2)_____.
   Customer: You're right. This is a detailed report about our financial status, credit standing and so on.
   Clerk: We'll _____(3)_____ and tell you our decision in a week or so.
   Customer: Thanks a lot.

3. Clerk: Good morning, _____(1)_____?

Customer: Yes, our plant is short of funds in foreign exchange. Could you supply a foreign loan to us?

Clerk: Well, as a regular customer with nice credit position of our bank, we'll consider this. _____(2)_____?

Customer: Dollars. _____(3)_____?

Clerk: We'd adopt a floating rate loan for your company. _____(4)_____?

Customer: US $100,000 for 12 months.

Clerk: Generally speaking, there should be no problem. Anyway, I have to check your recent Balance Sheet and Profit and Loss Statement again. Do you have them?

Customer: Here you are.

Clerk: OK. _____(5)_____ and tell you our decision in a week or so.

Customer: Thank you very much.

Listening exercises

■ **Listen to the following sentences and choose the best answer to each of the sentence you have just heard. Each of the sentences will be only read once.**

1. A. We need your debit authority next Monday.
　　B. You have enough money to debit our authority.
　　C. You're very kind to debit our account.
　　D. We need you to debit our authority next month.

2. A. The company got a loan of USD 800.00.
　　B. The company can borrow up to USD 8,000,000.00.
　　C. The company can borrow up to USD 800,000.00.
　　D. The company will provide a loan of USD 800,000.00.

3. A. It is a rule to check the documents and make payment.
　　B. Our rule is to check the documents while effecting payment.
　　C. We make it a rule to check the documents and then effect payment.
　　D. We usually make payment after checking the documents.

4. A. We only accept cash payment for bill.
　　B. We can only accept your credit card for payment of bill.
　　C. It doesn't matter for us if you pay cash or with your credit card.
　　D. It is not allowed to pay bills with the credit cards.

5. A. You're required to secure the money you borrowed.
   B. You're required to show your credit rating.
   C. You're required to offer a security for a loan from bank.
   D. You're required to improve the security.

6. A. This company is worth of financing.
   B. This company is highly rated in credit status.
   C. This company is rated lower in credit standing.
   D. This company runs a greater risk to make loans.

7. A. Overseas business is also protected by the Bank Act just like the domestic business.
   B. Depositors and commercial ads for institutional deposit are supervised by the Bank Act.

8. A. Banks and non-financial firms face different kinds of risks.
   B. Non-financial firms do not face any kind of risk.

9. A. Interest rate risk is a normal part of banking operations.
   B. Interest rate risk is a terrible threat to banking operations.

10. A. Some borrowers are engaged in undesirable activities which are considered immoral.
    B. Some lenders are engaged in undesirable activities which are considered immoral.

■ **Listen to the following conversations from a woman and a man, after each conversation there will be a question or a few questions. Find out the correct answer to the question you have heard. Each conversation will be read once.**

1. A. Immediate payment.
   B. Deferred payment.
   C. Invoice.
   D. US $1,000.

2. A. This week.
   B. A week ago.
   C. At the end of this week.
   D. This month.

3. A. Husband and wife.
   B. Bank clerk and customer.
   C. Credit officer and customer.
   D. Estate agent and house buyer.

4. A. Letter of credit must be a favorable way.
   B. The issuing bank should be a big one.
   C. A confirmed irrevocable L/C will be acceptable.
   D. The L/C should be in terms of US dollar.

5. A. A contractual arrangement.
   B. A counterpart.
   C. Many types of risks.
   D. Credit risk.

6. A. Earnings.
   B. Profit.
   C. A big threat.
   D. Capital base.

7. A. Representatives.
   B. Agencies.
   C. Branches.
   D. Subsidiaries.

8. A. In 1844.
   B. In 1814.
   C. In 1694.
   D. In 1496.

9. A. Federal Reserve System.
   B. International Monetary Fund.
   C. World Bank.
   D. International Bank for Reconstruction and Development.

10. A. In Federal Reserve System.
   B. With the branches.
   C. At Commercial banks.
   D. At the Federal Reserve Bank.

UNIT 2 LOANS

■ **Listen to the short passage and choose the best answer to the question you have heard after each of the passage. You will hear the passage only once.**

Passage One

1. A. They would like to lend it out for a longer time.
   B. They would like to put it in the banks as long as possible.
   C. They would like to get it back whenever they wish.
   D. They would like to charge the banks interest at higher rate.

2. A. They would like to pay the money back over several years.
   B. They would like to pay the bank interest at a higher rate.
   C. They would like to investigate whether a loan would be safe.
   D. They would like not to pay the money back at all.

3. A. It would like to accept more money from depositors.
   B. It would like to make an investigation whether the loan would be safe.
   C. It would charge the borrower interest at the highest rate.
   D. It would build up considerable expertise.

Passage Two

1. A. When you countersign before the cashier.
   B. If the cheques are stolen.
   C. If the cheques are accidentally lost.
   D. When you are on the spot.

2. A. Every purchaser is provided with a booklet.
   B. Refunds are obtainable around the world.
   C. The points make immediate refunds for any amount.
   D. Any remaining balance can be settled quickly.

3. A. It is the second one in the world.
   B. It is the first one in the world.
   C. It gives people a passport to travel.
   D. It is free of charge.

10 Make conversations with the information given below, taking into account the logical relationship of the content.

1. Mr. Sun is a bank clerk of the mortgage department of Bank of China, Beijing Branch. Mr. Martin has decided to buy a house and he wants to get it through a mortgage loan.

Mr. Sun	Mr. Martin
Greeting	Greeting
How much is the loan?	Apply for a mortgage loan
15% percent down payment.	8,000,000
Repayment schedule	Twenty years
Collateral	Other property interest rate.
3.8 per annum	Thanks, think it over.

2. The customer is the manager of Food Import and Export Company. He'd like to expand his business, but he's having some difficulties with a working capital for the expansion.

A bank clerk	A customer
Greeting	Greeting
Applying for a working capital	Look into credit standing before making decision
Latest copies of balance sheet and operating statement.	Check it over
When to tell your decision.	Call in three days.
Wait for good news.	May offer a loan in five days.

3. Mr. Smith wants to get the overdraft from the bank, he is asking the bank clerk about the loan period and the interest.

Mr. Smith	Clerk
Greeting	Greeting
In need of money	What's your proposition?
Need another $200	What sort of period could you repay us in?
Within 3 months	
Ok	Charge 5% interest
Fill in the form	

11 Make conversations according to the cases given below.

Case 1
Mr. Johnson wants to buy a house. He goes to a branch of the Industrial and Commercial Bank of China to inquire about the procedure of applying for a loan.

Case 2
The manager of the credit department and the president are going to examine and approve the loan application submitted by Mr. Johnson.

Case 3
Some bank managers are having a discussion on the lending and the risks of non-repayment.

Case 4
A representative of ABC company come to the bank to apply for the foreign exchange loan.

Supplementary Reading: The Inter-bank Market

The inter-bank lending and borrowing market is very important to banks, financial companies, insurance companies, pension funds and the government, because it  provides a means by which financial institutions can utilize and adjust their liquidity positions in the quickest possible way. Moreover, through the lending and borrowing activities, the government can extend its influence to affect money market conditions.

The inter-bank market has developed because it provides a mechanism for the movement of deposits among banks in a rather smooth fashion suitable to the need and requirement of the banking sector and other financial institutions.

Inter-bank lending is traditionally unsecured and always involves the taking and lending of substantially large bank deposits for a short period of time. Since inter-bank lending involves lending among banks, they have their own special procedures with regard to the interest rate charged and the way they handle the transactions. The deals are usually arranged by telephone calls; and the inter-bank lending rate varies from time to time, reflecting the overall fluctuations in liquidity in the banking sector as a whole. Therefore, if liquidity in the money market is extremely tight, the rate may go up, sometimes as high as 15% to 20%, while the normal saving interest rate at the same time could be 5% to 6%.

Unit 3
Foreign Exchange

AIMS

- Exchanging currency
- Handling reconversion
- Inquiring about rates of exchange
- Purchasing foreign currency
- Encashing a traveller's cheque

Information bank

Foreign Exchange Dealings for Account of Individuals refers to the firm foreign exchange dealings conducted by the individuals through the service personnel behind the counter or through other electronic banking service methods within the time for dealings set by the Bank. Long service time for dealings: Business hours of each branch vary with different conditions. The longest dealing lasts 18 hours each day, covering business hours of the main international financial markets. The banks make offers according to the quotations of the international foreign exchange market and in line with international practices. Affected by various kinds of political and economic factors in the world and by contingencies, the exchange rates often show radical fluctuations. As a result, risks and opportunities co-exist in foreign exchange dealings for account of individuals.

Spot Transaction of Foreign Exchange refers to the foreign exchange transaction settled on the second bank working day after the foreign exchange transaction has been concluded. The settlement day is the value date. The value date will be postponed if it falls out of the bank working day or during the holidays. The rate of Spot Transaction of Foreign Exchange is called Spot Rate. The Bank of China can conduct foreign exchange dealings concluded on the same day with interest being calculated or dealings concluded on the same day with the interest being calculated on the next day.

Introduction to Spot Transaction of Foreign Exchange

Spot Transaction of Foreign Exchange is the most essential form in foreign exchange dealings. It has the three main functions as follows:

1. Spot Transaction of Foreign Exchange can meet the needs of the customer to make temporary payment. Through Spot Transaction of Foreign Exchange, the customer can convert a kind of foreign currency on hand into another kind of foreign currency duly to deal with the foreign exchange settlement in import and export business, tendering and overseas project contracting, etc or to pay back the foreign exchange loans. For example, a company will return one million US dollars of loans on Wednesday to a foreign bank and the company has Japanese Yen, then the company can buy from our Bank USD one million on Monday as per the spot rate of USD 1= JPY 130.00 and sell the Yen at the same time. On Wednesday, the company pays JPY 0.13 billion to the credit our Bank by transfer; while our Bank gives USD 1 million to the company. Then the company can remit the US dollars to pay back the loans.

2. Spot Transaction of Foreign Exchange can help regulate the set-up of the customer's foreign currencies on hand. For example, by following the principle of "not putting all the eggs into the same basket" and through Spot Transaction of Foreign Exchange, a company can convert 15% of all its foreign exchange from the US dollar into euro and 10% into yen to divert the foreign exchange risks by this combination.

3. Spot Transaction of Foreign Exchange is an important instrument for foreign exchange speculation. This speculation can give rise to rich profits as well as huge losses.

1 **Retell the functions of Spot Transaction of Foreign Exchange in your own words.**

Function 1:

Function 2:

Function 3:

Conversation 1: Exchanging Currency

Linda: Is this Bank of China? Could you change some money for me, please?
Bank Clerk: Certainly. What kind of currency and how much do you want to change?
Linda: Only five hundred Canadian dollars.
Bank Clerk: Would you mind showing me your passport?
Linda: Not in the least. Here you are. What is the Canadian dollar going for today?
Bank Clerk: The buying rate of Canadian dollar notes is 550 yuan per hundred dollars.
Linda: Thank you. How much Reminbi Yuan shall I get for five hundred dollars?
Bank Clerk: Let me see. Five hundred Canadian dollars make 2,750 yuan.
Linda: I hope you'll give me twenty 100-yuan notes and five fifties.
Bank Clerk: Here are the cash and exchange memo. Check them, please.
Linda: It seems there is some change in the rate. I got 2,200 yuan for 500 Canadian dollars when I was staying in Shanghai last month. I think the rate of the Canadian dollar against the Renminbi has risen again, hasn't it?
Bank Clerk: Yes, it certainly has.
Linda: OK. Thank you very much.
Bank Clerk: It's my pleasure.

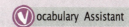ocabulary Assistant

the buying rate 买进价格
exchange memo 兑换水单

2 **Translate the phrases into Chinese.**

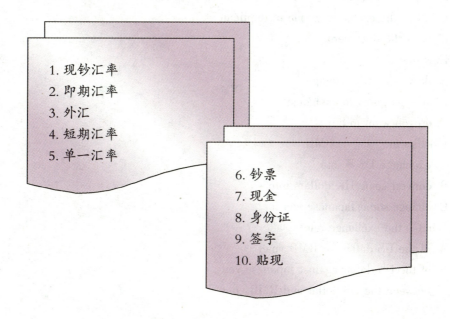

1. 现钞汇率
2. 即期汇率
3. 外汇
4. 短期汇率
5. 单一汇率

6. 钞票
7. 现金
8. 身份证
9. 签字
10. 贴现

Conversation 2: Handling Reconversion

Bank Clerk: Hello. Are you Mr. Smith? You were here last month and exchanged US $1,000 into RMB.
Mr. Smith: Yes. Good memory. I'm here to trouble you again.
Bank Clerk: No trouble at all. What's the matter this time?
Mr. Smith: I've got about RMB ¥1,500 unused. Can I convert it back into US dollars?
Bank Clerk: Yes, of course. Your exchange memo, please.
Mr. Smith: Here you are.
Bank Clerk: Today's exchange rate is at just the same as the one in your memo. So RMB ¥1,500 mean $180. Please check.
Mr. Smith: Exactly right. Thank you very much. Good-bye!
Bank Clerk: Good-bye!

Vocabulary Assistant

unused 未使用过的
convert 转换,兑换

3 Substitution drills and try to translate each sentence into Chinese.

1. Here is your money. Please _____.
   A. count it   B. check it   C. check the amount

2. Please _____.
   A. copy the material
   B. fill in the exchange memo in duplicate
   C. print the document

3. How much _____?
   A. do you want to change
   B. are you going to exchange
   C. do you want to buy

4. I'd like to _____ RMB.
   A. exchange US $ into
   B. convert some HK dollars into
   C. change some Japanese yen for

5. What's the exchange rate _____?
   A. of the US dollar for RMB yuan
   B. of the US dollar against Japanese yen
   C. between the US dollar and RMB yuan

Conversation 3: Inquiring about rates of exchange

Bank Clerk: Can I help you?
Customer: Yes, I'd like to change some money to cover my expenses here. What's today's rate of the US dollar against the RMB yuan?
Bank Clerk: Let me see, the buying rate is RMB ¥73.28 per one hundred dollars. How much would you like to change?
Customer: Two hundred dollars altogether.
Bank Clerk: Would you mind showing me your passport?
Customer: Here it is. And how much Renminbi shall I get?
Bank Clerk: Let me see. Two hundred dollars makes RMB ¥1462. Here is the cash and the exchange memo. Please check it.
Customer: That's correct. Thank you very much.

Vocabulary Assistant
cover 弥补,负担支付
expenses 费用

4 Try to translate the following sentences into Chinese and pay more attention to the words in black.

1. According to our Regulation on Foreign Exchange Administration, any amount of Renminbi exceeding RMB ¥20,000 is **forbidden** to be taken abroad.

2. Please go to **counter** No.6 for service.

3. I'd like to change some money to cover my **expenses** here.

4. But I'll go back to USA in a week when the **vacation** starts.

5. I still have two thousand Renminbi yuan unused from my **wages**.

6. According to the current **provisions** of our foreign exchange administration regulations...

7. Yes, but where am I to **countersign**?

8. The words "countersign here in presence of paying agent (or **cashier**)" are printed there.

Take Foreign Currency to Go Abroad

The bank's client with foreign currency deposit account need withdraw foreign exchange and take foreign currency to go abroad after his successful application for settling down abroad or visiting families, traveling, investigating or studying is approved, he can make an application to the original business office. The bank is to issue a "Foreign Exchange Holding Permit for Going Abroad" to the client according to provisions.

Banks can handle the exchange between RMB and foreign currencies at current quotations on the day. Convertible currencies include US dollar, Australian dollar, Euro, Canadian Dollar, Japanese yen, Singapore dollar, HK dollar, English pound, Swiss franc, etc. The banks can handle foreign exchange purchase for official foreign visit groups. You are only required to take the exit paper approved by the Administration of Foreign Exchange for the bank's examination before acquiring foreign exchange. Foreigners leaving the country can convert the unused RMB, which were converted when they entered the country, into foreign currencies according to their passports and original foreign currency conversion receipts within six months.

Vocabulary Assistant

US dollar 美元	Australian Dollar 澳元
Euro 欧元	Canadian Dollar 加元
Japanese yen 日元	Singapore Dollar 新加坡元
HK Dollar 港元	Swiss Franc 瑞士法郎
English pound 英镑	

5 Match the following terms with their respective explanations.

note of small denomination	报价单，行情表
counter signature	取款单
foreign exchange certificate	浮动汇率
quotation	法定汇率
floating rate	复签，
official exchange rate	会签小额钞票
withdrawal slip	外汇券

6 In this section you'll hear a short paragraph. There are some words or phrases missing in the paragraph. It can be read three times. The first time you just listen, and the second time, you'll have a break of 20 seconds. During the break, you can write down the missing words. The third time is for you to check your writing. Now let's begin.

  Companies operate and expect to be paid in the currency of the countries in which they're ___(1)___. That means anyone wanting to ___(2)___ from a firm in another ___(3)___ has to acquire some of that country's currency first. For example, if a US company that operates department stores wants to buy ___(4)___ wool sweaters from a British ___(5)___, it has to pay the bill in ___(6)___, not US dollars. But the American firm has only dollars, not pounds. Clearly, to make the purchase, it has to ___(7)___. We also say the firm buys pounds for dollars. The purchase is accomplished in ___(8)___ market, which is organized for the purchase of exchanging currencies. The foreign exchange market operates much like other ___(9)___, but isn't located in a specific place like ___(10)___. Rather, it's a network of brokers and banks based in financial centers around the world. Most commercial banks are able to access the market and provide exchange services to their clients.

Conversation 4: Purchasing Foreign Currency

Bank Clerk: How do you do, sir? What can I do for you?
Customer: How do you do? I've been a foreign teacher for two years in Beijing University. But I'll go back to USA in a week when the vacation starts. I still have two thousand Renminbi yuan unused from my wages. Can I change them into US dollars?
Bank Clerk: Yes, you can if you have the relation personal certificates like your Foreign Experts Certificate, etc.
Customer: It so happens that I have them.
Bank Clerk: That's good. According to the current provisions of our foreign exchange administration regulations, you can convert your Renminbi notes not more than RMB ¥2,400 per month while you're staying in China. Well, by the way, have you ever bought foreign currency at present?

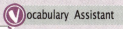ocabulary Assistant

vacation 假期 wages 薪水,工资
provisions 规定 convert 兑换

Customer: No, I haven't.
Bank Clerk: So I think it's no problem for you to buy US dollars with your two thousand Renminbi yuan.
Customer: Can you tell me what's the exchange rate today?
Bank Clerk: The selling rate is seven hundred and twenty-three Renminbi yuan (RMB ¥723) against one hundred US dollars (USD$100). You'll get two hundred and seventy-seven US dollars.
Customer: That's clear. I want to buy now.
Bank Clerk: Please go to counter NO.10. You can have the service there.
Customer: Thank you very much.
Bank Clerk: You are welcome.

7 Try to translate the following sentences into English and fill in the blanks.

1. 我要兑换一些钱。
   I want to _____ some money.
2. 这是兑换水单。
   This is the exchange memo for your _____.
3. 这是500英镑(钞票)和兑换水单。
   Here are the _____ and the memo.
4. 你的意思是汇率经常在变。
   Do you mean it changes _____?
5. 是的，外币的兑换率每天都在上下浮动。
   Yes, the exchange rates _____ every day.
6. 好像支票更合适。
   It sounds like cheques have a more _____ rate.
7. 但兑换这笔外币,您得另付0.75%的手续费。
   But you have to pay 0.75% _____ on this money exchange.
8. 我还有大约1500元人民币还没有用完。
   I've got about RMB ¥1,500 _____.
9. 您能把我这些钱再兑换成美元吗？
   Can I _____ it back into US dollars?
10. 我可以将其中一部分换成美元，另外一部分作为纪念品带回国吗？
    Can I change some of them back into American dollars, and take some away to my home as a _____?

Conversation 5: Encashing a Traveller's Cheque

George Brooke: Excuse me. Can you encash these Canadian dollar traveler's cheques of George Brooke.

Bank Clerk: Certainly. How much do you want to cash?

George Brooke: Only six hundred Canadian dollars to meet my living expense before the remittance comes. Here are the cheques.

Bank Clerk: Would you mind showing me your passport?

George Brooke: Certainly. Here it is.

Bank Clerk: It's a banking practice that traveler's cheques must be countersigned at the bank when you cash them. I'm afraid you'll have to sign here again.

George Brooke: All right. What rate are you giving today?

Bank Clerk: The buying rate for notes is 550 yuan for 100 Canadian dollars. With traveler's cheques a quarter percent interest charges will be deducted from the proceeds after conversion.

George Brooke: Well, how much can I get in RMB currency?

Bank Clerk: Let me see. It comes to RMB 2,475 yuan. Here are your money and exchange memo. Keep them well. You'll need the memo if you have some RMB left and have to convert it back into foreign currency upon leaving China.

George Brooke: Thank you for the information.

Bank Clerk: Not at all.

Vocabulary Assistant

encash 兑换
traveler's cheques 旅行支票
remittance 汇款
countersign 会签

42 UNIT 3 FOREIGN EXCHANGE

8 Complete the following conversations.

1. Clerk: Hello. ___(1)___ ?

Customer: Yes, please. I've just ___(2)___ in China and I want to ___(3)___ American dollars ___(4)___ RMB.

Clerk: All right. How much ___(5)___ ?

Customer: ___(6)___ US dollars first. What is today's ___(7)___ ?

Clerk: Well, today's ___(8)___ is RMB ¥723 to one hundred American dollars. You ___(9)___ on the Electronic Rate Board over there.

Customer: Thank you. ___(10)___ back soon.

2. Customer: Excuse me, Miss. Can you help me?

Clerk: Yes?

Customer: I want to change some Dollars into Renminbi.

Clerk: ___(1)___ ?

Customer: Let me see. Five hundred dollars.

Clerk: ___(2)___ ?

Customer: Yes, I've got my passport.

Clerk: OK. Would you please write down on this form ___(3)___ (兑换金额) ___(4)___ (全名) in capital letters, your ___(5)___ (永久住址), your ___(6)___ (国籍), and your ___(7)___ (护照号码) here?

Customer: OK.

Clerk: Let's see, five hundred pounds altogether.

Customer: Exactly. Here you are.

3. Customer: Excuse me, but is this where you exchange foreign money for RMB yuan?

Clerk: Yes, Madam. ___(1)___ ?

Customer: I want to have some dollars changed into RMB yuan.

Clerk: All right. ___(2)___ ?

Customer: Five hundred dollars.

Clerk: ___(3)___ ?

Customer: Forty one hundreds, and the rest in tens, please.

Clerk: Here is your cash.

Customer: Thank you very much.

FOREIGN EXCHANGE UNIT 3

 Listening exercises

■ **Listen to the following sentences and choose the best answer to each of the sentence you have just heard. Each of the sentences will be only read once.**

1. A. The two currencies are different both in name and in value.
   B. The two currencies are the same in name and different in value.

2. A. If the exchange rate of GBP/USD is 1/1.8723, the exchange rate of USD/GBP is the reciprocal of it.
   B. If the exchange rate of GBP/USD is 1/1.8723, the exchange rate of USD/GBP is the same as that.

3. A. The US company has to exchange dollars for pounds to make settlement for the goods imported from UK.
   B. The US company must exchange some pounds for dollars before the transaction is made.

4. A. The foreign exchange market operates much the same like other financial markets.
   B. There's no physical market place such as stock exchanges for the foreign exchange transactions.

5. A. Payments in international trade are often made in the currencies of the seller's countries as they expect.
   B. Companies can use the currency of their own country to make the purchase directly in other countries.

6. A. Once importing goods from other countries you can use the currency of your own country to make the purchase.
   B. The international trade makes merchants use foreign currencies rather than their own.

7. A. A customer wants the sum of GBP to be transferred as soon as possible.
   B. A customer wants to make a spot transaction by buying US dollars for pounds.

UNIT 3 FOREIGN EXCHANGE

8. A. No, impossible.
   B. That will be troublesome.
   C. Yes, if it can be proved true.
   D. There is no such a case.

9. A. You should carry money with you when traveling abroad.
   B. You'd better carry travelers' cheques when traveling abroad.
   C. You are recommended to travel with foreign currency.
   D. When you travel, you'll have to carry enough money in a travelers' cheque.

10. A. I always confuse the difference between the buying rate and the selling rate.
    B. The buying rate and the selling rate are always a problem.
    C. It is proper for me to differ the buying rate from the selling rate.
    D. The buying rate is just the selling rate.

■ **Listen to the following conversation from a woman and a man, after each conversation there will be a question or a few questions. Find out the correct answer to the question you have heard. Each conversation will be read once.**

Conversation 1
1. A. 880 yen.
   B. 794 yen.
   C. 719 yen.
   D. 888 yen.

Conversation 2
2. A. Dollar.
   B. Mark.
   C. Franc.
   D. Swiss franc.

Conversation 3
3. A. USD 508.09.   B. USD 58.9.
   C. USD 500.89.   D. USD 50089.
4. A. RMB 8.2639/USD. B. RMB 8.3629/USD.
   C. RMB 8.0639/USD. D. RMB 8.6239/USD.
5. A. RMB 1,431.95.   B. RMB 4,131.95.
   C. RMB 3,141.95.   D. RMB 1,131.59.

Conversation 4

6. A. Counter No.12. B. Counter No.6.
   C. Counter No.15. D. Counter No.16.
7. A. 700 yuan. B. 600 yuan.
   C. 650 yuan. D. 750 yuan.
8. A. The customer. B. The airport.
   C. The bank. D. None of the above.

■ **In this section, you will hear a long passage, at the end of the passage, some questions will be asked on what you've just heard. The passage and the questions will be spoken only once. After each question, there will be a pause. During the pause, you must read the four suggested answers marked A, B, C and D, and decide which is the best answer.**

1. A. He should come to the foreign exchange market to buy or sell currencies.
   B. He should find the counterpart to complete the transaction.
   C. He should go to require his agent to do the business for him.
   D. He should enter the trade with the bank's dealing department.

2. A. By phone. B. by mail.
   C. By ticket. D. By signature.

3. A. In the bank's dealing department.
   B. In the bank's operations department.
   C. In the back room of the company.
   D. In the manager's office of the bank.

4. A. Expected changes in macroeconomic activity.
   B. Growth in gross domestic product.
   C. Expected inflation rates.
   D. Specific place of a market.

5. A. 30, 90, 180 days.
   B. 30, 60, 180 days.
   C. 1, 2, 3 months.
   D. 1, 2, 3 years.

10 Make conversations with the information given below, taking into account the logical relationship of the content.

1. The customer needs to exchange US dollars for RMB.

Clerk	Customer
Greetings	Convert US $ into RMB
How much	200 US dollar/Today's rate
1:7.23	How much RMB
Passport	Denomination?

2. A bank clerk helps a foreigner to change back his/her remnant RMB into foreign currency he/she wants.

Clerk	A foreign traveller
Greetings	
Right here	Exchanging department
Amount	Change RMB back into pound
Exchange memo/passport	RMB 375.58
Reconversion memo/check farewell	Correct.

3. A foreigner comes into a branch of Bank of China to buy a traveller's cheque.

A bank clerk	A customer
Greetings	Buy a traveller's cheque
Which traveller's cheques	American Express
Denominations	Ten hundreds, twenty fifties, thirty
Sign a cheque	twenties,
One percent of total amount of purchase	and rest tens
US $3,030 altogether	Cost of cheques
Thanks	Thanks

11 Make conversations according to the cases given below.

Case 1
Mr. Johnson goes to the Dealing Department of Guangzhou Branch, Bank of China. He wants to make a 28 days forward contract with the bank because he needs to make the payment in US dollars to the American exporter.

Case 2
Mr. Johnson meets Professor William at the airport. He talks with his teacher of the financial situation of China and the change in exchange rates of Renminbi against US dollars.

Case 3
Mr. Johnson is the manager of an import company. He goes to the bank to consult with an expert about methods of hedging exchange risks.

Case 4
Mr. Johnson goes to the bank to inquire about foreign exchange rate.

Supplementary Reading

Futures

The first important thing to realize about foreign currency futures is that when you have a futures contract, you do not own foreign exchange. A futures contract instead represents a pure bet on the direction of price (exchange rate) movement of the underlying currency. What this means is that the futures price is not a monetary amount you pay to anyone.

Rather, the futures price is the variable about which you are betting. You can bet either that the price will go up or that it will go down. If you buy a futures contract (go along), and the futures price goes up, you make money. If the futures price goes down, you lose money. Thus if you total FX portfolio consisted of a long position in FX futures, you would be betting that the price would go up. If you sell a futures contract (go short) and the futures price goes down, you make money. If the futures price goes up, you lose money.

Options

Currency options may have two kinds of value, intrinsic value and time value. If and to the extent that an option would currently be profitable to exercise, it is said to have intrinsic value. In the case of a call, if the spot price is higher than the option exercise price, the option has intrinsic value. In the case of a put, if the spot price is less than the option exercise price, the option has intrinsic value. Such options are said to be 'in-the-money'. If the opposite is true of either calls or puts, they have no intrinsic value and said to be 'out-of-the-money'. For example, if the spot price for the Euro is $0.43, a Euro 40 call—the strike price—has intrinsic value of $0.03/Euro, whereas a Euro 40 put has no intrinsic value. Time value is what traders are willing to pay above the intrinsic value. Time value evaporates as the maturity date nears and is zero at expiration date.

A buyer of an option pays a premium for the option—paid in advance by the buyer of an option. In the over-the-counter market, premiums are quoted as a percentage of the transaction amount. For listed options, they are quoted in currency units. The total premium is the amount of the option in units times the premium.

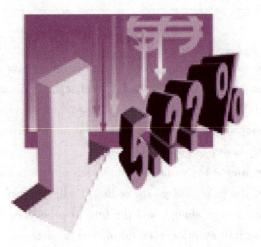

Unit 4

Bank Cards

AIMS

- Inquiring about a debit card
- Applying for a card
- Using a credit card
- Cashing with a foreign credit card
- Reporting a loss of a credit card

Information bank

Today, more and more people in the world are using credit cards instead of money to buy the things they need. Almost anyone who has a steady income and a continuous work record can apply for a credit card. There are many credit cards available: American Express, VISA, and Master Card are some of the most popular.

If you have a credit card, you can buy a car, eat a dinner, take a trip, and even get a haircut by charging the cost to your account. In this way, you can pay for purchases a month later, without any extra charge. Or you may choose to make your payments over several months and pay only part of the total amount each month. If you do this, the credit company, or the bank that sponsors the credit card, will add a small service charge to your total bill. This is very convenient for the customer.

With the credit card in your wallet or purse, you don't have to carry much cash and worry about losing money through carelessness or theft. The card user only has to worry about paying the final bill. This, of course, can be a problem, if you charge more than you can pay for. In the recent years, credit cards also appear in China. The Great Wall credit card and the Peony credit card are the pioneer cards sponsored by the Bank of China and the Industrial and Commercial Bank of China, respectively.

Many of us believe that it will only be a matter of time before credit cards replace cash and checks for both individuals and businesses.

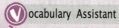

ocabulary Assistant

American Express 美国运通卡 VISA 维萨卡
Master Card 万事达卡 sponsor 发行

Introduction of a Debit Card

The debit card deposit is defined as one that does not have a definite term, which is based on the current passbook account opened in the bank. It can't be overdrawn. With one current passbook, only one debit card can be opened. You can apply for the debit card without any guarantee.

The functions of the card include deposit or withdrawal, account transferring between the cards, inquiry of the remaining amount, modification of password and consumption on the POS, etc. The cardholder can report loss, freeze, cancel the report of loss, cancel the freeze of the debit card. All these don't influence the use of the basic account.

Debit card deposit is the most basic and conventional method of bank deposit. A client may make deposits or withdrawals at any time. For its free and flexible use of funds, the debit card deposit is taken as the basis of clients' financial asset managements.

Aside from the functions of deposit and withdrawal, a debit card deposit account also has the following functions:

1. To apply for a debit card with which you may handle such banking services as withdrawals and transfer on an ATM, and consumption at the specially engaged shops;
2. To handle the salary payment service on agency;
3. To apply for a telephone banking service;
4. To make an automatic banking.

A debit card may be issued to you at the same time at any savings office after you transact the deposits and deposit a certain amount of cash (RMB 1 yuan at least) at the card issuing institution.

Vocabulary Assistant

debit card 借记卡　　　　　　overdraw 透支
guarantee 担保　　　　　　　POS (point of sales) 消费终端
conventional 常规的　　　　　financial asset managements 理财活动
specially engaged 特约　　　　automatic banking 通存通兑

1 Answer the following questions briefly.

1. What functions does a debit card have?
2. How to apply for a debit card?

Conversation 1: Inquiring about a Debit Card

Clerk: Could you tell me something about your Peony Debit Card?
Customer: Yes, of course.
Clerk: What service advantages does a peony card possess?
Customer: Oh. First of all, we have interconnected our service offices throughout the country. In more than 320 card-issuing cities, there are over 28,000 savings offices and 100,000 special units.
Clerk: How can I get the benefits from a personal debit card?
Customer: First of all, it saves more money to use a credit card than to use cash. So it is very helpful for families to finance. In addition, the card-issuing offices will count interests for the deposits with the debit card.
Clerk: Is it convenient to use?
Customer: Of course. Any ATM provides 24-hour online self services. It is very convenient to do cash withdrawal, accounts checking, cipher amending and funds allocating, etc.
Clerk: Can I buy things with it?
Customer: Yes, you can. A slight sweep over the POS terminal with your Peony Card and several punches on the keyboard will effect your payment for consumption immediately.
Clerk: That's good.

Vocabulary Assistant

interconnect 联网   special units 特约单位
online self services 自助服务   cipher 密码
funds allocating 划拨资金

2 Translate the phrases into English.

1. 借记卡
2. 信用卡
3. 信用额度
4. 授权
5. 透支
6. 发行
7. 兑换水单
8. 宽限期

■ Introduction of Credit Cards

Credit cards are instruments issued by banks to customers (card-holders) to enable them to acquire goods, services or currency (where regulations allow) on credit.

First, the customer will be provided with a card carrying a line of credit that, ranging from several hundred to several thousand dollars, varies according to the credibility of the customer.

Then, the customer can obtain goods or services by showing his/her card to a store, a hotel or a restaurant that has a pre-arrangement with the issuing bank to accept credit cards. Having examined the validity of the card, the supplier will complete a sales slip. The following information will then be processed to the slip together with the credit card through an imprinter supplied by the issuing bank:

the customer's account number and name,

expiration date of the card, and

the merchant's account number and name.

Finally, the customer has to sign the sales slip which is then compared with the signature on the card. In some cases, the card issuing bank may approve the exceeding of each sale amount above the card ceiling limit.

After the sale or service, the merchant will return the card and a copy of the sales slip to the customer, keep another copy for the file and send a third to the issuing bank for reimbursement within three business days after the transaction date.

On the other side, the customer will monthly receive a bill from the bank for payment of his/her purchase. Usually, he/she is allowed a grace period of 25 days.

Vocabulary Assistant

credibility 信用额度   validity 有效性
sales slip 签购单据   imprinter 压卡机
expiration date 到期日   reimbursement 追索
grace period 宽限期

Conversation 2: Applying for a Card (1)

Clerk: Good morning, sir. What can I do for you?

Customer: Good morning. I want to apply for a personal RMB Credit Card issued by your bank. Can you explain how to get it?

Clerk: All right. But may I have a look at your identity card, please?

Customer: Yes, of course. Here you are.

Clerk: Good. Please take it back. Now let me have some details about your personal creditworthiness, such as your monthly salary and other professional income. Of course all this information is kept strictly confidential.

Customer: To be frank with you, I'm now engaged in a high technical position. So I have a fixed salary income of RMB 8,000 yuan every month, which is paid into your bank. I think my salary qualifies me for consideration of a RMB card.

Clerk: Ok. In consideration of your salary, you have quite a good credit standing at present. But I'm afraid you are required to provide a guarantee by your company.

Customer: Oh, yes. A guarantee is required. And what documents do I need to supply?

Clerk: For a personal card, we also need a copy of your identity card.

Customer: No problem, I think.

Clerk: As for the concrete procedures, please go to the clerk at Counter No.5 for service.

Customer: Thank you very much.

Vocabulary Assistant

creditworthiness 信誉   confidential 保密的

Conversation 3: Applying for a Card (2)

Clerk: Good afternoon, sir. Can I help you?
Customer: Yes. I want to have a Peony Card from your bank, but I don't know what kind of cards is best for me.
Clerk: Well, we have a big Peony Card family, including Peony Credit Card, Money-link Card, Peony Debit Card, Peony International Card, Peony Special Card, etc.
Customer: What is Money-link Card?
Clerk: It is a versatile card that links a lot of business together.
Customer: "Versatile"? What does that mean?
Clerk: You may either make deposits and withdrawals at any savings office or make transfers and inquiries at any ATM with this card.
Customer: Anything else?
Clerk: With this card, you may also enjoy services like consumption at POS terminals of all special merchants, payroll service and payment for power and gas, etc.
Customer: Oh, it's convenient for me.
Clerk: By the way, it has a matched passbook.
Customer: That's just what I wanted.

Vocabulary Assistant

Money-link Card 灵通卡   versatile 多用途的
payroll 工资   power 电
gas 煤气

---

3 **Read the following sentences and decide them true or false. Write T for true and F for false.**

(　　) 1. The debit card can't be overdrawn.

(　　) 2. You should provide a guarantee if you want to apply for a debit card.

(　　) 3. The credibility of a customer is in relation to his or her salary income.

(　　) 4. Should a credit card be overdrawn, the cardholder should repay the outstanding balance without any delay.

Conversation 4: Using a Credit Card

Clerk: Good morning.
Customer: Good morning. I've opened a Peony Card account recently. Now I want to cash some money, how can I do it, please?
Clerk: You can use it to draw money from the ATM, but the withdrawal amount is limited within RMB 1,000 yuan each time. You can also use it at the counter to get much more money, if you want.
Customer: For what amount do you need authorization?
Clerk: For any amount exceeding the line of credit, we'll have to.
Customer: How about paying my expenses with the card?
Clerk: You don't need to get authorization if your expenses are in line with the credit given by the issuing bank.
Customer: OK, I see. Thank you for your assistance.
Clerk: You're welcome.

Vocabulary Assistant
cash 取现
the line of credit 信用额度

Conversation 5: Cashing with a Foreign Credit Card

Clerk: Good morning. Can I help you?
Customer: Good morning. This is the first time I've traveled in China. Could I cash some money with my Master Card?
Clerk: Yes, we can do it for you after we contact the Master representative office for authorization.
Customer: Then, how about the service charge?
Clerk: It's 4% of your withdrawals. But I have to remind you that there's only one time you can draw cash from our bank within a day, no matter whether your requirement is accepted or not.
Customer: You mean I'll have to come here another day if my requirement is refused one day?
Clerk: Exactly. But another point to be mentioned: you can only cash amount equivalent to RMB 1,500 yuan or more each time.
Customer: Ok. Thank you for your explanation.
Clerk: Not at all. We're always at your service.

4 Translate the following sentences into English.

1. 您需要填写信用卡申请表格，并提供以下证明文件。
2. 银行会根据您交的保证金数额给您相应的透支额度。
3. 保证金和您的透支额度之间的比例为 10:1。
4. 消费透支您可以享受 20 到 50 天的免息期。
5. 透支利息按每天万分之五计算。
6. 我们会自动从您的卡中扣除手续费 3%。
7. 我需要申请授权，请您稍等。
8. 您的卡在 POS 机上显示通讯故障。
9. 由于两家银行的通讯中断造成我行没有收到您银行发出的授权号码。
10. 我的银行卡被自动提款机吞了。

5 Listening exercises

■ **Spot Dictation:** In this section you'll hear two short paragraphs. There are some words or phrases missing in each paragraph. Each paragraph will be read three times. For the first time you just listen and for the second time, you'll have a break of 20 seconds. During the break, you can write down the missing words or phrases. The third time is for you to check your writing. Now let's begin.

1

The UK Government stated in a White Paper ___(1)___ "A Post Office Giro" published in August 1965 that, ___(2)___ those studies, the Government had concluded that a Post Office Giro, ___(3)___, would be a ___(4)___ addition to the existing media for transmitting ___(5)___. For many people with simple ___(6)___ and no bank accounts, ___(7)___, run by a familiar institution, for the ___(8)___ of bills, the sending of money and, if described, the ___(9)___ of their pay.

2

The banker must pay cheque ___(1)___ on him by his customer in legal form on presentation during ___(2)___ or within a reasonable ___(3)___ after the bank's advertised closing time at the branch of the bank where the ___(4)___ is kept, provided that (a) the customer has there sufficient ___(5)___ to his credit, ___(6)___, and (b) there are no legal bars to payment. The ___(7)___ to honor cheques is the most important of the banker's duties. The breach of this duty may ___(8)___ the banker in a claim for ___(9)___.

Complete sentences: In this part you will hear 6 sentences. Each sentence will be read twice. For the first time you just listen and for the second time, you'll have a break of 10 seconds following each sentence. During the break, try to complete the sentences according to what you have just heard. Please watch your spelling.

1. A credit card is a plastic card to be used upon presentation by the cardholder to _____.
2. Credit card customers are given _____.
3. Banks normally set different credit lines _____.
4. Every time the cardholder uses a credit card for purchasing _____.
5. Each month the cardholder receives a statement from the bank, _____.

6 Match the following terms with their respective explanations.

credit card	amount of money by which a bank account is overdrawn
cipher	card that allows its holder to buy goods and services on credit
credit rating	secret writing in which a set of letters or symbols is used to represent others
overdraft	assessment of how reliable somebody is in paying for goods bought on credit
credit-worthy	accepted as safe to give credit to, because reliable in making repayment

7 Translate the following sentences into Chinese.

1. Banks offer account statement on a monthly basis to facilitate your wealth management.
2. Different saving accounts can be opened with the debit card in our bank, which renders convenience of deposits and withdrawals, avoiding the trouble of many passbooks and deposit certificates.
3. All types of the credit cards issued by our bank measure up the international standard and combine the RMB and USD account into one card that can be accepted around the world.
4. The application forms are available in every branches of our bank, and can also be downloaded from our websites.

Conversation 6: Report a Loss of a Credit Card

Customer: Excuse me, madam, I lost my credit card this morning and I'd like to report the loss now.

Clerk: Take it easy, sir. Please show me your passport.

Customer: Here you are. Well, can you have a quick check and see if there's any withdrawal or charges made on my card?

Clerk: What's your number, please?

Customer: Here it is.

Clerk: Please wait a moment. Let me check it for you. Well, sir, there is no withdrawal record on the account, and I don't find any expenses record on it, either. Usually it's impossible for one to use a card falsely. Don't worry about it.

Customer: That's good. I hope so.

Clerk: Now please fill out the application for reporting the loss.

Customer: All right. But how long will it take to have a new one?

Clerk: In three days. And we'll charge you RMB 70 yuan for your report of the loss.

Customer: No problem. Here you are. Thank you.

Clerk: You're welcome.

8 Complete the following conversations.

1. A: Hello, may I ___(1)___ some money with the Visa Card?

   B: Yes, please show me your ___(2)___.

   A: Here it is.

   B: Very well. We can ___(3)___ a certain sum of money ___(4)___ your credit card. How much do you want to ___(5)___?

   A: Is it possible for me to ___(6)___ US $500?

   B: Yes, that can be ___(7)___.

   A: Please ___(8)___ it for me. This is my passport.

   B: Very well. Please fill in this ___(9)___ memo.

2. A: Could you ___(1)___ my Master Card?

B: Yes, of course. How much do you want to ___(2)___?

A: US $1,000.

B: According to the Authorization Center's rule of the Master Card, every encashment must be ___(3)___ by the Center no matter how much the amount is.

A: Is that so? How long does it take to ___(4)___ the encashment?

B: About one day.

A: OK, please ask the center for US $1,000. I'll come back tomorrow morning.

B: All right. Please fill in this ___(5)___ and see you tomorrow.

3. A: For what amount do you need authorization?

B: For the amount exceeding ___(1)___, we will have to.

A: How about the ___(2)___ for the services available in other cities?

B: The service charge is 0.1% of the cash amount to be deposited, while 1% of the amount to be withdrawn.

A: Can a transfer be done in other cities?

B: Of course, but a service ___(3)___ will be charged for that.

A: Is there any other fee?

B: Yes, there's ___(4)___ commission required by the issuing bank.

4. A: Good morning, sir. I'd like to cash my personal checks ___(1)___ by American Express Card.

B: ___(2)___ would you like to cash?

A: ___(3)___ US dollars.

B: I'm sorry, sir. You can't cash so much according to the ___(4)___ Center's rule of AE Card. Its maximum amount cannot ___(5)___ five hundred US dollars.

A: Really? Then may I have four hundred US dollars ___(6)___ instead of five hundred?

B: Certainly. Please fill out this ___(7)___ slip. And your ___(8)___, please.

A: OK. This is my ___(9)___. By the ___(10)___, do I have to pay any charge?

B: No, sir. Here is your money and your ___(11)___. Please check them.

Listening exercises

Direction: Listen to the following conversation from a woman and a man, after each conversation there will be a question. Find out the correct answer to the question you have heard. Each conversation will be read once.

1. A. On his card. B. On the goods.
   C. On a sales slip. D. On the invoice.

2. A. They are different. B. They are the same.
   C. They are similar. D. They are reversed.

3. A. The credit limit. B. The monthly statement.
   C. The overdraft. D. The way of repayment.

4. A. Immediately after the statement is received.
   B. Within the time limit.
   C. Within a month.
   D. At any time.

5. A. The credit line will be lower than usual.
   B. The credit line will be higher than usual.
   C. The credit line will be as usual.
   D. The credit line will be indefinite.

6. A. $2,350. B. $3,460.
   C. $4,700. D. $1,110.

7. A. A simple interest. B. A rate of 5%.
   C. A rate of 0.05%. D. A compound interest.

8. A. You should have enough money in your bank account.
   B. You should use it to pay for goods and services.
   C. The card should be debited to a current account.
   D. No credit is involved.

9. A. A POS terminal. B. A computer. C. A network. D. An ATM.

10. A. Cheque cards. B. Credit cards. C. Debit cards. D. Smart cards.

■ **Listen to the short passage and choose the best answer to the question you have heard after each passage. You will hear the passage only once.**

Passage One

1. A. Cash machines. B. Credit cards.
   C. Tellers' cages. D. Clearing systems.

2. A. Cards. B. Credit and Debit cards.
   C. Check stands. D. Personal checks.

3. A. Card readers. B. Computer connection.
   C. Tellers' cages. D. Personal checks.

Passage Two

1. A. Supermarkets. B. Gas stations.
   C. Stores. D. Newspaper stands.

2. A. Current account. B. Deposit account.
   C. Savings account. D. Personal loan account.

3. A. Secure. B. Portable.
   C. Durable. D. Golden.

10 **Make conversations with the information given below, taking into account the logical relationship of the content.**

1. A bank clerk is telling Mr. William something about Peony Credit Card.

Clerk	Mr. William
Peony card	Want to have a card
Money-link card	What is a... card?
Links a lot of business	That's great
Make deposits and withdrawals	Anything else
ATM, POS terminals	Just what I wanted
Convenient	

2. Mrs. Allen wants to cash money with her Visa Card in a bank.

Clerk	Mrs. Allen
How much	US $1200
The rule	How long?
One day	OK.
Cash slip	Tomorrow
Of course	Identification

3. A bank clerk helps a customer to use ATM.

Clerk	Customer
Insert card	Have a trouble
PIN number	How to use...?
Press number	Can you explain it to me?
Enter the amount required	I see.
A maximum RMB ¥1,000	Thank you

11 Make conversations according to the cases given below.

Case 1
Mr. Johnson comes to Guangzhou Branch of Bank of China, enquiring about the credit card because he wants to issue a Great Wall credit card. Mr. Zhang, the manager of the Credit Card Department, gives him reception and they are talking about the details of the bankcards.

Case 2
Mr. Smith is at a check stand of a store to pay for his purchases with his credit card, but he is told his card can't be used because his credit limits have been used up.

Case 3
Ms. Green lost her bank card, she comes to Beijing Branch of China Construction Bank, reporting the loss.

Case 4
Ms. Bush wanted to withdraw some money in an ATM, but her card was stuck by the ATM. She comes to the bank asking for help.

Supplementary Reading: The Great Wall International Card

Great Wall International Card is an indispensable pass for your (or your friends' or relatives') international activities like traveling abroad, studying abroad, business trips, investigations and exchanges, etc. What the card offers you is an easy and free life beyond borders.

▪ Universal Card

- **Free to spend and easy to withdraw cash in 256 countries, 19 million merchants**

- Great Wall International Card, made by international standard, is accepted by over 19 million VISA or MasterCard merchants in 256 countries and regions; with the card, you may make your spending for shopping, traveling, traffic and hotel accommodation. It can be used to obtain cash at member banks, or at ATMs marked with [PLUS] or [CIRRUS] throughout the world.

▪ Convenient Card

- **Cash withdrawal for spending and automatic currency exchange ensure a delightful world tour**

- In whichever country where you want to make payments or withdraw cash, the bank will effect settlement in the same currency as that deposited in your card, since the local currency is automatically exchanged at the rate quoted by the International Credit Card Organization. You will enjoy a pleasant global tour without regard to the currency of the country where you pay the bill.

▪ Fashionable and Flexible Card

- **Consumption before repayment, plus a 50-day interest-free credit period, gives you much flexibility for arrangement by yourself**

- Great Wall International Card is a credit card featuring consumption before repayment. There's no need for prior deposits; rather, the Bank will authorize a line of credit appropriate to your credit status, within which the cardholder may make payment or withdraw cash, or enjoy successive spending or withdrawals. The card supplies the revolving credit and offers an interest-free repayment period up to 50 days. If you pay up the credit in this period, the Bank will levy no interest or charges. Repayment options provided by the Bank include voluntary, automatic and minimum repayment.

Unit 5 Intermediary Services

AIMS

- Renting a safe deposit box
- Payroll account service
- Charge agency service
- Commission insurance
- E-banking service

Information bank

Commercial banks perform many functions, some central to their main role in the economy and others more peripheral. Although lending and deposit taking have been the epicenter of commercial banking, the last few years have witnessed a general surge in both the types and the volume of bank services. This surge has been induced in part by government deregulation, but most importantly by competitive pressures.

The three main functions of commercial banks are interrelated: the creation of money, accomplished through lending and investing activities; the holding of the deposits; and the provision of a mechanism for payments and transfer of funds. They all relate to the critical role in the overall management of the flow of money and credit through the economy.

In addition, intermediary services are offered primarily to draw customers by providing complete money management and ancillary services through a single institution. Some of these services, such as settlement, trust management, leasing, agency service, E-bank service, bank card, factoring and safe deposit box, guarantee service as well as personal finance arrangement, may themselves be profitable.

A bank in China, acting as an agent, currently provides safe deposit box; banking@home, which is a new generation of personal Internet banking integrating banking, investment, and financing services; fee-based businesses such as paying fees, giving pay packets, handling stock fund transfer service, handling securities trading settlement, handling insurance service. All these are intermediary services of the bank.

Safe Deposit Box Service

Safe deposit box is a kind of service rendered by the bank that keeps valuables for the renter in the form of renting a safe deposit box. Usually safe deposit boxes are metal compartments stored within the bank vault. This arrangement gives the customer both control over access to the stored valuables and privacy.

A renter aged 18 or above may apply for renting a safe deposit box against his or her valid credentials (for a unit renter, with the seal of the unit and signet of its legal representative affixed), filling in the Application for Renting Safe Deposit Box, and voluntarily signing a Box Renting Contract with the bank.

Vocabulary Assistant

renter 租户
privacy 隐私
application 申请文
legal representative 法人代表
vault 保险库
credentials 证件
valuables 贵重品

1 Retell the main points for a safe deposit box in your own words.

Point 1:

Point 2:

Point 3:

2 Select the answer that correctly completes the sentences.

1. Safe deposit box is a kind of service rendered by the bank that keeps valuables for the _____.
   A. rich   B. banker   C. clerk   D. renter
2. In future, money will be in the form of _____.
   A. cash
   B. notes and coins
   C. electronic money
   D. paper gold

3. A bank should sign _____ for customer's payroll agency service.
   A. an entrustment agreement
   B. a loan agreement
   C. a passbook
   D. a guarantee letter
4. _____ is a new generation of personal Internet banking integrating banking, investment, and financing services
   A. Banking@home
   B. Payroll agency
   C. Insurance
   D. Credit card
5. You should have a _____ when you use e-banking.
   A. passbook
   B. debit card
   C. specimen signature
   D. password
6. _____ is a kind of transfer settlement service in which the bank collects as agent of fee collectors fees from their users.
   A. Bill payment service
   B. Deposit service
   C. Insurance
   D. Bank card

Conversation 1: Renting a Safe Deposit Box

Customer: Good morning, sir! Can I rent a safe deposit box in your bank?
Clerk: Yes, madam. You can rent safe deposit boxes in our bank for safekeeping your precious assets.
Customer: How much is the rental fee, per month, please?
Clerk: It depends on the size. We have got three sizes of boxes. What size do you want, madam?
Customer: I'm not sure, but I'm going to put in it some securities and jewelry, what size do you think is suitable?
Clerk: I think a small size will do.
Customer: How much do you charge for renting a small one?
Clerk: We would charge you 80 yuan for one year and 80 yuan for keys.
Customer: Well, I'll rent it for one year.
Clerk: Very well, madam. May I have your signature here?
Customer: Certainly. Thank you.
Clerk: It's my pleasure.

Vocabulary Assistant

safe deposit box 保管箱   safekeeping 保管
rental fee 租金   securities 证券
charge 收取

Conversation 2: Payroll Account Service

Customer: Hello, Mr. Wang. What is the payroll agency service of your bank?
Clerk: Well, based on entrustment agreement, our bank may pay the employees' salaries for any corporations.
Customer: That's great. What payment methods do you provide?
Clerk: We have your real-paid salaries entered into your employees' real-name accounts in compliance with your instructions.
Customer: Is there any alternatives?
Clerk: We may make payment in cash, that is to say, the employees get their salaries directly at the counter of our bank, or the employees' salaries are transferred to any appointed current savings accounts.
Customer: Then which method is suitable for our corporation?
Clerk: We shall make various payments for your needs based on different conditions of your corporation.
Customer: We'll sign the agreement with you tomorrow.
Clerk: Thank you for selecting our bank.

 ocabulary Assistant

payroll agency service 代发工资业务
entrustment agreement 委托协议
real-name account 实名账户

3 Translate the phrases into English.

1. 中间业务
2. 代理业务
3. 委托业务
4. 代理保险业务
5. 电话银行
6. 手机银行
7. 网上银行
8. 银证通
9. 工资账户
10. 工资存折

4 Match the following terms with their respective explanations.

commission	banking transaction that income is gained by providing services
discount	a person who is trusted to manage a trustor's property
dividend	the amount paid or payable, for an insurance policy
premium	a part of a company's profit that is divided among the people who have shares in the company
fee banking	to deduct or subtract from a cost or prices
fiduciary	a fee or percentage allowed to a sales representative or an agent for services rendered

5 Listening exercises

■ **Spot Dictation:** In this section you'll hear two short paragraphs. There are some words or phrases missing in each paragraph. Each paragraph will be read three times. For the first time you just listen and for the second time, you'll have a break of 20 seconds. During the break, you can write down the missing words or phrases. The third time is for you to check your writing. Now let's begin.

1

___(1)___ has radically changed the way customers can do banking. Before-banking, checking an ___(2)___ required the customer to either go to customer service or the ___(3)___. Now, there are many methods available. For example, ___(4)___ banking which gives access to a broader range of services. These services include changing account details like address, and ___(5)___, ___(6)___, arranging ___(7)___ on direct debits, and performing ___(8)___.

2

___(1)___ and social insurance welfare business is a business whereby any ___(2)___ institution of ICBC conducts batch ___(3)___ hrough the advanced computer networked system, automatically transfers relevant ___(4)___ into a ___(5)___ account designated by a ___(6)___, and pay his/her salary on behalf of the ___(7)___ /institutional unit or pay his/her social insurance welfares on behalf of the social insurance ___(8)___.

■ Complete sentences: In this part you will hear 6 sentences. Each sentence will be read twice. The first time you just listen and the second time, you'll have a break of 10 seconds following each sentence. During the break, try to complete the sentences according to what you have just heard. Please watch your spelling.

1. This would reduce their _____ and improve the operational efficiency.
2. You will leap from the conventional finance management to the era of _____.
3. However, without the appropriate security measures, people will hesitate at paying their money _____.
4. The agency _____ by transfer is an efficient, safe and expedient mode.
5. That's because the ICBC has joined in the _____ International Organization in Feb.,1990.
6. Any depositor can pay public _____ and other expenses due at any networked savings office of ICBC.

Conversation 3: Charge Agency Services

Customer: Good morning, Xiao Wang!
Clerk: Good morning, Mr. Brown!
Customer: Will you please tell me what the charge agency service is?
Clerk: You may entrust us as an agent to pay the charges of your water, power, coal gas, telephone, etc. Then you will have nothing to worry about.
Customer: That's great. But how can I have it?
Clerk: Please fill out the Application Form of Entrustment Agreement for Charges with a copy of your ID card and your Charge Card number.
Customer: OK. Is that all right?
Clerk: All right. You should also provide your Current One-for-All passbook or credit card.
Customer: This is my passbook of your bank. Here it is.
Clerk: Be sure that you have enough money in your account.
Customer: I remember.
Clerk: You'll enjoy yourself with the charge agency services through our bank next month.

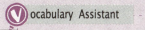
Vocabulary Assistant

current one-for-all passbook 活期一本通

Banking@home

Banking@home is a new generation of personal Internet banking integrating banking, investment, and financing services. It has 12 functions and 58 sub-functions, and is able to meet the needs of multi-level clients for various financial services and provide highly safe and individualized services for you. You can make account inquiry or inter-account transfer, self-help registration card addition, self-help sub-accounts linkage and other operations on all your accounts (including deposit book, money-link card, Elite Club account, quasi credit card, credit card and business card account) registered at the Internet banking or conduct intra-bank remittance, inter-bank remittance and batch account transfer.

Toll station

It provides payment agent services for mobile phone fee, local telephone fee, Internet fee, tuition, etc., and all-roundly meets various payment needs of the clients. The clients at different regions can also enjoy the payment services with different local features.

Personal financing

To meet the needs of the clients for sustaining property appreciation and enable the clients to control their own properties at any time or place, "Personal Financing" provides various financing services with unique features for you, i.e. designing financing plans, applying for financing services, entering into various financing agreements, tailor-making financial information, pre-engaging services, etc.

Vocabulary Assistant

Money-link card 灵通卡　　　　　　　toll station 缴费站
Elite Club account 理财金账户　　　　quasi credit card 准信用卡
batch account transfer 批量转账　　　pre-engaging services 预约服务

6 Retell two types of Banking@home in your own words.

Type 1:

Type 2:

Conversation 4: Commission Insurance

Customer: Excuse me. Can I transact Bank-Insurance Link business in your bank?
Clerk: Yes, you can.
Customer: How can I buy an insurance policy?
Clerk: You should make a choice of the insurance companies, the insured amount and the insurance period by yourself.
Customer: I prefer a policy of Bonus-for-Thousand-Happiness of Ping An Insurance Company.
Clerk: All right. Have you got a current account in our bank?
Customer: Yes, I have got a "Current One-for-All" passbook. Here you are.
Clerk: Please fill out the application form of insurance with the amount and period on it. Write your ID card number clearly.
Customer: I will... Is that so?
Clerk: Pass me your ID card, please. I'll check them up.
Customer: Here it is.
Clerk: No problem. Here is your insurance document and your card. You will receive a policy from Ping An Insurance Company next month.
Customer: Thank you very much.
Clerk: You are welcome.

ocabulary Assistant

Bank-insurance link 银保通
Bonus-for-Thousand-Happiness 千禧红

7 Select elements from columns A, B and C to make at least five sentences. Be sure that the sentences you form make sense.

A	B	C
(1) The bank	(1) have to open	(1) safe-deposit boxes for rent.
(2) A customer	(2) may enjoy	(2) the box before customer
(3) The bank workers	(3) has got	(3) e-banking services
	(4) can provide	(4) agency insurance
		(5) personal finance service

72 UNIT 5　INTERMEDIARY SERVICES

8　Listen and complete the following conversations, each conversation will be read three times.

1. A: Good morning, sir. _____(1)_____?
   B: Good morning. I'm a customer of your bank. I've heard that your bank has opened a service called _____(2)_____.
   A: Oh, yes. It's a deposit account that links to your _____(3)_____.
   B: I see.

2. A: Let me show you around the service center of _____(1)_____, telling you the services available to the customers now.
   B: Thank you very much.
   A: Well, here you can see, this service center has been designed for three different departments—_____(2)_____, a reception house and a business management office to meet the different requirements of the customers.
   B: Yes, the conditions and environment here seem to be _____(3)_____. But what can I do when I need your service?
   A: You can have _____(4)_____ from any one of the clerks here.

3. A: What services do you offer?
   B: You can read the balance of your account and the result of transactions, get information about interest rates, kinds of deposit, _____(1)_____ of foreign exchange set by the bank, sell or buy foreign exchange or _____(2)_____ etc.
   A: It sounds interesting. I may do my personal finances whenever I want.
   B: Yes, _____(3)_____. It is very convenient for the customers.
   A: Thank you for your explanation.
   B: You are welcome.

4. B: Please fill out the _____(1)_____ with the amount and period on it. Write your ID card number clearly.
   A: I will.... Is that so?
   B: Pass me your ID card, please. I'll _____(2)_____.
   A: Here it is.
   B: No problem. Here is your insurance document and your card. You will receive a policy from Ping An Insurance Company _____(3)_____.

5. A: Good morning! Can I make my mobile phone funded through your bank?

B: Yes. Will you fund it in cash or through your savings account?

A: I don't think I have an _____(1)_____ for charge with you, and I'll pay it in cash this time.

B: OK! May I know your mobile phone number?

A: _____(2)_____.

B: How much do you fund it?

A: 500 yuan. Here it is.

B: Here is the _____(3)_____ for you to sign.

A: Sign it here?

B: This is the receipt of charge for you. Keep it well, please.

A: I will.

Conversation 5: E-banking Service

Clerk: May I help you, sir?

Customer: Yes. I want to know something about your e-banking service, could you tell me?

Clerk: OK. If you have a personal computer connected to our e-bank through the internet, you can have the personal or company banking services from our bank, and make payment on the internet.

Customer: But I wonder if it is safe to do that?

Clerk: Don't worry. If you enter the net, you're requested to input your password. That's a protection.

Customer: I see.

Clerk: Thanks. Just a moment, please. I'm now doing the transfer for you.

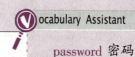

password 密码

9 **Listening exercises**

■ **Listen to the following sentences and choose the best answer to each of the sentence you have just heard. Each of the sentences will be only read once.**

1. A. The minimum charge is $20.   B. The minimum charge is $40.
   C. The minimum charge is $30.   D. The minimum charge is $35.

2. A. We'll charge 5% interest on it.   B. We'll pay 5% interest on it.
   C. We'll charge 3% interest on it.   D. We'll charge 3% interest on it.

3. A. The phone number doesn't coincide with the one you give us.
   B. The card number doesn't coincide with the one you give us.
   C. The account number doesn't coincide with the one you give us.
   D. The code number doesn't coincide with the one you give us.

4. A. You are requested to provide your passport.
   B. You are requested to input your password.
   C. You are requested to provide your passbook.
   D. You aren't requested to input your password.

5. A. I want to put some securities and valuables in it.
   B. I want to rent a safe deposit box.
   C. I want to put some stocks and bonds in it.
   D. I want to put some securities only in it.

6. A. Besides insurance, you can also get more or less interests.
   B. Besides insurance, you can also get more or less dividends.
   C. Besides insurance, you can also get more or commissions.
   D. Besides insurance, you can also get more or less goods.

7. A. It will mature two months from now.
   B. It does not mature until now.
   C. It will mature one month from now.
   D. It doesn't mature now.

8. A. It will be credited to your account automatically.
   B. It will be debited to your account automatically.
   C. It will be credited to your stock account directly.
   D. It will be debited to your stock account directly.

9. A. What size do you want to rent? B. What account do you want to open?
   C. What card do you want to use? D. What's the yearly rental fee?

10. A. Our bank is open everyday from 8:00 a.m. to 5:00 p.m.
    B. Our bank is open everyday from 8:00 a.m. to 3:00 p.m.
    C. Our bank is open everyday from 8:00 a.m. to 4:00 p.m.
    D. Our bank is open everyday from 8:00 a.m. to 6:00 p.m.

■ **Listen to the following conversations from a woman and a man, after each conversation there will be a question. Find out the correct answer to the question you have heard. Each conversation will be read once.**

1. A. 95580. B. 95888. C. 95588. D. 95858.

2. A. Bank Link. B. Securities Link.
   C. Stock Link. D. Bank-Securities Link.

3. A. Not less than RMB 300, 000 yuan. B. Less than RMB 300, 000 yuan.
   C. Not more than RMB 300, 000 yuan. D. More than RMB 300, 000 yuan.

4. A. At the bank. B. At home.
   C. On internet. D. At insurance Co.

5. A. Dividend. B. Deposit amount.
   C. Policy amount. D. Deposit interest.

6. A. He wants to apply for a credit card. B. He wants to deposit money.
   C. He wants to open an account. D. He wants to pay the electricity charge.

7. A. 70. B. 68. C. 2. D. 17.

8. A. The insurance agency service.
   B. The telephone deducting agency service.
   C. The wage account service.
   D. The gas agency service.

9. A. 120,000. B. 27,000. C. 2,700. D. 12,000.

10. A. Passbook. B. Card number.
    C. Password. D. Account number.

UNIT 5 INTERMEDIARY SERVICES

■ Listen to the short passages and choose the best answer to the question you have heard after each passage. You will hear the passage only once.

Passage One

1. A. Open an account (basic account or settlement account) with the BOC.
   B. Deposit some money with the BOC.
   C. Open an account of foreign exchange with the BOC.
   D. Deposit some foreign exchange.

2. A. At the head office of the Bank of China.
   B. At the foreign exchange department.
   C. At the loan department.
   D. At the local office of the Bank of China.

3. A. Internet agreement.
   B. Application form.
   C. Loan agreement
   D. Bank card.

Passage Two

1. A. ICBC.   B. BOC.   C. ABC.   D. BBC.

2. A. 120,000.   B. 130,000.   C. 140,000.   D. 150,000.

3. A. refund   B. deposit   C. loan   D. collection

10 Make conversations with the information given below, taking into account the logical relationship of the content.

1. A clerk helps a new customer with a safe deposit box.

Clerk	Customer
Safe deposit boxes for rent	I wonder
Depends on the size	Rental fee
On the rack of the desk	Put some securities and jewelry
A small one	Where can I have it?
It is in the vault	

2. A clerk helps a businessman to transact e-bank services.

Clerk	Businessman
What can I do for you?	I need e-banking.
Provide a range of e-banking services.	Could you give me more details?
Check balance, transfer money, get some information	It's so convenient.

3. Mr. Zhang wants to know commission insurance.

Mr. Zhang	Clerk
Commission insurance	Bank-insurance link
What can I benefit from it?	Dividend-participated insurance
Difference between deposit and dividend-participated insurance	Deposit interest is fixed
	Dividend depends on operation result

11 Make conversations according to the cases given below.

Case 1
A customer comes to Shanghai Branch of the Bank of China. He asks for renting a safe deposit box offered by the bank. Make a conversation between the bank clerk and the customer.

Case 2
Mr. Li is an accountant in a company, he is talking to a bank clerk about the payroll account service. Then they sign an agency agreement for payroll.

Case 3
Miss Zhang wants to buy a policy of Bonus-for-Thousand-Happiness of Ping An Insurance Company through a bank, a clerk named Li Ming receives her.

Case 4
Mr. Li works in a foreign-funded firm, he comes to a bank in order to know about the personal finance management. Make a conversation between the bank clerk and the customer.

Supplementary Reading: Agency Service

A bank, acting as an agent, currently provides such fee-based businesses as paying fees, giving pay packets, handling stock fund transfer service, handling securities trading settlement and handling insurance services. All these are intermediary services of the bank.

1. Bill Payment Service   Bill payment service is a kind of transfer settlement service in which the bank collects as agent of fee collectors (such as postal, power, gas and water supply departments) fees from their users. All the fee collectors and their users shall open current accounts with the agent bank. On every day of fee collection provided in the agreements, the bank regularly debits the accounts of the users with the amounts listed in the fee collection sheets of the collectors and brings them to the credit of the accounts of the collectors, and also takes commissions according to the number of payments by the users. The clients may also pay such fees, say, fixed telephone charges, mobile phone charges, traffic violation fines, insurance premiums, etc., in cash across the bank counters.

2. Automatic Deposit Service   Automatic deposit service is a kind of service in which the bank grants with the trust of state organs, public institutions and enterprises pays directly to their staff members and workers through their current accounts opened with the bank. The handling procedures are as follows: after consultations between the bank and the pay issuer, the latter shall fill in and give a letter of authorization for pay giving on commission to the bank, each staff member of the pay issuer shall open a current account with the bank who in turn issues to them passbooks or ATM cards with which they may withdraw their deposits. This kind of business changes the traditional practice of clients and is more convenient for the clients as it changes the practice of "use before depositing" to "use after depositing".

3. Commission Insurance   Bancassurance service is available now from a bank, an agent for insurance companies, such as Ping An. A client may complete the whole range of insurance operations from effecting insurance and paying premiums to getting policy and preservation at a savings outlet of the Bank of China.

4. Selling and Redeeming Book-entry Treasury Bonds on Commission   All savings outlets of the bank sell and redeem book-entry treasury bonds on commission.

5. Transfer Service For Security Company   Currently, the bank's main agency services for stock trading include banking-securities transfer service and stock trading settlement service on commission.

Unit 6 Remittance

AIMS

- Inward remittance
- Outward remittance
- Telegraphic transfer
- Cashing a term draft
- Collecting bills
- Discounting a bill of exchange

Information bank

Remittances are part of a bank's international services. The remitting bank, at the request of a remitter, sends the required funds to a payee or beneficiary by the means instructed by the remitter, through a paying bank (its overseas branch or its corresponding bank). Remittances are divided into two categories, inward and outward. An inward remittance is where a foreign bank sends funds to a domestic bank with an instruction for the bank to pay the funds to the payee. An outward remittance is where a domestic bank sends funds to its overseas branches, subsidiaries or corresponding banks with an instruction for the receiving bank to pay a certain amount to the nominated payee. Inward and outward remittances are usually carried out by a mail transfer (M/T), demand draft (D/D), or telegraphic transfer (T/T). The T/T and the D/D are the most common methods used. The T/T is the quickest and most efficient remittance method available.

You can conveniently and swiftly remit your foreign exchange fund to any account of other cities or foreign countries. You can select a method from T/T, M/T and D/D on the basis of your own needs. Your relatives and friends in other cities or foreign countries can remit the foreign exchange funds to the bank who will safely and timely send the funds to you.

ocabulary Assistant

payee 收款人	beneficiary 受益人	corresponding bank 代理行
inward 汇入	outward 汇出	domestic 国内的
subsidiary 子公司	nominated 特定的	M/T 信汇
D/D 票汇	T/T 电汇	

International Remittance-Inward & Outward

International Remittance-Inward

■ **How to Timely Receive Proceeds of Remittance from Abroad?**

The client shall open a current account in foreign exchange with the receiving bank or its subsidiaries, and then inform the remitter abroad of the account number, the name of the account holder (in standard Chinese phonetic alphabet), the name of the depository bank, its address, and the SWIFT CODE.

■ **Handling Methods of the Bank when the Inward Remittance Currency Is Different from the Currency of Your Account**

If the currency of inward remittance is different from the currency of the inward remittance account you designates, say, an inward remittance is in Canadian dollar while your account is a US dollar account, it will be entered into the account after the proceeds are converted into the US dollar according to the exchange rate for the current day. If the inward remittance is in Renminbi, it cannot be converted into a foreign currency but entered direct into the account; if the inward remittance is in a foreign currency, it can be entered into a Renminbi account after conversion.

International Remittance-Outward

■ **Tariff for Personal Outward Remittance**

● Commissions: One per thousand of the amount remitted, with the highest at RMB 250 and the lowest at RMB 20.

● Spread charge: about 3% of the amount remitted for cashing foreign banknotes (no such charge for spot exchange).

● Telegraphic charge: RMB 150 yuan (RMB 80 for a remittance to Hong Kong and Macao regions).

■ **Relevant Provisions of the State Administration Exchange Control Personal Outward Remittances of Foreign Exchange Used as Expenditures under Current Account:**

1. If spot exchange less than USD 10,000 or equivalent is remitted outward in a lump sum from an account of personal spot exchange deposit, or cash foreign banknotes less than USD 2,000 or equivalent are remitted outward in a lump sum from foreign banknote holding or from an account of personal foreign banknote deposit, the outward remittance procedures may be followed directly at the bank.

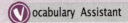

Vocabulary Assistant

phonetic alphabet 拼音字母
converted 兑换   tariff 费率
provisions 规定   lump sum 大额

2. If spot exchange of more than USD 10,000 (USD 10,000 inclusive) but less than USD 50,000 is remitted outward in a lump sum, or foreign banknotes valued at more than USD 2,000 (USD 2,000 inclusive) but less than USD 10,000 or equivalent are remitted outward in a lump sum, an application shall be filed with the local state administration of exchange control by presenting the certificate materials for current account expenditures and related customs declaration for inward foreign exchange or bank documents or bank certificates. After examination of truthfulness by the state administration of exchange control, outward remittance procedures may be followed at the bank against the certificate of approval issued by the state administration exchange control.

3. If spot exchange valued at USD 50,000 (USD 50,000 inclusive) or more is remitted outward in a lump sum or equivalent, or foreign banknotes valued at USD 10,000 (USD 10,000 inclusive) or more are remitted outward in a lump sum, the local administration exchange control shall report it to the State Administration of Exchange Control for examination and approval, and the outward remittance procedures may be followed at the bank against the certificate of approval issued by the local state administration of exchange control.

1 Answer the following questions briefly.

1. How many parties are involved in the remittance? What are they?
2. What are the ways of remittance? Which one is the quickest?

Conversation 1: Inward Remittance

Clerk: Can I help you?
Customer: Well, my friend sent me 1,000 US dollars through Bank of America, New York three days ago. I want to know if the money has arrived.
Clerk: Let me check it for you. Please tell me your name and show me your passport.
Customer: My name is Petersen, and here is my passport.
Clerk: Oh, here are 1,000 US dollars for you from New York. Will you withdraw the cash?
Customer: Yes, I will.
Clerk: Mr. Petersen, here you are, 1,000 US dollars. Please count it.
Customer: That's it. Thank you.
Clerk: Not at all. Hope to see you again.

2. Translate the phrases into English.

1. 电汇
2. 信汇
3. 票汇
4. 汇款单
5. 付款行
6. 汇款人
7. 收款人
8. 托收
9. 兑现
10. 远期汇票
11. 贴现
12. 承兑
13. 拒付
14. 追索

Conversation 2: Outward Remittance

Customer: I'd like to send some money to my sister in California. And I hope she can get it as soon as possible. Can I wire the money to her?

Clerk: Yes. We have a telegraphic transfer service for outward remittance. We can make arrangement to send it by cable if you like. But first of all, we want to see your personal certificates and documents presented by you to the bank.

Customer: What are they, please?

Clerk: Your passport with a valid visa, a certificate for your personal income, or the other original documents for receipt if you have.

Customer: So I see, the foreign exchange control system is applied in your country. But now I want to be assured the remittance by telegraphic transfer would be fast, wouldn't it?

Clerk: Yes, either a regular or an urgent cable would be faster than a check by post or a mail transfer from us to her bank. As your request is so urgent today, we can manage to send it by SWIFT.

Customer: Thank you very much.

Clerk: It's my pleasure.

Vocabulary Assistant

wire 电汇 visa 签证
original documents 原始凭证

3 Match the following terms with their respective explanations.

remit	exchange sth for cash
draft	sending money to a person or place
negotiate	written order to a bank to pay money to sb
cash	get or give money for cheques, bonds, etc.
drawer	buy or sell a bill of exchange for less than it will be worth when due
dishonor	a person who draws a cheque, etc.
discount	refuse to cash a cheque, etc.

Conversation 3: Telegraphic Transfer

Clerk: Hello! May I help you, sir?

Customer: Yes, I hope so. I want to send some money to New York. Is it handled here?

Clerk: Yes, it is. How much would you like to remit?

Customer: Ten thousand yuan in RMB.

Clerk: How would you like to remit, sir?

Customer: I beg your pardon?

Clerk: Do you want to remit the money by air or by cable, sir?

Customer: By cable, please. How much do you charge for a cable transfer to New York?

Clerk: We charge you RMB ¥150 for the cable. As for our handling commission, it depends on how much you send.

Customer: How does it count?

Clerk: We will charge you 0.1% of the amount you remit for bank commission. But the minimum charge is RMB ¥20 while the maximum is RMB ¥200.

Customer: Thank you for your explanation. I'd like to remit it by cable.

Clerk: That's all right. Please fill out this remittance slip.

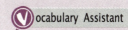
Vocabulary Assistant

remittance slip 汇款单

4 Translate the following sentences into English.

1. 我想给在纽约的朋友汇款 5000 美元。

2. 您需要填写一张汇款单。

3. 我想查一下汇款有没有到账。

4. 请出示您的护照好吗？

5. 请问哪种汇款方式最快？

6. 请问汇款到东京最快需要几天？

7. 您能帮我兑现一张远期汇票吗？

8. 请问托收这张汇票需要多长时间？

9. 请问汇款 5000 美元到法兰克福的手续费是多少？

10. 电汇是所有汇款方式中最快的一种。

5 Listening exercises

Spot Dictation: In this section you'll hear two short paragraphs. There are some words or phrases missing in each paragraph. Each paragraph will be read three times. For the first time you just listen and for the second time, you'll have a break of 20 seconds. During the break, you can write down the missing words or phrases. The third time is for you to check your writing. Now let's begin.

1

As a general rule, a bill of exchange must be ___(1)___ presented for payment, and if it is not so presented, the ___(2)___ and endorsers are discharged. This is a ___(3)___ rule. There are many cases where the ___(4)___ of a bill has lost his rights completely as ___(5)___ the drawer and endorsers, merely because he ___(6)___ observe the very strict rules relating to presentment for payment. The acceptor, ___(7)___ remains liable on a bill accepted generally, even if it is not presented for payment.

2

A foreign exchange account is an account to ___(1)___ money sent from abroad and a foreign ___(2)___ account is one to deposit and withdraw cash in ___(3)___. When you send money from different types of accounts, the ___(4)___ are different. For example, if you want to ___(5)___ some money from your foreign exchange amount, there're two kinds of fees: ___(6)___ and ___(7)___. Whereas, if you use a foreign cash account, there is an extra charge for ___(8)___ cash abroad.

■ **Complete sentences: In this part you will hear 5 sentences. Each sentence will be read twice. For the first time you just listen and for the second time, you'll have a break of 10 seconds following each sentence. During the break, try to complete the sentences according to what you have just heard. Please watch your spelling.**

1. If there is no direct banking relationship between the remitting bank and the beneficiary bank, the remitting bank _____.
2. The beneficiary bank is entitled to credit the money wired from abroad to the client's account based only on _____.
3. A bank draft _____ which is issued by a bank.
4. A foreign exchange account is _____.
5. A bill may be drawn upon any person, whereas a check must _____.

■ **Collection from Abroad**

■ **Handling Procedures**

1. Presenting valid credentials of the principal; if the principal is absent, present valid credentials of his own / her own and the agent.
2. The name of the beneficiary on the bill must be consistent with the name on the valid credentials of the beneficiary. If the name of the beneficiary on the bill is written in Chinese phonetic alphabet, it must conform to the name of the credentials; if not, in view of the interest protection of the beneficiary, a certificate issued by the working unit or sub-district executive office, or a law firm or notary office is necessary so as to confirm the real name of the beneficiary.
3. When collection is handled, a collection application in duplicate shall be filled in, with one copy returned to the client for serving as the certificate for proceeds obtaining.

■ **Time Needed for Bill Collection**

● In accordance with the geographical locations of the drawee and the different places for currency clearing, bill collection usually needs about 40 days. It needs a longer time for some places, say, about 60 days for collection of USD bills whose payments are made in Canada as they need to be cleared in the United States.

■ **Bills for Which Only Collection Is Permitted** (Personal Checks Abroad)

● For a personal check in foreign currency, regardless of different amounts, the actual proceeds are collected from the drawee bank abroad according to the trust of the client before related deposit and withdrawal procedures can be handled at the requests of the client.

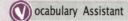

credentials 证件   principal 委托人
geographical 地理的

Conversation 4: Cashing a Term Draft

Customer: Excuse me, may I ask how to cash my term draft?

Clerk: Sure. Would you please show me your draft?

Customer: Here it is.

Clerk: I'm sorry to tell you that your draft can't be cashed right now because it was issued five months ago. There is still one month to go for the expiry date. In order to make payment safe, I think I'd better collect it for you.

Customer: I have no idea of cashing draft. Therefore, I agree with you. But how long will it take to have my draft collected?

Clerk: About one month.

Customer: That's quite a long time. Anyway, please collect for me.

Clerk: So please tell me your telephone number so as to enable us to advise you of the result of collection in time.

Customer: This is my business card. You can call the number on it. Thank you.

Clerk: You're welcome.

Vocabulary Assistant

cash 兑现　　　　term draft 远期汇票
collect 托收

6 Fill in the blanks.

1. According to _____ _____, a traveler's cheque can only be accepted with the buyer himself or herself holding their own _____ _____.
   根据国际惯例，办理旅行支票必须本人出示其有效的护照。

2. The traveler's cheque must be _____ in _____ of the bank clerk.
   旅行支票必须在银行柜台进行复签。

3. A _____ _____ account is an account to receive money sent from _____.
   外币现汇账户是指由境外汇入的款项。

4. If you use demand draft, you will _____ 150 RMB of _____ _____.
   如果您用票汇将节省150元的电报费。

Conversation 5: Collecting Bills

Customer: Can you help me cash this check?

Clerk: Let me see. Oh, I'm sorry, but we can't cash it immediately.

Customer: Why not?

Clerk: You see this is a personal check. If it was a bank's check, we could cash it right now. But for this personal check, we must first send it to the paying bank for collection.

Customer: Then how many days will it take to collect this check?

Clerk: It will take two months.

Customer: Two months? Oh, my God! I can't wait that long. Isn't there any way to make it shorter?

Clerk: Well, we can instruct your bank to send the money by telex after the check's collected. But in that case, you will have to pay the telex charge.

Customer: I don't mind that, as long as it can be cashed earlier. I'm badly in need of money.

Clerk: Well, if you want money urgently and don't mind paying some telex charges, why don't you send a cable and instruct your bank to send the money? We could send a cable for you.

Customer: That's a good idea. Could you do that for me?

Clerk: No problem. If we send a telex message through our New York Office, we might get a return telex tomorrow morning.

Customer: Thank you very much. I appreciate your help.

Clerk: You're welcome.

Vocabulary Assistant

paying bank 付款行   appreciate 感激

Conversation 6: Discounting a Bill of Exchange

Clerk: Bank of China. Can I help you?

Customer: Yes, please. I'd like to get some information about discounting a bill of exchange. Do you know that?

Clerk: Yes, sir. We can handle the discounting of bills of exchange if they meet certain criteria. Can you tell what kind of a bill you have?

Customer: Yes, it's a ninety-day bill for $6,000. It matures about two months from now. I didn't think we'd have to discount it, but I need the working capital right now. How do I discount it?

Clerk: Well, we can discount certain trade and commercial bills and certain trade acceptances in addition to most bankers' acceptances. The discount rate depends on the terms of the bill, the amount, the reputation of the drawee and the drawer.

Customer: Why does it depend on the drawer's reputation or financial status?

Clerk: Well, we discount most bills on a full recourse basis. Should the bill be dishonored, it will be returned on recourse to the drawer.

Customer: I see. Is it difficult to handle the paperwork? I'm not sure just what I should do.

Clerk: Well, the best thing is to come in and talk with our discount officer. He will give you all the information you need.

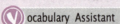ocabulary Assistant

discount 贴现　　　　　　　criteria 标准
working capital 流动资金　　commercial bills 商业票据
acceptances 承兑　　　　　drawee 受票人
recourse 追索　　　　　　dishonor 拒付
paperwork 手续

7 Translate the following sentences into Chinese.

1. Telegraphic transfer, the quickest settlement tool, facilitates the exporters to speed up cash flow.

2. Compared with the letter of credit and collection, the remittance has the characteristics of simple formality and low charge.

3. Inward remittances from abroad represent a mode of financial settlement, by which an overseas remitter transmits payment in foreign currencies to a domestic recipient through a bank.

4. While making an exchange, the draft-holders are required to endorse the draft with their chop or signature on the back of the draft.

8 Complete the following conversations.

1. A: ___(1)___ you tell me where the counter for inward ___(2)___ is?
   B: Yes, here it is. Can I help you?
   A: I have an advice of drawing from Bank of America. I want to know whether the money ___(3)___?
   B: Ok. I'll ___(4)___ for you. Please tell me your ___(5)___ and show me your ___(6)___, please.
   A: My name is Peterson. This is my passport.
   B: Good. Wait a minute. I'll ___(7)___.

2. A: Good morning. I want to ___(1)___ some money to Paris.
   B: No problem. Do you ___(2)___ the money by T/T, M/T or D/D?
   A: Which is the fastest way?
   B: It's ___(3)___. It only takes about two hours.
   A: I'll take T/T. ___(4)___ is the commission?
   B: 20 yuan, please.
   A: Here is the ___(5)___.
   B: Ok. Please sign the ___(6)___ slip.

3. A: May I cash a traveler's cheque here?

   B: Of course. We'd be happy to ___(1)___.

   A: Well, may I ___(2)___ these three cheques of American Express for $100 each? I think that will be enough.

   B: Yes. Would you please countersign them here?

   A: Ok. Here you are.

   B: Could you show me your ___(3)___?

   A: Here it is.

   B: Ok. I will fill in the exchange memo for you now. Why not take a seat over there for a moment?

   A: I would like to. Thanks.

 Listen to the following conversations from a woman and a man, after each conversation there will be a question. Find out the correct answer to the question you have heard. Each conversation will be read once.

1. A. To endorse his cheques.
   B. To show his passport.
   C. To cash some traveler's cheques.
   D. To open a checking account.

2. A. He lost a cheque and the thief cashed it.
   B. He opened an cheque account.
   C. A chief stole the money from the bank.
   D. He cashed the cheque but the money was stolen by a thief.

3. A. The drawee bank will refuse to pay the draft.
   B. The drawee bank will issue another draft to the customer.
   C. The drawee bank will investigate into the case first.
   D. The drawee bank will pay the draft immediately.

4. A. On August 8th.
   B. On August 6th.
   C. On August 7th.
   D. On August 9th.

5. A. How to present the bill for payment.
   B. The presentation of bills for payment.
   C. The solution to the injured drawer.
   D. The payment of the cheque.

6. A. The customer is required to write his name on each traveler's cheque in the presence of the issuing bank.
   B. The customer is required to countersign each instrument in the presence of the correspondent.
   C. The customer is required to countersign each instrument in the presence of the collecting bank.
   D. The customer is required to countersign each instrument in the presence of the bank who buys the cheque.

10 Make conversations with the information given below, taking into account the logical relationship of the content.

1. A bank clerk helps Mr. Smith remit money abroad.

Clerk	Mr. Smith
Greetings	Money to New York
How much?	US $3,000
Fill up	T/T
T/T, M/T, D/D	Passport
Charge	Low

2. A bank clerk helps Mrs. White with the encashment of remittance from abroad.

Clerk	Mr. White
Greetings	Advice of Drawing from Paris
Currency/Amount?	Euro 5,000
Fill in	In figures or in words?
Identification?	Passport
Deduction from	Service charge?

3. Mrs. Smith wants to send some US dollars to her son.

Mr. Smith	Clerk
Outward remittance	How much?
US $2,000 urgent	Which way?
The amount of charge?	By cable?
How long?	A little bit high
Form filled out	Name, address, passport number, etc.

11 Make conversations according to the cases given below.

Case 1
A lady comes to Bank of China. She wants to check her inward remittance. Make a conversation between the lady and the bank clerk.

Case 2
Mr. Smith wants to remit some money to his friend who is now in New York. Make a conversation between Mr. Smith and the bank clerk.

Case 3
Mr. Johnson has got a usance draft from his foreign customer for the purchase of shoes made by the foreign company. He has to accept the draft, so he goes to his bank to ask Mr. Li, Manager of the International Settlement Department, about the acceptance of bills. Make a conversation between Mr. Johnson and Mr. Li.

Supplementary Reading

Inward Collection

Definition

Upon reception of entrustment from the foreign correspondent bank, in accordance with instructions received, the bank collect payment from the importer and deliver the relevant commercial documents to the importer.

There are two types of inward collection. Under D/P terms, import documents are released to the importer upon payment. Under D/A terms, documents are released to the importer against acceptance.

Functions and Features

1) Low Cost-helping the importer to save expense and control cost.

2) Convenient and Simple-easy to operate, convenient and feasible as compared with letter of credit.

3) Little capital occupied-no prepayment is required at the preparation and shipping stage of the exporter so that no capital is occupied, the importer can obtain the documents and dispose the goods upon payment or acceptance.

4) Improve cash flows-under D/A terms, the importer can obtain the commercial documents and dispose the goods upon acceptance of the bill, and the payment can be made after the goods are sold out and cash inflow realized. There is almost no capital occupation, so that liquidity is improved.

International Factoring

Definition

When you accept purchase orders from buyers from foreign countries (or overseas) under the payment terms of O/A, you may worry about the safety of the receivable and need funds. Banks are in the position to protect you from payment risk, to help collect receivables, to provide funding and maintenance services as well.

Functions and Features

Risk guarantee

The bank will pay you 100% of the invoice amount when your buyer is insolvent or default in his payment.

The bank and its partners will remind your buyers to pay on time and enable you to focus on your business development.

Financing

You no longer have to wait until the end of the credit period to receive your money. The bank will fund you against the receivables.

The bank will provide you the regular report on the status of the ledger and enable you to keep fully informed about the performance of your buyers.

Unit 7

Letter of Credit

AIMS

- Types of letters of credit
- Opening irrevocable letters of credit
- Confirming letters of credit
- Extending letters of credit
- Amending and canceling letters of credit

Information bank

A letter of credit, also called an L/C, is a written undertaking by the issuing bank given to the seller (exporter or beneficiary), at the request of the buyer (importer or applicant), to pay at sight or at a future date up to a stated sum of money. The L/C is only good for a stated period of time (through the expiration date) and is payable upon presentation of stipulated documents. The issuing bank is substituting its credit for that of the buyer. The advantage of the L/C is that it minimizes the financial risk to overseas customers. L/Cs may be confirmed or unconfirmed.

Put simply, the letter of credit is a promise by the bank to pay the seller when the seller has met conditions stipulated in the letter of credit. Payment by letter of credit is a kind of bank credit instead of commercial credit.

The feature common to all kinds of L/C is that the buyer arranges with a bank to provide finance for the exporter in the country of the latter on delivery of the shipping documents. On presentation of the shipping documents, the banker will pay the purchase price, normally by paying a sight bill on presentation or by accepting a time bill drawn on the buyer.

1. What is UCP600?

The terms UCP is an acronym referring to the Uniform Custom and Practice for Documentary Credits. It is an internationally accepted legal document that provides guidelines and reference for the bank operations regarding documentary credits. The UCP was developed by the ICC (International Chamber of Commerce) and is updated from time to time. The latest version is ICC Publication No.600, for which it is called UCP600.

2. Why Is It Called a Documentary Credit?

The documentary credit is the most widely used form of letter of credit. When the exporter negotiates payment against a letter of credit with the bank, he has to provide the documents required by the letter of credit. That is why it is called the documentary credit. This is similar to the documentary bill of exchange.

Vocabulary Assistant

the Uniform Custom and Practice for Documentary Credits 跟单信用证统一惯例规则
International Chamber of Commerce 国际商会
documentary credit 跟单信用证

---

1 **Select the answer that correctly completes the sentences.**

1. Will you please remit the extra charges to the Citibank New York _____ our credit?
   A. by   B. for   C. across   D. over

2. Please _____ your bank _____ the establishment of your L/C without delay.
   A. approach, for   B. get in touch, for
   C. approach, so as to   D. get contact with, concerning

3. The stipulations of the L/C should _____ those of the contract.
   A. agree to   B. agree in   C. agree on   D. agree with

4. _____ was developed by the ICC and is an internationally accepted legal document that provides guidelines and reference for the bank operations regarding documentary credits.
   A. Incoterms 2000   B. UCP
   C. WTO   D. ICC

Conversation 1: Types of Letters of Credit

Mr. Oven: Hello! Is this Bank of China? This is Sam Oven speaking, could you help me?

Operator: Hold on, please. I'll call the person to talk with you.

Clerk: Hello. Can I help you?

Mr. Oven: Hello, this is Sam Oven. I want to open a Letter of Credit.

Clerk: Oh, what kinds of credit do you want to open?

Mr. Oven: What are the kinds of Letters of Credit?

Clerk: There are several ways of division. For example, we may divide Letter of Credit into documentary credit and clean credit according to whether it is attached to shipping documents or not. And the former one is frequently used in international trade.

Mr. Oven: International trade? OK, now on mentioning L/C hereinafter, we refer to documentary credit.

Clerk: Certainly. And all credit must state whether they are irrevocable or revocable. The irrevocable L/C could not be modified or cancelled within its validity term unless the concerned parties of the L/C are unanimously agreed to do so.

Mr. Oven: Oh, I think the irrevocable L/C is more suitable for me. Could you help me to open it?

Clerk: Sure, will you come over here? I'll open it for you.

Mr. Oven: Thanks. See you later.

Clerk: See you then.

Vocabulary Assistant

clean credit 光票信用证
shipping documents 运输单据
hereinafter 以下
irrevocable L/C 不可撤销信用证
unanimously 一致地

2 Match the following terms with their respective explanations.

Irrevocable L/C	the beneficiary may collect the purchase price from the bank against sight draft.
Confirmed L/C	the bill of exchange attached by the L/C drawn by the seller should be accompanied with shipping documents.
Clean L/C	the credit is guaranteed by a bank other than the issuing bank.
Sight L/C	the credit can't be amended or canceled without the permission from the beneficiary of the credit.
Documentary L/C	the bill of exchange attached by the L/C is a clean bill.

Conversation 2: Opening Irrevocable Letters of Credit

Charles: Hello, may I speak to Chen Yang?
Chen Yang: Speaking.
Charles: This is Charles, General Bank. Thank you for your timely L/C sent to us.
Chen Yang: That's all right. That's what we should do to promote our co-operation.
Charles: Yes. However, we have observed that it is the practice of your bank to mail only the original copy of your credit, with no other copy to follow.
Chen Yang: We have done it in this way for two years. Is there anything wrong?
Charles: Everything is OK. Chances are that the original might fail to reach us, as the possibilities of miscarriage or having gone astray during transmission.
Chen Yang: Do you have a solution?
Charles: We would suggest that your good bank should send us the original and a copy of the credit issued by first airmail and have another copy sent by next airmail, so that its final arrival might be better ensured.
Chen Yang: Thank you for your suggestion. I'm expecting a better cooperation between us. Bye-bye.
Charles: Bye-bye.

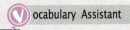Vocabulary Assistant

original copy 正本   miscarriage 误投

3 Translate the phrases into English.

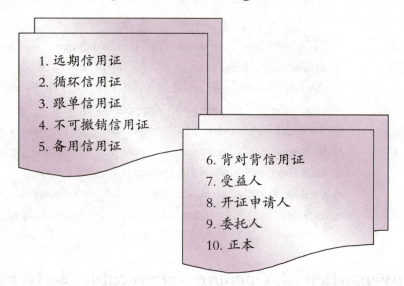

1. 远期信用证
2. 循环信用证
3. 跟单信用证
4. 不可撤销信用证
5. 备用信用证
6. 背对背信用证
7. 受益人
8. 开证申请人
9. 委托人
10. 正本

4 Fill in the blanks with the proper words or phrases given below.

| L/C | down | interest | tie-up |
| 6,000 | concession | deal | sight draft |

Mr. Bush plans to purchase some silk from China. Mr. Bush comes to China and has a talk with Mr. Wang, representative of China Textiles I & E Corporation, Chengdu Branch. They are having a face-to-face discussion on payment.

Wang: In payment terms, would you like to accept ___(1)___?

Bush: I'm sorry. I have to think it over. As you know, the money condition is tight and the bank ___(2)___ is high.

Wang: I understand your position. But this is the first ___(3)___ between us, and I hope we can trade on customary terms, i.e., letter of credit available against ___(4)___.

Bush: Letter of credit at sight indeed costs us a great deal. From the moment to open credit till the time our buyers pay us, the ___(5)___ of our funds lasts about four months. At the moment, I do have some difficulty. Could you make some ___(6)___, say, to accept D/P?

Wang: I would like to bend the rules a little if possible, but we only accept D/P only if the amount is under US $3,000.

Bush: But the amount of this transaction is US $___(7)___. Would you accept payment half by L/C and half by D/P?

Wang: If you can give us a 10% ___(8)___ payment, we can accept your payment terms.

Bush: 10%? That's all right.

Wang: Then that's settled.

Parties Involved In L/C

There are several parties involved in the use of an L/C: the L/C applicant; the L/C beneficiary; the L/C opening bank; the L/C advising bank; the L/C negotiating bank; the L/C paying bank; the L/C confirming bank and the L/C accepting bank. A detailed explanation of the role of the main parties involved in L/C are as follows:

Applicant (the Buyer or the Importer)

The applicant applies to his bank to open a letter of credit for the seller. The bank will normally require the applicant to have sufficient funds on deposit in the bank to cover at least a part of the amount covered by the L/C.

Issuing Bank (the buyer's bank)

The issuing bank is the bank that opens the letter of credit and makes payment against the L/C when it receives the documents required by the L/C. The issuing bank is usually the buyer's bank in the buyer's country.

Advising Bank (the seller's bank)

The advising bank is the bank that is asked by the buyer or the issuing bank to notify the seller of the arrival of the L/C. It is generally in the seller's country and has a business relationship with the seller. And it may provide other services, such as L/C examination, checking the credit of the importer, providing the seller with loans for shipment of the goods and so on.

Beneficiary (the seller or the exporter)

The seller is the beneficiary of the letter of credit. He is entitled to draw the contracted amount from the letter of credit. To get payment, the seller must first obey absolutely the conditions contained in the letter of credit.

Role of the bank

In documentary credit, the banks just deal in documents instead of the goods under contract. A drawback is that the goods actually shipped may not conform to the contract even though the documents provided do conform to the special wording of the documentary credit.

Vocabulary Assistant

applicant 开证申请人 issuing bank 开证行
advising bank 通知行 beneficiray 受益人

5 Translate the phrases into Chinese

1. issuing bank
2. collecting bank
3. insurance policy
4. S/C
5. client
6. paying bank
7. acceptance
8. port of discharge
9. port of loading
10. international practice
11. Invoice
12. freight clause
13. transshipment
14. extension
15. reimbursement

Conversation 3: Confirming Letters of Credit

Mr. Harden: Good morning, Miss Wu.

Miss Wu: Good morning, Mr. Harden.

Mr. Harden: I received your L/C of Feb 2, 2006. There are some items I want to make sure.

Miss Wu: OK, what's that?

Mr. Harden: First, you didn't write in the unit price of the goods.

Miss Wu: $280 for each..

Mr. Harden: Where is the port of discharge?

Miss Wu: The destination is Shanghai.

Mr. Harden: What is the latest date of shipment?

Miss Wu: The shipment should be on or before May 16, 2006.

Mr. Harden: Is transshipment allowed?

Miss Wu: Not allowed.

Mr. Harden: OK, that's all. I hope you make everything clear next time.

Miss Wu: Thank you for your coming and reminding.

Mr. Harden: You are welcome. Good-bye.

Miss Wu: Bye-bye.

Vocabulary Assistant

unit price 货物单价　　port of discharge 卸货港
destination 目的港　　transshipment 转运

In this section, you'll hear two short conversations. There are some words or phrases missing in each paragraph. Each conversation will be read three times. For the first time you just listen and for the second time, you'll have a break of 20 seconds. During the break, you can write down the missing words or phrases. The third time is for you to check your writing. Now let's begin.

Conversation 1

Clerk: Can I help you?
Wu Ming: Yes, I want to ___(1)___.
Clerk: OK. Please ___(2)___ this form first. (After a while...)
Wu Ming: It's done. Is it all right?
Clerk: Let me see, there is something you should make sure. First, you must fill in the ___(3)___. That's the most important of all.
Wu Ming: The amount is $105,000.
Clerk: Second, you should write in details about the ___(4)___, quantity and ___(5)___ of your goods.
Wu Ming: 10 warm air blowers, $10,500 per set.
Clerk: Last, you should specify the ___(6)___.
Wu Ming: I'll call my manager to make it sure. Thank you very much.
Clerk: You are welcome.

Conversation 2

Cao Yang: Hello, may I speak to Brain?
Brain: This is Brain speaking.
Cao Yang: This is Cao Yang. Good afternoon, Mr. Brain.
Brain: Good afternoon.
Cao Yang: I received your L/C No.3687 yesterday. Is it a ___(1)___ or ___(2)___ L/C?
Brain: It is confirmed.
Cao Yang: But the credit is not signed "confirmed", and I can not find the ___(3)___.
Brain: Hold on, I will check it up. (After a while...) Yes, you are right. In accordance with the ___(4)___, it is a "confirmed" credit, and we forgot to ___(5)___ you.
Cao Yang: So I hope you can send us an ___(6)___ as soon as possible.
Brain: Sure. I'll send it to you right now.
Cao Yang: Thank you. Good-bye!
Brain: Bye.

Conversation 4: Extending Letters of Credit

Chen Hao: Hello, can I speak to Xie Ying?
Clerk: Please hold on for a moment.
Xie Ying: This is Xie Ying speaking.
Chen Hao: This is Chen Hao, Wing Lung Bank. We want an extension of your L/C No. 8313.
Xie Ying: I remember we sent it on Feb 22, 2006. There was enough time for the exporter to settle the shipment.
Chen Hao: Yes, but we received it on March 26, 2006, and as the latest shipment date falls on March 29, 2006, only two or three days left for shipment after their receipt of notification, it doesn't seem possible for the beneficiary to effect shipment on or before that date.
Xie Ying: How many days of extension do you think is suitable?
Chen Hao: What about 10 days?
Xie Ying: That's feasible. I'll send you an amendment tomorrow. Good-bye!
Chen Hao: Thanks a lot. Bye.

Vocabulary Assistant

extension 展期　　effect shipment 装船
beneficiary 受益人，一般指出口方

7 Try to make a telephone call according to this business letter to extend the L/C.

Dear Sirs,

As we specified in our S/C SD781, shipment should be made before 9 November, but your letter of credit reached us only today. It is, therefore, impossible for us to effect delivery on time. Please extend the shipment date and the validity of your L/C to the end of November and December 15, 2003 respectively and arrange the amendment to L/C to reach us by 20 November.

We anticipate an early arrival of your amendment advice.

Yours faithfully

Conversation 5: Amending and Canceling Letters of Credit

Xing Bin: Good afternoon, Mr. Zhou.
Zhou Yi: Good afternoon, Mr. Xing. Sit down, please.
Xing Bin: We received your L/C, dated Jan 31, 2002 for $20,000. We want an amendment in it.
Zhou Yi: What's that?
Xing Bin: We want the sentence "Signed by the steamship agent" deleted.
Zhou Yi: Oh, let me see. The purpose of this request is not clear to us, since in the past, in all our credits through you, the same expression was used and there was no difficulty in negotiating the documents.
Xing Bin: Yes, but this time we want the bill of lading to be signed by means of chop instead of the usual manual signature.
Zhou Yi: I see. And that is the usual practice in China for bills of lading to be signed. We have no objection to complying with your wishes.
Xing Bin: Thank you very much. We look forward to our further cooperation. Bye-bye!
Zhou Yi: Bye!

Vocabulary Assistant

bill of lading 海运提单   chop 盖章

8 Complete the following conversation.

A: May I come in?
B: ___(1)___.
A: Good morning, Miss Anna.
B: ___(2)___.
A: I opened the L/C No. 4297 last month.
B: Yes, what's the matter?
A: I regret to say, ___(3)___, I want to cancel the L/C.
B: Oh... The L/C is signed "irrevocable", and the cancellation of the L/C must be authorized by many authorities. First, ___(4)___. It's really a complicated process. We'll notify you at least three days later.
A: So I can cancel it three days later?
B: That's not necessarily the case. ___(5)___, you can cancel it; ___(6)___, the L/C is still available.
A: I see. Thank you. See you.
B: See you then.

9 Listening exercises

■ Listen to the following sentences and choose the best answer to each of the sentences you have just heard. Each of the sentences will be only read once.

1. A. a sight draft B. a usance draft
   C. an overdraft D. a clean draft

2. A. The company changed idea.
   B. The company preferred an L/C to collection.
   C. The company did not want an L/C.
   D. The company applied for documentary collection.

3. A. back-to-back credit
   B. reciprocal credit
   C. documentary credit
   D. stand-by credit

4. A. We'll have the faxed L/C from you.
   B. We can get the L/C through fax.
   C. You'll have the L/C faxed from us.
   D. We'll send the L/C to you by mail.

5. A. The amount has been paid to your Head Office account.
   B. You have credited the amount to our account.
   C. We have received the amount from your account.
   D. Your Head Office account has been debited with the amount.

6. A. Banks will deal with the documentary credit along with the sales comtract.
   B. Banks take no care of the sales contract while dealing with the documentary credit.
   C. The documentary credit and the sales contract are both important to banks.
   D. Banks will care for either the documentary credit or the sales contract.

7. A. To benefit, all the documents are to be combined with the credit.
   B. All the documents are to be made by the beneficiary for the credit.
   C. All the documents are to be made out in conformity with the terms and conditions of the credit.
   D. The beneficiary will make the documents combine with the terms and conditions of the credit.

8. A. Bank extends the validity of the L/C to the customer.
   B. Bank effects the issuance of an L/C to the importer.
   C. Bank offers a financial support to the importer by issuing an L/C.
   D. Bank issues an L/C to make money from the importer customer.

9. A. An irrevocable L/C can not be committed to amendment.
   B. An irrevocable L/C can not be canceled without permission.
   C. An irrevocable L/C can not be canceled or amended.
   D. Neither cancellation nor amendment without permission can be made to the irrevocable L/C.

10. A. You are the advising bank and the possible confirming bank.
    B. You are the beneficiary of the L/C.
    C. You are the advising bank only.
    D. You are required by the beneficiary to confirm the L/C.

■ **Listen to the following conversation from a woman and a man, after each conversation there will be a question or a few questions. Find out the correct answer to the question you have heard. Each conversation will be read once.**

1. A. Invoice.   B. Shoes.
   C. Carriage.   D. Error.

2. A. A month ago.   B. A week ago.
   C. Two weeks ago.   D. Two months ago.

3. A. Bills of lading.   B. Consular invoice.
   C. Insurance policy.   D. Certificate of origin.

4. A. Investment department.
   B. Accounting department.
   C. Settlement department.
   D. Safe department.

5. A. Citibank, New York is one of our correspondent banks.
   B. We can advise this L/C through the Citibank, New York.
   C. We will send the advice of the L/C directly to the beneficiary.
   D. Another bank will be chosen as the advising bank of this L/C.

106　UNIT 7　LETTER OF CREDIT

6. A. Collection Order.　　　　　　　　B. Bill of Lading.
   C. Letter of credit.　　　　　　　　　D. Certificate of Origin.

7. A. The issuing bank.　　　　　　　　B. The bank's correspondent.
   C. The advising bank.　　　　　　　　D. The bank in the importer's country.

8. A. The principal.　　　　　　　　　　B. The remitting bank.
   C. The drawee.　　　　　　　　　　　D. Both A and B.

9. A. In the advising bank.　　　　　　　B. In the exporter's company.
   C. In the issuing bank.　　　　　　　　D. In the importer's office.

10. A. Documentary credit.　　　　　　　B. Documentary collection.
    C. Payment in advance.　　　　　　　D. Open account.

■ **In this section, you will hear a long passage, at the end of the passage, some questions will be asked on what you've just heard. The passage and the questions will be spoken only once. After each question, there will be a pause. During the pause, you must read the four suggested answers marked A, B, C and D, and decide which is the best answer.**

1. A. The buyer.　　　　　　　　　　　B. The seller.
   C. The advising bank.　　　　　　　　D. The issuing bank.

2. A. Dongfang.　　　　　　　　　　　B. Ben.
   C. The correspondent bank.　　　　　　D. The issuing bank.

3. A. A documentary credit.　　　　　　　B. A personal credit.
   C. A standby credit.　　　　　　　　　D. A negotiation credit.

4. A. It is an unconditional payment promise of the issuing bank.
   B. It is a conditional payment promise of the issuing bank.
   C. It is a conditional payment order of the issuing bank.
   D. It is an unconditional payment order of the issuing bank.

5. A. They must state whether they are irrevocable or revocable.
   B. They must state whether they are negotiable or irrevocable.
   C. They must state whether they are transferable or negotiable.
   D. They must state whether they are documentary credits or back-to-back credits.

10 Make conversations with the information given below, taking into account the logical relationship of the content.

1. The customer wants to open an irrevocable L/C with the Bank of China, but their balance of account is not enough.

A customer	A bank clerk
Greetings	Greetings
Open an L/C for our company	What kind of L/C?
An irrevocable L/C at sight	Total amount of the money
RMB 4,000,000 yuan	The balance of your account is not enough
Ask for suggestion	
Think it over	Offer some mortgage
Thank you	You are welcome

2. The customer wants to extend the L/C because the beneficiary can't effect shipment before the fixed date in the L/C.

A customer	A bank clerk
Greetings	Greetings
Extend the L/C	Why? The exporter has enough
But we receive the L/C late	time to effect shipment
	How many days of extension do you
About 10 days	think is suitable?
bye	Ok, it's feasible

3. The customer wants t oamend the L/C because of some mistakes in the L/C.

A customer	A bank clerk
Greetings	Greetings
Amend the L/C	What's that?
We want the sentence "Signed by	Not clear
the steamship agent" deleted	I see, it's practical
We want B/L	
Thank you	

UNIT 7 LETTER OF CREDIT

11 Make conversations according to the cases given below.

Case 1
Mr. Johnson is a young merchant. He is required to issue a letter of credit as the means of payment, but he does not know the procedure of issuance of a credit. So he comes to consult with Mr. Zhang, an expert of the Department of Settlement, Guangdong Branch of Bank of China.

Case 2
Mr. Johnson is informed by his bank that a letter of credit in favor of him has arrived. He goes to the bank and examines the terms and conditions of the credit with the help of Mr. Zhang.

Case 3
Mr. Johnson has shipped goods and obtained all the shipping documents. He goes to the bank to present for payment, but he is refused. He approaches Mr. Zhang and wants to know why and how to deal with it.

Case 4
Mr. Johnson is the representative of a large Chinese manufacturing company. He discusses the modes of payment with bank clerk and asks which mode of payment benefits the buyer.

Supplementary Reading: Procedures of L/C

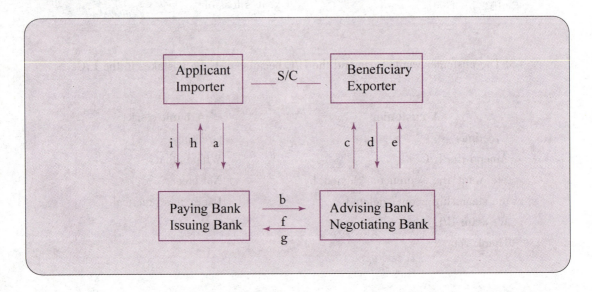

a. The importer applies to a local bank for opening an L/C in favor of the exporter and provides a certain amount of deposit and formality fees.
b. The opening bank sends the L/C opened to the advising bank.
c. The advising bank transfers the L/C to the exporter.
d. After examining the L/C, the exporter delivers the goods according to the stipulations of L/C. After shipment, the exporter makes out a draft and draws up the documents in accordance with the L/C, and delivers them to the negotiating bank within its validity.
e. If the documents are in conformity with the L/C, the negotiating bank will advance the purchase price to the exporter.
f. The negotiating bank transfers the draft and documents to the opening bank or the bank appointed by the opening bank applying for payment.
g. The opening bank will pay to the negotiating bank after examining the documents.
h. The opening bank informs the applicant of the same and asks him to make payment so as to get hold of the shipping documents.
i. The applicant makes payment to get hold of shipping documents, and takes delivery of the goods against the documents.

Unit 8 Insurance

AIMS

- Inquiring about insurance
- Auto insurance
- Home insurance
- Personal insurance
- Cargo transportation insurance

Information bank

As the saying goes, in nature there are unexpected storms and in life there are unpredictable vicissitudes. In daily life, something unforeseen will occur at any time and anywhere, natural calamities and accidents may result in property damage or bodily injury or even loss of life.

Insurance is a necessity for everyone in our society because it provides financial protection against unexpected misfortune.

There are many types of insurance and insurance contracts, such as property insurance, motor vehicle insurance, marine insurance, personal insurance and reinsurance. A licensed insurance agent is a valuable source of information and advice on matters dealing with insurance protection.

When you purchase insurance, you are provided an insurance contract called a policy. An insurance policy is an agreement between you and the insurance company. It describes what is being insured and the conditions under which protection is to be provided. The policy also states the limits of the protection. The insurance company which provides the protection is known as the insurer. The person or business purchasing the insurance is known as the insured or the policy-holder. The insurer and the insured are known as parties to the contract. According to the insurance policy, the insured should pay insurance premium which is a sum of money to the insurer, in return the insurer undertakes to indemnify the insured in the event of loss from an insured risk.

Insurance organizations also employ specialists called actuaries who prepare the data upon which insurance rates are based, and for persons who are interested in law there are many positions in the legal department handling claims against the company.

Principles of Insurance

1. Principle of indemnity is one of the most important precepts for many types of insurance, particularly for property insurance. According to this principle, the insured may not collect more than the actual loss in the event of damage caused by an insured peril. This principle serves to control moral hazards that might otherwise exist.

2. Principle of insurable interest holds that an insured must demonstrate a personal loss or else be unable to collect amount due when a loss caused by an insured peril occurs.

3. Principle of subrogation grows out of the principle of indemnity. Under the principle of subrogation one who has indemnified another's loss is entitled to recovery from any liable third parties who are responsible.

4. Principle of utmost good faith requires a higher standard of honesty is imposed on parties to an insurance agreement than is imposed through ordinary commercial contracts. The principle of utmost good faith has greatly affected insurance practices.

Vocabulary Assistant

principle of indemnity 赔偿原则
principle of insurable interest 可保利益原则
principle of subrogation 代位追偿原则
principle of utmost good faith 最大诚信原则

1 Retell the principles of insurance in your own words.

Principle 1:

Principle 2:

Principle 3:

Principle 4:

2 Select the answer that correctly completes the sentences.

1. _____ is a necessity for everyone in our society because it provides financial protection against unexpected misfortune.
   A. Insurance	B. Security	C. Investment

2. When you purchase insurance, you are provided an insurance contract which is called a _____.
   A. deposit certificate	B. bank card	C. policy

3. The person or business purchasing the insurance is known as the _____.
   A. insurer	B. insured	C. premium

4. The principle of _____ is one of the most important precepts for many types of insurance, under which the insured may not collect more than the actual loss in the event of damage caused by an insured peril.
   A. indemnity
   B. insurable interest
   C. subrogation

5. _____ is paid to the insurer by the inured under the terms and conditions of insurance contract.
   A. The premium
   B. The interest
   C. The dividend

Conversation 1: Inquiring about Insurance

Clerk: Hello. Servicemember's Group Life Insurance office.

Customer: Hello. I'm a full-time member on active duty. I wonder if there's some proper life insurance for me.

Clerk: SGLI, Servicemembers' Group Life Insurance.

Customer: What does SGLI provide?

Clerk: SGLI provides group life insurance. When you die, money will be paid to the person you designate to receive the insurance. The beneficiary can use this money to pay expenses related to your death or invest the money to help replace your salary.

Customer: Who can I designate to be the beneficiary?

Clerk: You may designate any person or any organization. Under the law, you have the absolute right to name and change the beneficiary at any time.

Customer: Good. And how much does SGLI cost?
Clerk: The monthly cost of SGLI is $20.00 for $250,000 of coverage.
Customer: How can I pay?
Clerk: This amount will be automatically deducted from your service pay.
Customer: Thank you very much.
Clerk: It's my pleasure.

Vocabulary Assistant

life insurance 人寿保险　　SGLI 军人人寿险
beneficiary 受益人　　　　invest 投资
coverage 保险

Conversation 2: Auto Insurance

Clerk: Good morning, sir. What can I do for you?
Customer: Thanks. My name is John. I am here to purchase insurance for my newly purchased car.
Clerk: How long have you been licensed?
Customer: About 5 years.
Clerk: Have you had any traffic violation or accident record in the past 3 years?
Customer: No. I've brought my driving record and insurance experience letter from my current insurer of another car.
Clerk: Thank you. They are clean. By the way, if you can let us insurance all of your vehicles, we'll give you a very favorable discount.
Customer: I was thinking of that, since I hear your rates are competitive.
Clerk: You bet. Which year is your new car?
Customer: 2006 Ford Freestar.
Clerk: What's it used for?
Customer: For pleasure or going shopping on weekends.
Clerk: How would you like your car covered?
Customer: What's your requirement for the third party liability?
Clerk: $200,000. But I recommend $1million. Should you cause bodily injury or property damage to the third party, probably the loss will be very great. So I don't think $200,000 provides you an adequate coverage.

Customer: Then $1million please. But I'm wondering whether my own bodily injury is covered suppose the accident is due to my own fault.

Clerk: You are also covered as well as passengers in your car and pedestrians involved. If you are not able to work for more than 7 days because of the accident, we'll pay for your income loss.

Customer: Sounds good. How about the physical damage of the auto?

Clerk: It's not covered unless you insure your car against collision or comprehensive risks. In most cases, a certain deductible applies.

Customer: You mean you can waive the deductible in some cases?

Clerk: Yes. In case your car is stolen, we pay for your actual cash value of your car without requiring the deductible.

Customer: I didn't know that.

Clerk: Before processing your application, let me give you a quote so that you can decide on the coverage.

Customer: Good idea.

Vocabulary Assistant

quote 报价　　rates 费率
third party liability 第三方责任

3 Translate the phrases into English.

1. 保险代理
2. 保险金额
3. 保险费率
4. 汽车事故
5. 人身伤害
6. 免赔额
7. 汽车保单
8. 撞车
9. 翻车
10. 理赔

4 Match the following terms with their respective explanations.

insurance policy	a payment for insurance protection
premium	a person who purchases insurance
the insured	a written agreement between an insurance company and a policyholder
claim	probability calculation of the likelihood of the occurrence of perils on which premiums are based
the law of large numbers	a request for payment
insurer	a person who sells insurance

5 Listening exercises

Spot Dictation: In this section you'll hear two short paragraphs. There are some words or phrases missing in each paragraph. Each paragraph will be read three times. For the first time you just listen and for the second time, you'll have a break of 20 seconds. During the break, you can write down the missing words or phrases. The third time is for you to check your writing. Now let's begin.

1

___(1)___ refers to all kinds of two or more than two wheeled power-driven vehicles. The ___(2)___ of motor vehicle insurance is motor vehicle and ___(3)___ in the main. The former belongs to ___(4)___ category in the narrow sense while the latter falls within ___(5)___. It should be stressed that the above-mentioned third party liability ___(6)___ is ___(7)___ in most countries of the world at present so that the benefit of the victim can be ___(8)___.

2

Application form is also known as ___(1)___. The following are the principle question headings common to most types of motor insurance proposal form: ___(2)___ name in full; Address; ___(3)___; Date of birth; Physical disabilities and ___(4)___; Ownership; ___(5)___; Previous insurance history; ___(6)___; Use to which the vehicle is put. Some insurers stress the application of certain questions to ensure that they obtain the ___(7)___ and conditions which the risk demands and this may be particularly important where the driver of the vehicle has an unsatisfactory record of ___(8)___.

UNIT 8 INSURANCE

■ **Complete sentences: In this part you will hear 6 sentences. Each sentence will be read twice. For the first time you just listen and for the second time, you'll have a break of 10 seconds following each sentence. During the break, try to complete the sentences according to what you have just heard. Please watch your spelling.**

1. You'd be eligible for a more _____ if you had one year's insurance experience.
2. If you insure your car against the third party liability only, _____ of your car doesn't affect the premium.
3. The insured of the auto policy include the driver, passenger and even _____ who are injured by the car.
4. We offer 20 percent _____ to those with 5 years' accident free experience.
5. _____ for the third party liability will pay for the bodily injury and property damage arising from the use or operation of your car.
6. _____ applies if you replace your windshield.

Conversation 3: Home Insurance

Clerk: Is there anything I can do for you, sir?

Customer: Yes, please. I just bought a new house. Could you tell me something about home insurance?

Clerk: Certainly, sir. Fire is a basic risk that any type home policy will cover, but flood is beyond the coverage of many policies. Besides fire, basic risks of a home policy also include lighting, explosion, smoke, falling object, impact by aircraft or land vehicle, riot, vandalism or malicious act, sudden and accidental water damage excluding flood, and windstorm or hail.

Customer: Do I have to buy insurance for my personal property?

Clerk: The home policy covers more than most people think. It covers personal liability happening at your home such as bodily injury you may unintentionally inflict on others. The property portion of the policy consist of four coverages: dwelling building, personal property, detached structure and additional living expenses.

Customer: Additional living expenses?

Clerk: Yes. If an insured peril makes your dwelling unfit for living, or you have to move out while repairs are being made, any necessary increases in living expenses are covered.

Customer: I didn't know that.

Clerk: Even the dwelling building is defined more than the building itself. It also includes the attached structure like the attached garage, permanently installed outdoor equipment, materials intended for use in repair of your dwelling, trees and other plants but the lawn is not included.

Customer: As for personal property, are my autos, computers, lawn mowers covered?

Clerk: Your autos are not covered by the home policy but lawn mowers are. Your computer and your other valuables may need specific personal effect policies. Or else, the home policy only reimburses you a limited amount for their loss or damage.

Customer: Thank you, I've got it.

Clerk: You're welcome.

Vocabulary Assistant

vandalism or malicious act 故意破坏或恶意为
attached garage 连体车库
reimburse 补偿

Personal Insurance

The subject-matter insured of personal insurance involves the personal life and body whereas the insurance perils refer to the living, death, injury, illness etc. Personal insurance usually comprises life insurance, health insurance and accident insurance etc. From the standpoint of the individual, life or health insurance may be defined as a contract, whereby for a stipulated consideration, called the premium, the insurer agrees to pay to the insured a defined amount upon the occurrence of death, disability, or some other specified event.

1. Life Insurance: The chief difference between life and other forms of insurance is that in the latter, the contingency insured against may or may not happen. While in life insurance, the event against death protection is unavoidable sooner or later. On the whole, the prevailing life insurance contracts in the world today are chiefly term insurance, whole-life insurance, endowment insurance and annuity insurance.

2. Health Insurance: Individual health insurance can be classified into two major categories, namely, disability income insurance and medical expense insurance. The former provides periodic payments when the insured is unable to work as a result of illness, disease, or injury. The basic benefit provided is a substitute income to replace at least a portion of the insured's earned income. Medical expense insurance supplies benefits for medical care.

3. Accident Insurance: Personal accident insurance refers to insurance for fixed benefits in the event of death or loss of limbs or sight by accident and / or disablement by accident. The so-called accident must be accidental, unexpected and unintentional.

Vocabulary Assistant

term insurance 定期保险
whole-life insurance 终身保险
annuity insurance 年金保险
disablement 残疾
endowment insurance 两全保险
medical care 医疗

6 Retell the types of personal insurance in your own words.

Type 1:

Type 2:

Type 3:

Conversation 4: Personal Insurance

Clerk: Good morning, sir. What can I do for you?

Customer: I'm leaving for South Africa next month. I will purchase insurance for the trip there.

Clerk: Oh, you are talking of the Personal Accident Insurance for Those Going Abroad. We have just introduced a program that is very fit for you.

Customer: What's the rate?

Clerk: The daily rate is only 0.01%.

Customer: Do you have any requirement for the minimum insurance amount?

Clerk: Yes, that's RMB 10,000 yuan. How much would you like it to be?

Customer: 500,000 yuan. How much should I pay for the insurance if my trip is 30 days?

Clerk: Just a moment, I'll work it out for you. It's 1,500 yuan.

Customer: The premium sounds reasonable. And what are the conditions?

Clerk: Simply put, if you are injured or even die within the validity, of course, we hope such things never happen, we'll compensate for the loss.

Customer: Can I appoint two or more beneficiaries?

Clerk: Sure. But you'd better specify what proportion you want each beneficiary to have.

Customer: How much will you pay if the insured dies?

Clerk: As much as the insurance amount.

Customer: If he or she is injured?

Clerk: It depends on many factors. Here is a detailed brochure which lists indemnity arrangements as well as the risks, insurance conditions, insurance amounts and premium rates.

Customer: Let me have a close study of it, the terms and conditions seem acceptable. Will you write me a policy?

Clerk: Yes, sir.

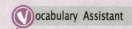

Vocabulary Assistant

compensate 赔偿　　　　indemnity 赔偿
beneficiary 受益人

7 Select elements from columns A, B and C to make at least five sentences. Be sure that the sentences you form make sense.

A	B	C
(1) The premiums	(1) was covered by	(1) exempt from taxation
(2) I'll	(2) is	(2) a whole life policy
(3) The indemnity of this insurance	(3) are guaranteed to	(3) workers' compensation insurance
(4) My injury	(4) issue you	(4) life protection
(5) Term insurance	(5) offers	(5) remain the same for the first ten years

8 Listen and complete the following conversations, each conversation will be read three times.

1. A: Good morning, Miss Chen. _____(1)_____?
   B: Could you tell me where _____(2)_____?
   A: Right here. I'll _____(3)_____ for you.
   B: Thanks a lot.
   A: _____(4)_____.

2. A: Hello. This is Century Insurance Associates, Inc.
   B: What's wrong?
   A: Don't worry. There's nothing wrong. I call to see if you may have some interests in our products.
   B: _____(1)_____?
   A: Employee benefits, major medical / life _____(2)_____, disability income, etc.
   B: Oh, I object to discussing about death and disability in the morning.
   A: _____(3)_____.
   B: I think maybe someone else may have interest in your topic. Bye!

3. A: Hello. This is Pacific Insurance. We specialize in _____(1)_____. Our belief is that all drivers be accepted regardless of record.
   B: _____(2)_____!
   A: But it is true. The motto of our company is that Pacific will when nobody will. And there is no _____(3)_____ for some accidents or violations.
   B: _____(4)_____. Thank you. It seems that that is the very thing I'm looking for.
   A: Pacific will find the very thing to _____(5)_____ our customers' unique demand.
   B: I will think about it. What's your phone number?

4. A: Fire department.
   B: I'd like to speak to someone about a fire I had last night on my farm.
   A: _____(1)_____?
   B: I do. That's why I'm phoning you now.
   A: Alright, sir. _____(2)_____?
   B: It's FM 7680.

5. A: I'm from auto _____(1)_____ department. Are you Mr. Melton?
   B: Yes.
   A: I'm deeply sorry for _____(2)_____.
   B: Thank you.
   A: _____(3)_____?
   B: Greg was in his car with some friends after school. The car was hit by a truck whose driver was drunk and at a high rate of speed. You see that damaged tree?
   A: I see. _____(4)_____.
   B: Thank you. Please handle it for me.

Conversation 5: Cargo Transportation Insurance

Clerk: May I help you, sir?
Customer: Yes. I want to ask something about cargo transportation insurance.
Clerk: Please.
Customer: Can the exporter always insure the goods himself?

Clerk: There may be the cases where a country requires incoming shipments to be insured locally, especially some developing countries. In that case, you can avoid losses by buying special contingency insurance.

Customer: The other day I heard someone speak of Open Cover Insurance. What is it?

Clerk: Open Cover gives you automatic protection on all your shipments. You get fixed conditions and fixed rates, and a maximum limit of protection for a shipment on any vessel. It can save you the trouble of insuring each individual shipment.

Customer: How are the conditions and rates determined?

Clerk: You can negotiate with the insurer to settle the terms.

Customer: What I can't understand is the jargon used in insurance. What was that paragraph I noted in a policy—something like, "Touching the perils which we the insurers are contented to bear and we…"

Clerk: "And we do take upon us in this voyage: they are of the storms, wars, fire, pirates, thieves, jettisons."

Customer: Yes, that sort of stuff.

Clerk: Well, perils of the sea means unusual situations such as storms, running aground—things like that.

Customer: I have learned so much from you. Thanks a lot.

Vocabulary Assistant

incoming shipments 进口货物
contingency insurance 意外事故保险
open cover 预约保险

9 Listening exercises

■ Listen to the following sentences and choose the best answer to each of the sentence you have just heard. Each of the sentences will be only read once.

1. A. The policy number is FM 8976.   B. The policy number is FN 7869.
   C. The policy number is FM 9876.   D. The policy number is FN 7140.

2. A. The premium is $2,000 each year.   B. The premium is $2,000 3 years.
   C. The premium is $2,100 each year.   D. The premium is $2,100 3 years.

3. A. She chooses life insurance.   B. She refuses life insurance.
   C. She chooses health insurance.   D. She chooses medical care insurance.

4. A. Life insurance is a means of shifting financial risks associated with death.
   B. Life insurance is a means of shifting financial risks associated with health.
   C. Life insurance is a means of financial risks associated with health.
   D. Life insurance is a means of shifting political risks associated with health.

5. A. Physical examination is necessary for this program.
   B. Physical examination is unnecessary for this program.
   C. Mental examination is necessary for this program.
   D. examination is necessary for this program.

6. A. Are you confident to handle all these claims?
   B. You cannot handle all these claims.
   C. Do you know about something about these claims?
   D. You have no right to handle all these claims.

7. A. There is charge for accidents.   B. There is charge for violations.
   C. There is charge for cars.   D. There is no charge for accidents.

8. A. This is Tony Smith, sales agent of Timmerman Insurance.
   B. This is John Green, sales agent of Timmerman Insurance.
   C. This is Tony Green, sales agent of Pacific Insurance.
   D. This is Tony Green, sales agent of Timmerman Insurance.

9. A. Can you give me the number of the phone?
   B. Can you give me the number of the policy?

C. Can you give me the number of the door?
D. Can you give me the number of the card?

10. A. This policy doesn't cover the livestock.
B. This policy doesn't cover the stock.
C. This policy doesn't cover the shop.
D. This policy does cover the livestock.

■ **Listen to the following conversations from a woman and a man, after each conversation there will be a question. Find out the correct answer to the question you have heard. Each conversation will be read once.**

1. A. $25,000.   B. $35,000.   C. $250,000.   D. $350,000.

2. A. Any person or legal entity.   B. Herself.
   C. Her parents.   D. Her children.

3. A. 11.   B. 12.   C. 13.   D. 14.

4. A. 5:00 p.m..   B. 6:00 p.m..   C. 7:00 p.m..   D. 4:00 p.m..

5. A. 3-year term.   B. 5-year term.   C. 6-year term.   D. 7-year term.

6. A. The deductible is higher than the premium.
   B. The premium is higher than the deductible.
   C. The higher the deductible, the higher the premium.
   D. The higher the deductible, the lower the premium.

7. A. Computer.   B. Mower.   C. Garage.   D. Auto.

8. A. Unmarried full-time students aged 4—24.
   B. Full-time students aged 4—24.
   C. Unmarried students.
   D. All students aged 4—24.

9. A. AIDS.   B. Suicide.
   C. AIDS and suicide.   D. Property.

10. A. 45.   B. 55.   C. 65.   D. 75.

INSURANCE UNIT 8 125

■ Listen to the short passages and choose the best answer to the question you have heard after each of the passage. You will hear the passage only once.

Passage One

1. A. either life insurance or non-life insurance B. marine insurance
   C. house insurance D. auto insurance

2. A. guarantee their interests
   B. protect policyholders
   C. comply with the law
   D. ensure a solvent standing for the benefit of the public

3. A. Interest.   B. Contract.   C. Premium.   D. Deposit.

Passage Two

1. A. to prevent insurance from becoming a gambling contract
   B. to remove a possible incentive for murder
   C. to mitigate the moral hazard
   D. All of the above

2. A. One can have an insurable interest in property and still not own the property.
   B. Ownership is the only evidence of insurable interest.
   C. Legal liability growing out of contracts establishes insurable interest in property.
   D. Insurable interest is limited to the extent of the pecuniary interest.

3. A. to control wagering with human lives
   B. to reduce the threat of murder
   C. to reduce the threat of willful destruction of property
   D. to increase the moral hazard

10 Make conversations with the information given below, taking into account the logical relationship of the content.

1. A customer is asking for something about home insurance.

Clerk	Customer
Greetings	Bought a new house
Coverage of home insurance	Have no idea about
Fire, gas explosion, water damage	Amount about indemnity
Theft and accident damage	Thanks for
1.5 million yuan per year	

2. A clerk helps a customer to handle medical care insurance.

Clerk	Customer
We provide medical care insurance	Is it difficult to make a claim?
Not at all.	I see.
Completed claim form	Monthly premium
Relevant supporting documents	Pound Sterling
110RMB yuan	Give me an enrollment.
Deposit term?	

3. A customer is asking for compensation, but the clerk thinks it's the customer's fault.

Clerk	Customer
There is nothing we can do for you.	Are you kidding?
In the proposal form	I lost everything.
Inflammable material	I burned my premises with drums.
You said "no"	I will sue you.
Store drums of petrol	

11 Make conversations according to the cases given below.

Case 1
Greg died of a car accident, his father phoned an insurance in which he insured. The clerk named Andy answered and asked some reasons causing the disaster.

Case 2
Mr. Smith bought a new private car, he is coming into auto department for insurance.
Miss Green introduces some details for auto insurance for him.

Case 3
Miss White will go to America for business by plane. Now she is inquiring for accident insurance.
Mr. Hill tells her some useful plans.

Case 4
Mr. Wood had fire last night, his house was burned down by this fire. Mr. Clark comes to the spot for investigation.

Supplementary Reading: Requirements of an Insurance Contract

A contract is an agreement embodying a set of promises that are legally enforceable. These promises must have been made under certain conditions before they can be enforced by law.

Insurance policies are contracts and must comply with the elements required of all valid contracts. In general, there are four requirements that are common to all valid contracts:

1. Agreement must be for a legal purpose. For insurance policies, this requirement means that the contract must neither violate the requirement of insurable interest nor protect or encourage illegal ventures.

2. Parties must have legal capacity to contract. Parties who have no legal capacity to contract include insane persons who cannot understand the nature of the agreement; intoxicated persons; corporations acting outside the scope of their charters, bylaws, or articles of corporation; and minors. Some states make exceptions for the last category, under which minors who have reached a certain age are granted the power to make binding contracts of insurance.

3. There must be a valid offer and acceptance. The general rule in insurance is that it is the applicant for insurance, not the agent, who makes the offer. The agent merely solicits an offer. When the contract goes into effect depends on the authority of the agent to act for the insurer in a given case. In property and liability insurance, it is the custom to give local agents authority to accept offers of many lines of insurance on the spot. In such cases, it is said that the agent will bind the insurer. If the insurer wishes to escape from its agreement, it may usually cancel the policy upon prescribed notice. In life insurance, the agent generally does not have authority to accept the applicant's offer for insurance. The insurer reserves this right, and the policy is not bound until the insurer has accepted the application.

4. Promises must be supported by the exchange of consideration. A consideration is the value given to each contracting party. The insured's consideration is made up of the monetary amount paid in premiums, plus an agreement to abide by the conditions of the insurance contract. The insurer's consideration is its promise to indemnify upon the occurrence of loss due to certain peril, to defend the insured in legal actions, or to perform other activities such as inspection or collection services, as the contract may specify.

Unit 9 Securities

AIMS

- Investing in stocks
- Trading in stocks
- Investing in funds
- Investing in treasury securities
- Investing in municipal bonds

Information bank

The capital market is the market in which long-term debt (generally those with original maturity of one year or greater) and equity instruments are traded. Firms that issue capital market securities and the investors who buy them have very different motivations than they have when they operate in the money markets. Firms and individuals use the money markets primarily to warehouse funds for short periods of time until a more important need or a more productive use for the funds arises. By contrast, firms and individuals use the capital markets for long-term investments. The capital markets provide an alternative to investment in assets such as real estate or gold.

Capital market trading occurs in either the primary market or the secondary market. The primary market is where new issues of stocks and bonds are introduced (by means of an IPO). Investment funds, corporations, and individual investors can all purchase securities offered in the primary market. The secondary market is where investors trade previously-issued securities without the involvement of the issuing-companies. The secondary market is what people are referring to when they talk about "the stock market".

The purpose of a stock market is to facilitate the exchange of securities between buyers and sellers, thus reducing the risks of investing. Just imagine how difficult it would be to sell shares if you had to call around the neighborhood trying to find a buyer. Really, a stock market is nothing more than a super-sophisticated farm market linking buyers and sellers.

Vocabulary Assistant

equity 股权　　　　　　　motivation 动机　　　　　　　　warehouse 持仓
real estate 房地产　　　　primary market 一级市场,发行市场　　IPO 初始公开发行
secondary market 二级市场,流通市场

Stock Trading

Most stocks are traded on exchanges, which are places where buyers and sellers meet and decide on a price. Some exchanges are physical locations where transactions are carried out on a trading floor. They are called organized exchanges. You're probably seen pictures of a trading floor, in which traders are wildly throwing their arms up, waving, yelling, and signaling to each other. The other type of exchange is a virtual kind, composed of a network of computers where trades are made electronically. It's called the over-the-counter (OTC) exchanges.

A bull market is when everything in the economy is great, people are finding jobs, GDP is growing, and stocks are rising. Things are just plainly rosy! Picking stocks during a bull market is easier because everything is going up. Bull markets cannot last forever though, and sometimes they can lead to dangerous situations if stocks become overvalued. If a person is optimistic, believing that stocks will go up, he or she is called a "bull" and said to have a "bullish outlook".

A bear market is when the economy is bad, recession is looming, and stock prices are falling. Bear markets make it tough for investors to pick profitable stocks. One solution to this is to make money when stocks are falling using a technique called short selling. Another strategy is to wait on the sidelines until you feel that the bear market is nearing its end, only starting to buy in anticipation of a bull market. If a person is pessimistic, believing that stocks are going to drop, he or she is called a "bear" and said to have a "bearish outlook".

Vocabulary Assistant

organized exchanges 有组织的交易所
over-the-counter 场外交易,柜台交易
bull market 牛市,股票行情看涨
overvalue 定价过高
bear market 熊市,股票行情看跌
recession 萧条
short selling 卖空,行情看跌时抛出股票
on the sidelines 旁观
anticipation 预期

1 There are five statements in this part. Decide whether the statements are true or false, and write T for true and F for false in the bracket.

(　　) 1. Firms and individuals use the capital markets for short-term investments.
(　　) 2. Investment funds and corporations can purchase securities offered in the primary market, but individual investors cannot.
(　　) 3. A secondary market is where the sale of previously issued securities takes place.
(　　) 4. There are two types of exchanges in the primary market for capital securities: organized exchanges and over-the-counter exchanges.
(　　) 5. A bull market means stock prices are rising whereas a bear market means stock prices are falling.

2 Select the answer that correctly completes the sentences.

1. The _____ is the place where long-term debt instruments and equity instruments are traded.
   A. money market
   B. capital market
   C. stock market

2. The _____ is where new issues of securities are created.
   A. primary market
   B. capital market
   C. secondary market

3. _____ are physical locations where transactions are carried out on a trading floor whereas the _____ a virtual one composed of a network of computers where trades are made electronically.
   A. Stock exchanges, OTC exchanges
   B. OTC exchanges, organized exchanges
   C. Organized exchanges, OTC exchanges

4. When there is a _____, you may make money by short selling.
   A. bear market
   B. bull market
   C. stock market

5. Picking stocks during a _____ is easier because everything is going up.
   A. bear market
   B. bull market
   C. stock market

6. If someone is considered to be bearish, where do they think the stock market is heading?
   A. Higher.　　　　　B. Lower.　　　　　C. Stagnant (Flat).

Conversation 1: Investing in Stocks

A: Hello! Black, you look pale. What has happened?

B: My uncle has just passed away.

A: I am sorry to hear that.

B: My sister and I have inherited a large sum of money. But we really don't know how to deal with it. You know both of us have no experience in investment. Could you give us some suggestions?

A: Of course, there are so many possible investments and the condition fluctuates so much nowadays.

B: We prefer stocks.

A: Ok, there are two ways to invest in stocks: long-term investment and short-term profit. First, you can put your money into the stable company with relative security perspective; second, you concentrate on buying stocks that promise a good and rapid growth rate and then resell them.

B: Both of the options are not very suitable. They need a lot of information and experience. You know we don't have so much time.

A: You are right. To invest in the stocks, you have to face the inflation and the devaluation, the government policy and so on. All the factors will affect the market.

B: Could you recommend some stocks?

A: The high-tech stocks have had high earnings.

B: I have heard that the market has been bearish lately. Is it a good time for investment?

A: Yes, but you can't buy stocks unless you make sure that the company you invest in can maintain their growth through difficult times. Otherwise, you will lose your money.

B: Thank you for your valuable suggestions.

A: My pleasure.

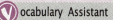
ocabulary Assistant

inherit 继承	fluctuate 波动
security 安全	perspective 前景
inflation 通货膨胀	devaluation 贬值
high-tech stocks 高科技股	earnings 收益
bearish 看跌的	

Conversation 2: Trading in Stocks

Clerk: Good morning, sir. What can I do for you?

Customer: Does your bank have the service on securities investments?

Clerk: Yes. We provide updated information of the stock market. You can watch the video monitors in our bank and get the instant prices of the stock you have bought. So, you can monitor share's performance closely.

Customer: Can I place my order by phone?

Clerk: Sure. You can simply call our securities hotlines. Our professionally trained staff will process your order at once by forwarding them to stockbrokers.

Customer: How to buy shares? I don't want to waste my time going to your bank to trade in securities.

Clerk: In fact, stock transactions can be directly done by account transfers, so it will save you extra trips.

Customer: That's nice.

Clerk: We also help clients to keep shares and transfer certificates. And we even offer service which can help clients to receive all the dividends and bonus shares.

Customer: Great! I'll think of it. Thank you very much.

Clerk: My pleasure. If you have further questions, you can visit our desk again or call our customer service hotline any time.

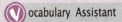ocabulary Assistant

updated 最新的	video monitor 电视显示器
instant 即时的	performance 业绩
place the order 委托	hotline 热线
stockbrokers 股票经纪人	account transfer 转账
certificate 凭证	bonus share 红利股票

Conversation 3: Investing in Funds

Customer: Good morning. I'm thinking of investing part of my money into other investment tools other than stocks and foreign currencies. May I have your suggestions?

Clerk: Yes, sir. Can I know the investment amount first?

Customer: I only have about fifty thousand dollars.

Clerk: That'll be fine. Have you ever heard about unit trusts and mutual funds?

Customer: No. Can you explain them simply to me?

Clerk: Certainly, sir. Both of them are investments where the combined resources of many investors are pooled together so as to provide the individual with a chance of diversifying his or her portfolio across a wide range of currencies, stocks, equities and bonds. These trusts or funds will be managed by professional fund managers.

Customer: I see. But how can your bank's service relate to these funds?

Clerk: Well, our investment service will help you to choose a Unit trust or Mutual fund among a range of possibilities and to evaluate them in terms of performance and risk.

Customer: What's the minimum investment amount for using this service?

Clerk: Sir, as long as you invest twenty thousand dollars or more in each fund, our bank can execute the buying, holding and selling of all your investment for you. In addition, we will provide you with the relevant prospectuses which state all the details of the various funds for your reference.

Customer: Can I know the charge for this investment service?

Clerk: Actually, our bank will not charge a fee for providing the above investment services but we will normally be paid a commission by the fund manager.

Customer: I see. I'm quite interested in your service.

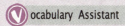ocabulary Assistant

unit trusts 单位信托　　　　mutual funds 互助基金
portfolio 投资组合　　　　　prospectus 招股说明书
fund managers 基金管理公司　commission 佣金

3 **Translate the phrases into English.**

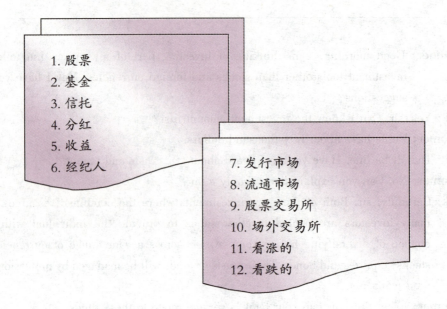

1. 股票
2. 基金
3. 信托
4. 分红
5. 收益
6. 经纪人
7. 发行市场
8. 流通市场
9. 股票交易所
10. 场外交易所
11. 看涨的
12. 看跌的

4 **Translate the following sentences.**

1. This morning Shenzhen Securities Exchange opened at 1605.08 p, up 21 p compared with the closing index of yesterday.
2. Most of the auto sector improved in a bullish market.
3. Sometimes it's very difficult to time the peaks and valleys of a stock.
4. Stocks with excellent performance are expected to rise in price.
5. There will be a quick recovery in the share price.
6. 股票市场是公众的投资场所之一。
7. 高科技股的市场价格突然下跌。
8. 股票价格的剧烈震荡是由于价格战所致。
9. 沪市收盘时上涨了20点。
10. 上星期沃尔玛的股票价格稍有下降。

Stocks and Bonds

A share of stock in a firm represents ownership. A stockholder owns a percentage interest in a firm, consistent with the percentage of outstanding stock held. This ownership is in contrast to a bondholder, who holds no ownership interest but is rather a creditor of the firm.

Investors can earn a return from stock in one of two ways. Either the price of the stock rises over time, or the firm pays the stockholder dividends. Frequently, investors earn a return from both sources. Stock is riskier than bonds because stockholders have a lower priority than bondholders when the firm is in trouble, the returns to investors are less assured because dividends can be easily changed, and stock price increases are not guaranteed. Despite these risks, it is possible to make a great deal of money by investing in stock, whereas that is very unlikely by investing in bonds. Another distinction between stock and bonds is that stock does not mature.

Bonds are securities that represent a debt owed by the issuer to the investor. Bonds obligate the issuer to pay a specified amount at a given date, generally with periodic interest payments. The par, face, or maturity value of the bond is the amount that the issuer must pay at maturity. The coupon rate is the rate of interest that the issuer must pay. This rate is usually fixed for the duration of the bond and does not fluctuate with market interest rates. If the repayment terms of a bond are not met, the holder of a bond has a claim on the assets of the issuer. Most bonds have maturities of between 10 and 30 years. Long-term bonds traded in the capital market include long-term government bonds, municipal bonds, and corporate bonds.

A common stock is, well, common. When people talk about stocks in general they are most likely referring to this type. In fact, the majority of stocks issued is in this form. Common shares represent ownership in a company and a claim (dividends) on a portion of profits. Investors get one vote per share to elect the board members, who oversee the major decisions made by management.

Vocabulary Assistant

ownership 所有权
bondholder 债券持有者
dividends 分红
distinction 区别
par 面值
municipal bonds 市政债券
common stock 普通股票
board 董事会

stockholder 股东
creditor 债权人
priority 优先权
periodic 定期的
coupon 息票
corporate bonds 公司债券
vote 投票权
oversee 监督

A preferred stock represents some degree of ownership in a company but usually doesn't come with the same voting rights. (This may vary depending on the company) With preferred shares investors are usually guaranteed a fixed dividend forever. This is different from common stocks, which has variable dividends that are never guaranteed. Another advantage is that in the event of liquidation preferred shareholders are paid off before the common shareholder (but still after debt holders). Preferred stocks may also be callable, meaning that the company has the option to purchase the shares from shareholders at any time for any reason (usually for a premium).

Vocabulary Assistant

preferred stock 优先股票　　liquidation 清算
callable 可赎回的　　　　　　premium 溢价

5 List the differences.

■ List the differences between bonds and stocks

- Ownership:
- Return:
- Priority:
- Maturity:

■ List the differences between common stocks and preferred stocks.

- Voting:
- Dividend:
- Priority:

6 Choose the best answer.

1. Stocks are also referred to as _____.
   A. securities
   B. equities
   C. shares
   D. A, B, and C

2. Which type of stock typically pays a higher dividend, but whose share price appreciates slower?
   A. Common stocks.
   B. Stock options.
   C. Preferred stocks.
   D. Commodities.

3. What is an advantage of investing in bonds? _____
   A. Bonds are generally of lower risk than stocks.
   B. Bonds offer a good source of income for retirees.
   C. Bonds issued by any stable country are almost risk-free securities.
   D. All of the above.

4. _____ have a higher priority than _____ when the firm is in trouble.
   A. Stockholders, bondholders
   B. Common stockholders, bondholders
   C. Bondholders, stockholders
   D. Preferred stockholders, bondholders

5. A key difference between bonds and stocks is that stocks _____.
   A. are tax-exempt
   B. represent ownership
   C. represent borrowing
   D. can be issued by state and local governments

6. The holder of preferred stocks has preference over the ordinary stockholders under the following circumstances:
   A. his voting rights are considered more important.
   B. he received his dividend before the ordinary stockholder.
   C. he has the greater right in choosing the board of directors.
   D. he has the right to buy ordinary shares more cheaply.

7. The holder of a bond is the _____.
   A. lender
   B. borrower
   C. debtor
   D. demander of credit

8. Business firms raise money by selling _____.
   A. currency
   B. cash
   C. both stocks and bonds
   D. demand deposits

7 Please read the following passages about The Dow Jones Industrial Average, and choose the best words or phrases to fill in the blanks.

Doctors always measure the heartbeat of a patient when examining the patient's health. The heartbeat of America's stock markets is the Dow Jones Industrial Average. No other measure of stock value is __1__ widely known. Sometimes it is simply called the Dow. It is published by the Dow Jones Company, an __2__ publisher of international financial news.

The Dow Jones Company is a product of Wall Street, the area in New York City that is the financial center of the United States. Three reporters, Charles Dow, Edward Jones and Charles Bergstresser, started the company in 1882. At first, they published a handwritten newsletter for financial workers. It was very successful. By 1889, the newsletter became the Wall Street Journal newspaper. The Dow Jones Company began publishing the Dow Jones Industrial Average in 1896. The list had twelve stocks. It represented the biggest industrial in the American economy at the time. Today, the Dow lists thirty stocks. They are often called "blue-chip" stocks. These stocks represent an ownership share in companies that are considered __3__. These well known companies include Coca-Cola, Eastman Kodak, McDonald's and General Electric.

When you read the Dow Jones Industrial Average, you quickly see that it is not the average price of thirty stocks. For example, the Dow recently increased to more than ten-thousand for the first time in more than eighteen months. Ten-thousand __4__ not seen like the average price of thirty stocks. In fact, the Dow Jones Industrial Average does not represent a price but a mathematical average. When the Dow goes up, it gains points, not dollars. The Dow Jones uses what __5__ a flexible divisor to keep changes in individual stock prices from affecting the whole average too much. The Dow system generally divides stock prices by the flexible divisor. The result is the number we see in newspapers and on television news reports.

Today, the Dow is just one of many stock averages. The Standard and Poor's Five-Hundred Index averages five-hundred stocks. Still others measure foreign stock exchanges. While stock averages are good research tools, many people consider them the heartbeat of finance.

1. A. as   B. that
   C. what   D. which
2. A. effective   B. affecting
   C. impactive   D. influential
3. A. strength   B. strong
   C. strongly   D. stronger
4. A. do   B. does
   C. is   D. are
5. A. calling   B. call
   C. called   D. is called

Conversation 4: Investing in Treasury Securities

A: Darling, have you decided how to invest the money Mother left us?

B: I think we should donate some to the charity; you said mother has mentioned that.

A: How about $ 50,000 to the Future Star Education Fund and $ 50,000 to Bright Fund for the Disabled?

B: I agree with you there. What shall we do with the rest?

A: I hear Treasury securities are good channels to invest in.

B: Why not corporate bonds? Corporate bonds offer better returns.

A: They do. But you'll have to face the risk of paying default if you don't choose the appropriate one.

B: We can refer to Moody's and Standard & Poor's to see which are most creditworthy. You see. The bonds rated AAA, AA and A are of high quality, those rated BBB or lower bear more risks of paying default. Those data make a good guideline.

A: Yes, AAA bonds are referred to as "gilt edge". They carry the smallest degree of risk. Which bonds can be considered gilt edge? What percentage of corporate bonds can be considered AAA? However, all the Treasury securities are AAA, whether they are Treasury bills, Treasury notes, or Treasury bonds. There is no risk of default unless the government stops issuing money.

B: That's for sure. What about the maturities of the government bonds?

A: Treasury bills are short-term with a maximum maturity of one year, and common maturities are 91 and 182 days. Treasury notes have a maturity of one to seven years. And Treasury bonds mature in 7 to 25 years or even longer. I don't think we can wait so long as 7 years.

B: No. Treasury bills are more suitable to us than the other two.

A: To get a reliable and profitable result, I propose that we ask our broker for advice.

B: Good. Let me call him.

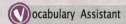
ocabulary Assistant

charity 慈善	Treasury securities 国库券
default 违约	Moody's 穆迪投资公司
Standard & Poor's 标准普尔	gilt edge 金边
Treasury bills 短期国库券	Treasury notes 中期国库券
Treasury bonds 长期国库券	broker 经纪人

Conversation 5: Investing in Municipal Bonds

A: Good morning, Mr. Harris. Come in. I was expecting you.

B: I'm terribly sorry I'm late. On the way I was held up by the traffic jam.

A: Doesn't matter.... Would you like tea or coffee?

B: Coffee, please. As I told you the other day, I've got $150,000 to invest.

A: These days stocks fluctuate too much, so I suggest you invest in bonds.

B: I hear bonds are tax-free.

A: Yes. Municipal bonds, for instance, are exempt from taxes.

B: Do you mean that I don't have to pay taxes on the money I invest in municipal bonds?

A: No. I don't mean the principal you invest in bonds. Rather, the interest you get on the investment is tax-free. May I know what's percentage of your income you pay to the Federal government as taxes?

B: 32 percent. I think taxes are too high.

A: That's one of the reasons why you need to some tax-free investment. Have you looked through the bonds quotes?

B: No. Could you recommend some to me?

A: The performance of the City of Los Angeles Bond is terrific. It's expected to work better.

B: How about its credit rating?

A: AA.

B: Terrific. I'll invest all the $150,000 in the City of Los Angeles.

A: Diversification is a strategy to spread investment risks. By diversification I mean that you should invest in a portfolio of more stocks or bonds rather than focusing your money on only one stock or bond.

B: I see. Are there any other AA municipal bonds you think suitable for me?

A: The City of San Francisco and the City of Detroit bonds can be ideal choices, I think.

B: Then I'll invest $50,000 in each of the three bonds. What do you think of it?

A: I think it's better than just investing in Los Angeles. Moreover the other two bonds offer higher returns.

B: Thank you so much for your help, Mr. Amis.

Vocabulary Assistant

bonds 债券
municipal bonds 市政债券
credit rating 信用等级
diversification 多样性

tax-free 免税的
quote 报价
performance 业绩
portfolio 投资组合

SECURITIES UNIT 9

8 Translate the following sentences.

1. 发行国库券是政府调节货币供给的一种手段。

2. 这种债券的利息收入是免征地方税的。

3. 客户除了买公司债券外,还可以买政府债券。

4. 通货膨胀是债券投资的又一风险。

5. 许多人并不把债券一直持有至到期日。

6. The level of interest payment on a bond is inverse to the credit rating.

7. Bonds floatation is a key channel for companies to finance some large-scale project.

8. It's a good idea to reduce the risk by also buying some nice, stable bonds at the same time.

9 You will listen to a telephone conversation. The conversation will be read only once. Listen carefully and decide whether the following statements are true or false. Mark T for true and F for false in the brackets in front of each statement.

(   ) 1. To buy and sell shares, one can simply go to a stock exchange.

(   ) 2. Brokers buy and sell shares on their own behalf.

(   ) 3. The requirements for opening an account include depositing a cash balance in the brokerage account.

(   ) 4. When you put in an order to buy shares, your broker will place your order on the market.

(   ) 5. When there are several bids at the price, the one with the largest amount will have priority.

10 **Make conversations with the information given below, taking into account the logical relationship of the content.**

1. A clerk helps a new customer with options on investment.

Clerk	Customer
Greetings	Have no idea about investment
Several options	Ask for differences between bonds and stocks
Advantages and disadvantages	Ask for more details on stocks
List two types of stocks	Interested in common stocks
Hope to be service of the customer	Thanks

2. A clerk explains to a businessman how to invest in funds.

Clerk	Businessman
Greeting and offer help	Want to invest in investments other than stocks
Ask the amount of investment	$100,000
Recommend mutual funds	Ask for the bank's related service
Explain the relevant information	Thanks

3. Mr. Johnson wants to invest in Treasury Securities.

Mr. Johnson	Bank's teller
Greeting	Offer help
Interested in Treasury Securities	Recommend corporate bnods
Worry about their default risk	Explain the bnds rating
Still prefer Treasury Securities	Explain the maturities of T. S.
Finally focus on Treasury Notes	Offer further services
Show appreciation	

11 Make conversations according to the cases given below.

Case 1
Mr. Johnson wants to invest $8,000 in stocks. He comes to a bank to get some relative information. Make a conversation between Mr. Johnson and the bank clerk.

Case 2
Mr. Smith wants to make an investment for $10,000. He can't decide to choose stocks or bonds. He comes to a bank to get some suggestions from the manager of investing department. Make a conversation between Mr. Smith and the manager.

Case 3
Miss Charles wants to open an account with Nanjing Branch of the Bank of China, helping her with her stock trading. Make a conversation between the bank clerk and Miss Charles.

Case 4
Mr. David has saved $10,000. He wants to invest in bonds since he doesn't have any time focusing on keeping close watch on the stock fluctuations. Suppose you're a bank clerk, develop a conversation with Mr. David, offering him some suggestions on the type of bond.

Supplementary Reading: What is NASDAQ

NASDAQ, acronym for the National Association of Securities Dealers Automated Quotation system, is one of the largest markets in the world for the trading of stocks. The number of companies listed on NASDAQ is more than that on any of the other stock exchanges in the United States, including the New York Stock Exchange (NYSE)  and the American Stock Exchange (AMEX). The majority of companies listed on NAS-DAQ are smaller than most of those on the NYSE and AMEX. NASDAQ has become known as the home of new technology companies, particularly computer and computer-related businesses. Trading on NASDAQ is initiated by stock brokers acting on behalf of their clients. The brokers negotiate with market makers who concentrate on trading specific stocks to reach a price for the stock.

Unlike other stock exchanges, NASDAQ has no central location where trading takes place. Instead, its market makers are located all over the country and make trades by telephone and via the Internet. Because brokers and market makers trade stocks directly instead of on the floor of a stock exchange, NASDAQ is called an over-the-counter market. The term over-the-counter refers to the direct nature of the trading, as in a store where goods are handed over a counter.

Since its inception in 1971, the NASDAQ Stock Market has been the innovator. As the world's first electronic stock market, NASDAQ long ago set a precedent for technological trading innovation that is unrivaled. Now poised to become the world's first truly global market, the NASDAQ Stock Market is the market of choice for business industry leaders worldwide. By providing an efficient environment for raising capital NASDAQ has helped thousands of companies achieve their desired growth and successfully make the leap into public ownership.

Unit 10 Banking Business Letters

AIMS

- Structure of banking business letters
- Format of banking business letters
- Rules of good writing

Information bank

A letter can be defined as a direct or personally written or printed message addressed to a person or an organization. Some dictionaries also define it simply as a written or a printed message.

A bank business letter refers to a letter about selling and buying of financial services such as depositing-taking, cheque-honoring, loan-granting, investment-consulting, etc.

When based on the identity of the addressee or your correspondent, there are private letters and business letters. When the classification is based on the purposes, there are many types of letters. To mention just a few, there are letters of thanks, letters of introduction, letters of complaints, letters asking for something, letters accepting something or refusing something, letters apologizing to somebody for something wrong, etc.

Strictly speaking, a business letter is composed of a standard envelope with the addressee's name, address and postal code on it and the letter itself.

The ways of the present communication in business world are quite different from the ways in the 1980s. Twenty years ago, business people kept in touch with each other by telegram, letters or something like that. Now most of the businessmen like to forward e-mails or transmit faxes in order to exchange information quickly. Compared with the old ways, faxes and e-mails are quite convenient, fast, flexible and simple.

Vocabulary Assistant

identity 本人　　　　　addressee 收信人　　　　private 个人的
classification 分类　　　complaint 抱怨

■ Structure of Banking Business Letters

A banking business letter consists of seven principal parts:

The letter head

Besides the name and address of the writer's firm, the letter head also includes telephone numbers, e-mail address, if any, and the kind of business carried on if this is not clear from the firm's name.

For companies registered in the United Kingdom with limited liability, the word Limited (or a recognized abbreviation of it) must form part of the name. Companies formed with limited liability in the United States use the abbreviation Inc., while Australian companies use (Pty) Ltd. as an abbreviation for Proprietary Limited.

The date

The date is often typed in full, in the logical order of day, month, year, thus: 12th October 2007.

To give the date in figures (e.g. 12/10/2007) may easily be confusing in correspondence with the United States, where it is the practice to give dates in the order of month, day and year.

The inside name and address

Generally, the inside name and address should include some or all parts of the following: the receiver's name and title, company name, street address, city, state/province, post-code and country. It appears on the left margin and usually starts two to four lines below the last line of the letter head.

The salutation

This is the greeting with which every letter begins. The customary greeting in a business letter is Dear Sir, but others are used as follows: Dear Madam (for both single and married women); Dear Sirs (when a partnership is addressed); Mesdames (when the partnership consists of women only, though the use of the less logical but more familiar Dear Sirs is permissible). When your correspondent is unknown to you and may be either a man or a woman, always use the form of Dear Sir.

The body of the letter

This is the part that really matters. Keep your sentences and paragraphs short and start a new paragraph for each new point you wish to stress. Short sentences and paragraphs provide easier reading and are easy to understand. There are often three paragraphs in a letter: the first paragraph makes an introduction or an acknowledgement if there has been previous correspondence; the second gives information and states the facts; the third refers to future actions.

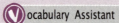
ocabulary Assistant

register 注册　　　　　　　liability 责任
abbreviation 缩写　　　　　confusing 混淆的
correspondence 函电　　　　salutation 称呼
acknowledgement 确认

The complimentary closure

The complimentary closure, like the salutation, is a matter of custom and a polite way of bringing a letter to a close. "Yours faithfully" and "Yours sincerely" are the mostly used complimentary closure.

The writer's signature

A signature must be the plain signature of the writer without a title. There is one exception to this: a woman writing to a stranger should indicate whether she is married or single and may do so by adding Mrs. or Miss in front of her signature.

Because many signatures are illegible, it is good practice to type the name of the signer and to place his manual signature above it.

Beside the above seven principal parts, there are some optional parts in a business letter:

"For attention" headings

These headings are used when it is desired to address a letter to a particular member of an organization. It is often typed above the salutation:

For the attention of Mr. T Warehouse

Dear Sir

Subject headings

The subject heading summarizes the theme of the letter and helps to ensure that the letter is passed without delay to the right person or department. It is often typed immediately below the salutation:

Dear Sir

Alterations to warehouse

References

Reference numbers enable replies to be linked with earlier correspondence and ensure that they reach the right person or department without delay. The best place for the writer's reference is at the beginning, in the upper left-hand corner, in line with the date, thus:

GBD/JB   25th January, 2008

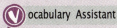
ocabulary Assistant

complimentary closure 结尾敬语   illegible 难辨认的
manual 手写的

Enclosures

If something is enclosed, note it below the reference notation.

Carbon Copy Notation/CC

If copies of a letter are sent to other parties, type CC below the enclosure.

Postscript/P.S

If the writer wishes to add something he forgets or for emphasis, he may usually add the postscript two lines below the carbon copy notation.

Format of Banking Business Letters

Basically there are two formats or styles used in writing business letters. One is indented letter style; the other is blocked letter style.

Indented style

Many people regard this as the most attractive of all letter styles. The blocked inside name and address is liked because it is compact and tidy. This style still appeals to readers. They like the indented paragraphing. They claim that it makes for easy reading. Others dislike the indentations because, they claim, they waste the typist's time.

Blocked style

This is also one of the main patterns in use at present. It can be subdivided into full block form and modified block form with indented paragraphs. Now a lot of businessmen prefer this form, because it can save time in typing the letter.

Vocabulary Assistant

enclosure 附件   Carbon Copy Notation 抄送
postscript 附言   indented style 缩进式
blocked style 齐头式

1 Answer the following questions briefly.

1. What major parts does a letter consist of?

2. What is the difference between British English and American English in writing the date of a letter?

3. What is the function of subject headings?

4. When are "for attention" headings necessary?

Specimen Letter 1: Indented Style of Letters

Directors: R B North M W Beevers
W D J Argent D A F Sutherland
Macdonald & Evans (Publications) Ltd
Estover Road Plymouth PL6 7PZ
Telephone: Plymouth (0752) 705251
Telex: 45635
Your ref.   Our ref.: RBN/ALV

                                                    20th September, 2007

Miss E. Hughes
100, South Street,
PURLEY Surrey
CR2 4TJ.
Dear Miss Hughes,

      This letter is typed in the traditional indented style. The inside name and address is typed in block form, but the paragraphs forming the body of the letter are all indented six spaces. Some typists prefer a deeper indentation and may use as many as ten spaces, though six are sufficient to show the separation of paragraphs clearly.

      Left-hand and right-hand margins of 30mm have been adopted. As in most letters typed in this style the date appears on the right-hand side, and is usually so placed that the last figure serves as a guide for the right-hand margin.

      This letter is of course typed in single line-spacing. The subject heading is centered two line-spacing below the salutation which in turn begins three line-spacing below the inside name and address. The paragraphs are separated by double line-spacing.

      The complimentary closure is typed to fall evenly across the center of the typing line, with the designation similarly centered. Some typists using this style prefer to place the complimentary closure to the right of the center rather than in the center.

                                                    Yours sincerely,
                                                    R B North
                                                    Managing Director

Specimen Letter 2: Blocked Style of Letters

Directors: R B North M W Beevers
W D J Argent D A F Sutherland
Macdonald & Evans (Publications) Ltd
Estover Road Plymouth PL6 7PZ
Telephone: Plymouth (0752) 705251
Telex: 45635
Your ref.   Our ref.: RBN/ALV

20th September, 2007

Miss E. Hughes
100, South Street,
PURLEY Surrey
CR2 4TJ.

Dear Miss Hughes,

This letter-style is very modern and has now become firmly established as the recommended way of setting out letters. Its main feature is that all typing lines, including those for the date, the inside name and address, the subject heading and the complimentary closure, begin at the left-hand margin.

Many firms who adopt this letter-style regard the date as an essential feature or the fully-blocked style and place it on the left, above the name and address and in line with it. Others prefer to place the date on the right, as in this example, because the right-hand position makes it easier to find particular letters in the file. It also gives the letter a more balanced appearance.

Yours sincerely,
R B North
Managing Director

Rules of Good Writing

1. Study your reader's interests
2. Adopt the right tone
3. Write clearly and to the point
4. Be courteous and considerate
5. Plan your letters
6. Pay attention to the first and last impressions
7. Check your letters

2. Decide whether the following statements are true or false. Put a T for true or F for false.

(   ) 1. There are numerous ways to lay out business letters, but the simplest, quickest and most widely used one is the full blocked style.

(   ) 2. In the body of a letter, several topics may be included in the same paragraph to save space and raise efficiency of communication.

(   ) 3. If you want to attach extra materials to a bank letter, you can put "C.C." at the end of the letter and indicate the content of the materials to be attached.

(   ) 4. In a bank letter, when you address somebody in a Salutation, you are now allowed to put the given name of the person addressed after "Dear".

(   ) 5. Although bank letters have become more and more informal and relaxed today, written language should always be more formal than that for oral communication.

(   ) 6. Long and complicated words and sentences can often be found in bank letters to show the characteristics of formality and strictness of bank letters.

Specimen Letter 3: Request to Open an Account

Dear Sir,

I have recently moved into this town and opened a bookstore at the above address. Having been recommended to your bank by Mr. James Currie, one of your customers, I wish to open a current account with you and should be glad if you would suggest a day and time when I may call on you to discuss the details. I will provide references should you require them.

Yours faithfully

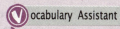

Vocabulary Assistant

reference 证明文书

Specimen Letter 4: Request for an Extension of a Loan

Dear Sir,

On 1st August last year you granted me a loan of $5,000. This loan is due for repayment at the end of this month and I have already taken steps to prepare for this. Unfortunately, however, due to a fire at my warehouse a fortnight ago, I have been faced with heavy unexpected payments. Damage from the fire is thought to be about $6,000 and is fully covered by insurance. But as my claim is unlikely to be settled before the end of next month, I should be glad if the period of the loan could be extended till then.

I am sure you will realize that the fire has presented me with serious problems and that repayment of the loan before settlement of my claim could be made only with the greatest difficulty.

Yours faithfully

Vocabulary Assistant

due 到期　　warehouse 仓库
claim 索赔

3 Match the banking terms in English in Column A with their Chinese equivalent in Column B.

Column A	Column B
transfer	余额
statement	订单
balance	偿付
order	对账单
reimbursement	转账

Column A	Column B
remittance	担保
proceeds	修改通知书
security	货款
countersign	汇款
amendment	会签

Specimen Letter 5: Open an L/C

Dear Sirs,

As instructed in your letter of 20th March, we are arranging to open a documentary credit with our branch in Sydney in favor of the North American Trading Company, valid until 30th September. You will find enclosed a copy of our telegram opening the credit and we shall be glad if you will check it to ensure that it agrees with your instructions. As soon as the credits are used we shall debit your account with the amount notified to us as having been drawn against them.

We shall take all necessary steps to make sure that your instructions are carefully carried out, but wish to make it clear that we cannot assume any responsibility for the safety of the goods, or for delays in delivery since these are matters beyond our control.

Yours faithfully

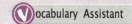ocabulary Assistant

documentary credit 跟单信用证
enclosed 随附的   assume 承担

4 Translate the following banking terms into English and give the equivalent English abbreviations for them.

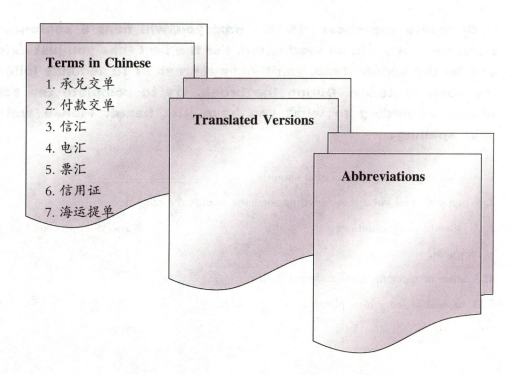

Terms in Chinese
1. 承兑交单
2. 付款交单
3. 信汇
4. 电汇
5. 票汇
6. 信用证
7. 海运提单

Translated Versions

Abbreviations

5 Listening exercises

■ **Spot Dictation:** In this section you'll hear two short paragraphs. There are some words or phrases missing in each paragraph. Each paragraph will be read three times. For the first time you just listen and for the second time, you'll have a break of 20 seconds. During the break, you can write down the missing words or phrases. The third time is for you to check your writing. Now let's begin.

1

A letter is really a ___(1)___ for a personally delivered ___(2)___. Your letter is your ___(3)___ to the person you can't talk to face to face. The tone of your writing shows your ___(4)___. You will want the tone and style of your letter to create a friendly ___(5)___ on the part of the receiver. Do not write when you are ___(6)___. If you do write, tear up and start over when you ___(7)___ "cool".

2

In any office there is much discussion and not always unanimous agreement on the ___(1)___ to be used in typing letters. To begin with, your company ___(2)___ should give the ___(3)___ about your company. The letter should not be difficult to read. Most business letters should be less than one page ___(4)___. Your readers expect to find a clear ___(5)___ of your ___(6)___, all the necessary information for them to act and a ___(7)___ to do.

■ **Complete sentences:** In this part you will hear 5 sentences. Each sentence will be read twice. For the first time you just listen and for the second time, you'll have a break of 10 seconds following each sentence. During the break, try to complete the sentences according to what you have just heard. Please watch your spelling.

1. A letter expressing appreciation should _____.

2. When you send out a letter inviting someone to attend a meeting, _____.

3. A letter of congratulations, _____, is always appreciated by the recipient.

4. A letter of recommendation should indicate _____.

5. A successful letter of application requires you _____.

6 **The following translated versions of the Chinese sentences are either not correct or not satisfactory, so please amend them properly.**

1. 感谢贵方 2007 年 12 月 12 日的来函邀请。

Thank you for 2005,12,12 letter of invitation.

2. 信用证一经使用，我行会立即按提取的金额借记你方账户。

The credit once is put into use, our bank will according to the drawn amount debit your account.

3. 我方已就标题下的货物与你方达成交易，感到非常高兴。

We have, on the cargo under the subject, with you reached agreement, feel very pleased.

4. 我们建议在货物备好待运时用电汇付款。

We suggest when goods are prepared and waiting for shipment use T/T to make payment.

5. 关于付款一事，我行将开出以你方为受益人的信用证，金额为全部货值。

Concerning payment, our bank will open as your bank beneficiary a letter of credit, the amount is all goods' worth.

7 Choose the correct answer from the four choices marked A, B, C and D to complete each of the following statements.

1. Please now _____ the first part of this order for items 1—8 by air, as these are urgently required by customers.
   A. mail   B. hand   C. dispatch   D. present
2. We regret to _____ that the goods shipped against your order No. 142 arrived damaged.
   A. inform   B. note   C. tell   D. say
3. We will appreciate it if you _____ your current brochure to us.
   A. offer   B. forward
   C. bring   D. make
4. In view of this above, we would like to propose that you should authorize us to _____ on one of your correspondents.
   A. rely   B. dwell
   C. fall   D. draw
5. We would be _____ if you would send us by airmail a copy of the packing lists included in each case to be sent by sea.
   A. please   B. flavored
   C. gratitude   D. obliged

8 Translate the following sentences into English.

1. 您还有4000美元的贷款未还。
2. 希望您能在12月31日之前结清贷款账户。
3. 您可能仅仅是忽略了这笔贷款，而不是有意要违反我们的信贷条款。
4. 我行随函附上一份有关该公司的报告，仅供贵行私下使用并参考。
5. 上述资料应严格保密。我们对其中的任何不实之处不负责任。
6. 请在核对2007年11月的账单后提出不符点。
7. 这笔应付款的到期日是2007年10月15日。
8. 在固定利率抵押贷款的情况下，银行在贷款的整个有效期内都按同样的利率收取利息。
9. 兹授权你方向本行开具金额为10,000美元的即期汇票，并附上以下单据。
10. 本信用证项下的远期汇票按即期议付，由本行贴现。贴现费或利息及承兑费由进口商承担。

Introduction of Telex, Fax and E-mail

Telex
● **Layout**
Telex No.（收电人电传号）
Urgent or Top Urgent（急件或特急件）
Date（日期）
To：（收电人公司名称及地址）
From：（发电人公司名称及地址）
Our Ref.：（我方发文编号）
Attn. Mr.（送××先生亲阅）
Re：（事由）
The Opening Sentences（开头语）
The Body of Telex（电传正文）
Paragraph 1：
Paragraph 2：
Paragraph 3：
Ending（结束语）
The Complimentary Closure（结尾语）
Name, Title & Telex No.（发电人姓名、职务及电传号）
Time（发电时间）
＋＋＋FIN＋＋＋（表示完毕）

电传的特点

1. 尽量选用短词，例如：
NOW（at present），DESPITE（in spite of）
2. 大量使用简化词和缩写词，例如：
URG（urgent），ASAP（as soon as possible）
3. 句法特点：
（1）动词 be 省略；冠词、介词以能理解为原则尽量省去，例如：
SMPLS UNRCVD SND DUPLICATE IMMDLY.
样品尚未收到，请补寄一份。
（2）we 做主语时尽量省去，必要时放在句子中间，例如：
我们尽力以最小亏损解决。
DOING UTMOST STTLE CLAIM LEAST LOSS.

（3）将来时用 will 或 -ing 表示；现在完成时和过去完成时统一用过去时表示；将来完成时用将来时表示，例如：
罐头沙丁鱼进口税将于 4 月底提高，请尽可能多来订单。
IMP DTY SARDING WILL BE RAISED BY END APL RUSH ODAS.
（4）开头语多用 TKS（THANKS）表示谢意；结尾语多用 RGDS（REGARDS）表示敬意。
（5）船名须用全称，而不用简化或缩写，例如：S.S. PRESIDENT "总统"号

Fax transmission is widely used nowadays. As to sending the messages, it is as fast as a telephone call whereas it is much cheaper because it takes less time. By putting any sheet of A4 paper through a fax machine, the sender could forward the message quite easily even if the company or the person doesn't have the computer.

And no special hardware or software is required to prepare a document that includes graphs, photographs or diagrams. Just photocopy them on a sheet of A4 paper. In this aspect, it is more convenient and flexible than e-mails.

● **Layout**

FAX TRANSMISSION
DATE:
TO:
FAX NUMBER:
NUMBER OF PAGES TRANSMITTED INCLUDING THIS COVER SHEET

_____

MESSAGE:
Body of the letter

_____

If any part of this fax transmission is missing or not clearly received, please call:
NAME:
PHONE:

● **Linguistic features**

The linguistic style of text in faxes is similar to that used in letters. A subject line is occasionally used, indicating the topic of the message or referring to previous contacts.

The useful expressions presented in business letters are also used in faxes. Sometimes, the differences between letters and faxes may only lie in their different means of transmission. However, faxes can sometimes be much more informal.

E-mail

Just as letters, telexes and faxes, e-mail is one of the ways of communication. It can send out quick notices to spread much more information, to a larger audience at one time. Compared with telephone, e-mail creates flexibility in the workplace; it reduces telephone interruptions. As another competitive advantage, e-mail produces documents to be filed, forwarded or retrieved.

- **Layout**

From: Peter Murray @ ix. Netcom.com
Date: Fri, December 23, 2007 15:35:08
To: Marilyn Patel @ Knowles.com
Subject: Offer sheets for 26 lanes of bowling equipment
C.C:

Attachment: offer sheets

Dear Marilyn,

    At your request, I am pleased to attach our offer sheets for 26 lanes of bowling equipment. Any questions please call us.

    Merry Christmas to you!

    Best regards,

    (the name of the company)

    Peter Murray

    Vice president

- **Linguistic features**

1. Compared with letters, faxes and telexes, e-mails tend to be more informal.
2. The e-mail message is composed of short sentences and short paragraphs. Normally speaking, there is only one idea for one paragraph, the vocabularies the writer use are simple and easy to understand.
3. People who communicate with each other by e-mail are often familiar with each other. So the tone of the message is conversational but professional. So what kind of tone you should use depends on the purpose of the e-mail, the relations and positions of the recipient.

9 Put the following telex into Chinese.

> RE S/C FA 1234 2000 CANNED BEEF EX MV DONGFENG ARVD QINGDAO SEPT 18TH UPON TAKING DLVRY FOUND 125 CTNS SHORT SHPG COMPANY TOLD US ONLY 1875 CTNS LOADED ON BOARD CARRYG VESSEL. SINCE THIS LOSS NOT NEGLIGIBL RQST MAKE UP 125 CTNS WHEN YOU DLVR LAST THREE ITEMS. PLS CHECK N MAKE SURE IF ALL 2000 CTNS LOADED ON BOARD VESSEL AT LOADPORT. TLX RPLY.

10 Write an e-mail according to the case given below.

> 我行已收到上述信用证之副本,现谨奉告贵行,经仔细查阅记录,我们并未收到该信用证之正本。
> 我行已凭此副本通知受益人,如正本不能及时送达,我行将凭副本议付。
> 期待你方早日答复。

11 Write banking letters according to the cases given below.

Case 1
请以招商银行信贷部的名义起草一封信给要求贷款的客户,表示你行同意按下列条件向其贷款:
(1) 贷款用途:建筑融资
(2) 贷款金额:50万元人民币
(3) 贷款方式:合约生效后一次性直接支付给贷款人
(4) 偿还期:10年
(5) 利率:优惠利率加1%
(6) 担保品:贷款人提交担保物
同时表示如果对方同意该条件,就在随附的复印件上签名并于2008年3月31日前寄回你行。

Case 2
写一封信给国外客户,介绍中国银行的情况:
(1) 中国银行是国际化程度最高的中资商业银行,也是唯一一家在亚、欧、澳、非、南美、北美六大洲均设有机构的银行,有强大的外币资金实力,基本形成了商业银行、投资银行和保险三大业务协同发展的格局,成为真正的全能银行。
(2) 在承担国家引进外资任务的过程中,具备多年外汇专业银行的丰富经验,在中国银行业培养和造就了一批精通国内及涉外业务的专业人才,并建立起了有高度竞争力的客户服务管理模式。

Case 3

以建设银行上海分行的名义给 Chase Manhattan Bank 写一封正式信函：

(1) 要求 Chase Manhattan Bank 开即期美元汇票以代替由其储户 Mr. Johnson 所开支票；

(2) 要求 Chase Manhattan Bank 将该汇票寄来；

(3) 要求 Chase Manhattan Bank 确认支票上受票人签名。

Supplementary Reading: How to Write a Good Letter

Writing Process

Whenever you write an email, memo, fax or letter, your readers are your customers. When you write, you need to provide good customer service and meet your readers' expectations.

If you want your writing to meet your reader's expectations and get results, your reader needs to

- understand your document easily and correctly
- respond to your document appropriately.

To meet their readers' expectations and get the results they want, most good writers follow a five-stage Writing Process. The five stages are:

- Plan
- Organise
- Draft
- Revise
- Edit

When you follow the Writing Process, you'll

- meet your reader's expectations
- be more efficient by doing first things first
- organise your documents logically
- revise your documents so that they are clear, concise and courteous
- edit your documents so that they are correct

Plan

"If you fail to plan, you plan to fail." Before you start to write, you have to plan what to write. You then write according to your plan.

Planning a letter involves three decisions. You decide

- Why you are writing (writer's purpose)
- What you want your reader to do (reader's response)
- What your reader needs to know (reader's information).

Organise

A well-organised letter, memo, fax or e-mail is easy to read and understand. If you organise the contents of your correspondence well, you are more likely to get the results you want.

To organise business letters, remember the saying "So far, so good".

Salutation	→	Dear Mr/Mrs/Ms/Miss...
Opening	→	Background + Purpose
Facts	→	Reader's Information
Action	→	Reader's Response

Draft

When you draft you should
- keep writing
- not edit

Revise

You should revise your documents to help the readers – your customers – more easily understand what you write. When your customers understand what you write, you can get the results you want.

Revise...	and make it
the DOCUMENT	Complete
each PARAGRAPH	Cohesive
each SENTENCE	Clear and Concise
each SENTENCE AGAIN	Courteous

Edit

Editing (or proof reading) puts the "finishing touches" on your document. Everything you write gives a lasting impression of your company and you as a writer. So, it's important to check your spelling, punctuation and grammar carefully. Missing commas, misspelled words and inaccurate grammar give a poor impression.

Vocabulary

A

abbreviation *n.* 缩写		unit 10
acceptance *n.* 承兑		unit 6
acknowledgement *n.* 确认		unit 10
actuary *n.* 公证人		unit 8
addressee *n.* 收信人		unit 10
agency *n.* 代理		unit 5
agreement *n.* 协议		unit 8
allowance *n.* 津贴		unit 2
amendment *n.* 修改(通知)书		unit 7
annuity *n.* 年金		unit 5
anticipation *n.* 预期		unit 9
applicant *n.* 申请人		unit 2
application *n.* 申请文		unit 8
appreciate *v.* 感激		unit 6
automatic *adj.* 自动的		unit 5

B

balance *n.* 余额		unit 1
batch *n.* 批量		unit 8
bearish *adj.* 看跌的		unit 9
beneficiary *n.* 受益人		unit 6
bill *n.* 账单		unit 5
board *n.* 董事会		unit 9
bonds *n.* 债券		unit 9
bonus *n.* 红利		unit 8

C

calamity *n.* 灾难		unit 8
callable *n.* 可赎回的		unit 9
cash *v.* 取现,兑现;*n.* 现金		unit 4
charge *v.* 收取;*n.* 手续费		unit 8
charity *n.* 慈善		unit 9
chop *v.* 盖章		unit 7
cipher *n.* 密码		unit 4
claim *v.* & *n.* 索赔		unit 10
classification *n.* 分类		unit 10
client *n.* 客户		unit 7
creditor *n.* 债权人		unit 9
collateral *n.* 抵押品		unit 2
collect *v.* 托收		unit 6
collection *n.* 托收		unit 6
commission *n.* 佣金,手续费		unit 4
compensate *v.* 赔偿		unit 5
complaint *n.* 抱怨		unit 10
complementary *adj.* 补充的		unit 10
confidential *adj.* 保密的		unit 4
confirmation *n.* 确认		unit 7
confusing *adj.* 混淆的		unit 10
contingency *n.* 意外事故		unit 5
conventional *adj.* 常规的,保守的		unit 4
convert *v.* 兑换		unit 6
correspondence *n.* 函电		unit 10
counsel *n.* 顾问		unit 9
counter *n.* 柜台		unit 1
countersign *n.* 会签		unit 3
cover *v.* 弥补,负担支付		unit 3
coverage *n.* 保险		unit 5
credentials *n.* 证件		unit 6
credibility *n.* 信用额度		unit 4
credit rating *n.* 信用等级		unit 9
criteria *n.* 标准		unit 6

D

default *n.* 违约	unit 9
demonstrate *v.* 证明	unit 8
denomination *n.* 票面额	unit 2
deposit *v. & n.* 存款	unit 1
deregulation *n.* 解除管制	unit 5
destination *n.* 目的地	unit 7
devaluation *n.* 贬值	unit 9
disablement *n.* 残疾	unit 5
discharge *v.* 卸货	unit 7
discount *v.* 贴现	unit 6
dishonor *v.* 拒付	unit 6
distinction *n.* 区别	unit 9
diversification *n.* 多样性	unit 9
dividends *n.* 分红	unit 9
domestic *adj.* 国内的	unit 6
draft *v.* 起草	unit 9
drawee *n.* 受票人	unit 6
drawn *v.* 提款	unit 7
duplicate *n.* 副本	unit 7

E

earnings *n.* 收益	unit 9
elite *n.* 精华	unit 8
embody *v.* 体现	unit 8
enclosure *n.* 附件	unit 10
endowment *n.* 捐赠	unit 5
entail *v.* 需要	unit 10
entrustment *n.* 委托	unit 8
equity *n.* 股权	unit 9
expenses *n.* 费用	unit 3
expiration *n.* 期满,终止	unit 4
extension *n.* 展期	unit 7

F

factoring *n.* 保理业务	unit 8
fine *v. & n.* 罚款	unit 5
floating *adj.* 浮动的	unit 2
forward *adj.* 远期的	unit 3

G

garage *n.* 车库	unit 5
geographical *adj.* 地理的	unit 6
guarantee *v. & n.* 担保	unit 4
guarantor *n.* 保证人	unit 2

H

high-tech stocks *n.* 高科技股	unit 9

I

identification *n.* 身份证	unit 3
illegible *adj.* 难辨认的	unit 10
imprinter *n.* 压卡机	unit 4
incoming *adj.* 进来的;*n.* 进来	unit 5
indemnity *v.* 赔偿	unit 5
in favor of... 以……为受益人	unit 7
inflation *n.* 通货膨胀	unit 9
inherit *v.* 继承	unit 9
installment *n.* 分期付款	unit 2
instant *adj.* 即时的	unit 9
institutional *adj.* 团体的	unit 9
insurer *n.* 保险人	unit 8
integrate *v.* 综合	unit 5
interest *n.* 利益	unit 5
interim *adj.* 临时的	unit 1
intermediary *n.* 中介;*adj.* 媒介的	unit 5
interrelated *adj.* 相关的	unit 5
intoxicate *v.* 激励	unit 8
invest *v.* 投资	unit 5
invoice *n.* 发票	unit 7

L

lease *v. & n.* 租借	unit 5
liability *n.* 责任	unit 10
liquidation *n.* 清算	unit 9

M

malicious *adj.* 恶意的	unit 5
manual *adj.* 手写的	unit 10
marine *adj.* 海洋的;*n.* 舰队	unit 8
mature *v.* 到期;*adj.* 到期的	unit 1
medical *adj.* 医疗的;*n.* 全身健康检查	unit 5
miscarriage *n.* 误投	unit 7
misfortune *n.* 灾祸	unit 8
Moody's 穆迪投资公司	unit 9
mortgage *v.* 抵押	unit 2
motivation *n.* 动机	unit 9

N

nominated *adj.* 被指定的	unit 6
note *n.* 钞票	unit 3

O

obliged *adj.* 感激的	unit 10
official *adj.* 官方的	unit 3
operational *adj.* 经营的	unit 2
original *n.* 正本	unit 7
overdraft *v. & n.* 透支	unit 4
oversee *v.* 监管	unit 9
ownership *n.* 所有权	unit 9

P

par *n.* 面值	unit 9
passbook *n.* 存折	unit 1
passport *n.* 护照	unit 1
password *n.* 密码	unit 1
paperwork *n.* 手续	unit 6
payee *n.* 收款人	unit 6
payroll *n.* 工资	unit 4
periodic *adj.* 定期的	unit 9
performance *n.* 业绩	unit 9
peripheral *adj.* 次要的	unit 5
placement *n.* 配置	unit 9
pledge *v.* 抵押	unit 10
portfolio *n.* 投资组合	unit 9
postscript *n.* 附言	unit 10
pre-engaging *adj.* 预约的	unit 8
premium *n.* 保费	unit 8
n. 溢价	unit 9
principal *n.* 委托人	unit 6
priority *n.* 优先权	unit 9
privacy *n.* 隐私	unit 8
private *adj.* 私人的	unit 10
privilege *n.* 优惠	unit 2
procedure *n.* 手续	unit 2
property *n.* 财产	unit 8
proposition *n.* 建议,想法	unit 2
prospectus *n.* 招股说明书	unit 9
provision *n.* 规定	unit 6

Q

quasi *adj.* 类似的	unit 8
quote *v.* 报价	unit 5
quotation *n.* 报价单,行情表	unit 3

R

rate *n.* 保险费率	unit 5
recession *n.* 萧条	unit 9
recourse *n.* 追索权	unit 6
redeem *v.* 赎回	unit 5
reference *n.* 证明文书,资信证明人	unit 10
register *v.* 注册	unit 10
reimburse *v.* 补偿	unit 5
reimbursement *n.* 追索,追偿	unit 4
reinsurance *n.* 再保险	unit 8
remit *v.* 汇款	unit 6
remittance *n.* 汇款	unit 6
renewal *n.* 更新	unit 4
rental *n.* 租金总额; *adj.* 出租的	unit 8
renter *n.* 租户	unit 8
repay *v.* 偿还	unit 2
representative *n.* 代表	unit 8
respectively *adv.* 分别地	unit 6

S

safekeeping *n.* 保管	unit 8
salutation *n.* 称呼	unit 10
securities *n.* 证券	unit 5
share *n.* 股份	unit 1
shipments *n.* 运输	unit 5
sidelines *n.* 场外	unit 9
sign *v.* 签字	unit 3
slip *n.* 凭条	unit 3
Standard & Poor's 标准普尔公司	unit 9
stocks *n.* 股票	unit 9
stockbroker *n.* 股票经纪人	unit 9
subrogation *n.* 代位追偿	unit 5
subsidiary *n.* 子公司; *adj.* 附属的	unit 6

T

tariff *v.* 费率	unit 6
terms *n.* 期限	unit 2
territory *n.* 领土	unit 6
transshipment *n.* 转运	unit 7
trustor *n.* 委托人	unit 5

U

unforeseen *adj.* 意外的	unit 8
unpredictable *adj.* 不可预测的	unit 8

unsecured *adj.* 无抵押	unit 2
unused *adj.* 未使用过的	unit 3
updated *adj.* 最新的	unit 9

V

vacation *n.* 假期	unit 3
valid *adj.* 有效的	unit 8
validity *n.* 有效性	unit 4
valuables *n.* 贵重品	unit 8
vandalism *n.* 故意破坏或恶意行为	unit 5
vault *n.* 保险库	unit 8
vehicle *n.* 车辆	unit 8
venture *v. & n.* 冒险	unit 8
versatile *adj.* 多用途的	unit 4
vicissitude *n.* 兴败	unit 8
violation *n.* 违背	unit 5
vote *n.* 投票权	unit 9

W

wages *n.* 薪水,工资	unit 3
warehouse *n.* 仓库	unit 10
v. 持仓	unit 9
withdraw *v.* 取款	unit 1
withdrawal *n.* 取款	unit 1
witness *v.* 目睹；*n.* 证据	unit 5

Tapescripts

Unit 1 Deposits

5 ■ *Spot Dictation: In this section you'll hear two short paragraphs. There are some words or phrases missing in each paragraph. Each paragraph will be read three times. For the first time you just listen and for the second time, you'll have a break of 20 seconds. During the break, you can write down the missing words or phrases. The third time is for you to check your writing. Now let's begin.*

1

Secondly, there are time deposits which always earn interest. The name time deposit arises because, in principle, these deposits may not usually be withdrawn without notice. The notice will be agreed between the bank and the depositor when the deposit is first opened. However, there is one group of time deposits called instant savings accounts where limited withdrawals may be made without any notice being formally required.

2

Some countries insure bank deposits but do not assess deposit premiums until bank has failed. This is the case in Turkey where only after a bank has failed are other banks asked to furnish the funds to pay depositors of the failed bank. In addition, the requirements to open a bank are very difficult, which makes it difficult for someone to enter the business of banking. Thus, Turkish banks tend to operate more safely since no fund for depositor payoffs exists until after a bank failure. The assessments made at that time may be very high, especially if a large bank were to fail.

■ *Complete sentences: In this part you will hear 6 sentences. Each sentence will be read twice. For the first time you just listen and for the second time, you'll have a break of 10 seconds following each sentence. During the break, try to complete the sentences according to what you have just heard. Please watch your spelling.*

1. Time is the period over which simple interest is calculated and is usually stated in years.
2. Making payments by writing cheques against cheque account deposits is popular, particularly when a high value of transactions is involved.

3. But the cheque itself is not "money"; it is only the amount of money in the relevant deposit account which is considered to be "money".
4. The balance standing to a customer's credit on current account is repayable on demand and he has the right to draw cheques.
5. There are three main types of bank deposits: sight deposits, time deposits and certificates of deposit.
6. Certificates of deposit are large deposits, usually over £100,000, and cannot be withdrawn until an agreed maturity date.

9 ■ *Listen to the following sentences and choose the best answer to each of the sentence you have just heard. Each of the sentences will be only read once.*

1. May I order a statement for my current account please? My account number is 30789410. And my name is Anita James.
2. The balance of your account of this month is three million six hundred seventy-four thousand five hundred ninety-three point zero one US dollars.
3. What will the bank do if it can't contact the customer who has overdrawn from his checking account?
4. May I have your passport please?
5. I would have opened a check account with your bank if I knew this.
6. With a current account, your money is immediately available.
7. Their account number is 173—272, and you put 173—227, with the last two numbers inverted.
8. Can I have your telephone number, so I can call you back?
9. Mr. Martin wishes he had opened the same kind of account as his colleague did.
10. The bank has a special obligation to depositors, because it makes profits from their money as well as its own.

■ *Listen to the following conversation from a woman and a man, after each conversation there will be a question. Find out the correct answer to the question you have heard. Each conversation will be read once.*

1. W: Will my deposit earn any interest?
   M: Certainly. The interest rate of savings account at the moment is 3% but if you opened a current account and deposit money, you wouldn't earn any interest.
   Q: What would the interest rate be if the woman opened a current account?
2. M: I'd like to draw two thousand francs on my account, please.
   W: I'm sorry, Sir. Your account has a balance of 427.20 francs.
   Q: How much is left to the account?
3. W: I don't need to hurry, the bank's open until six on Fridays.
   M: Yeah, but your deposit will only be credited if it's in by three.
   Q: What time should the woman go to the bank today?

4. W: I want to deposit some money on Sunday, but I don't know whether the bank opens or not.
   M: Oh, it opens just as usual. The business hours on Sunday are from 9 to 12 in the morning and 3 to 6 in the afternoon.
   Q: When does the bank close on Sunday?
5. W: Mr. Jones, this is Mr. Yamaha, our manager. Mr. Yamaha, this is Mr. Jones of the British Embassy in Tokyo. He has just opened an account with us.
   M: How do you do, Mr. Jones? It's a pleasure to meet you.
   Q: Who has opened an account?
6. M: All you need to open a savings account is $20. But in order to earn reasonable interest you should maintain a balance of at least $2,000.
   W: I only have US $200 but I'll open an account anyway.
   Q: What information does the man tell the woman?
7. W: Well, yes. What about interests on those accounts? I'm interested in fixed time deposits accounts.
   M: There are three kinds of fixed deposits, Madame. Three-month, six-month and twelve-month deposits. The interest on a three-month deposit is 4.5% per annum, on six-month 5%, on twelve-month 5.5%.
   Q: What is the interest rate on a six-month deposit?
8. M: How would you like your money, madam?
   W: Why? I like it very much.
   M: Oh, no. I mean, do you like your money in hundreds or in tens?
   W: Let it be in hundreds.
   Q: How would the woman like her money?
9. M: When would you like your time deposit to mature?
   W: Well, I'd like a monthly deposit, automatically renewed if I don't give the bank further instruction.
   Q: What maturity did the woman choose for her time deposit?
10. W: I want to put some money in my account.
    M: Please write down the amount, your name and the account number on this slip, Madame.
    Q: What is the woman NOT going to write down?

■ *Listen to the short passage and choose the best answer to the question you have heard after each of the passage. You will hear the passage only once.*

Passage One

There are two main types of bank account in the UK: current accounts and deposit accounts. A current account allows you to use cheque book, but your money doesn't earn interest. There are bank charges for current accounts, but if your account remains in credit you need pay no charges at all. You must keep a certain amount in credit in your current account to avoid charges. This amount changes from time to time.

A deposit account earns interest, but it doesn't allow you to use a cheque book. The rate of interest fluctuates. For example, in one year it dropped from 11% to 3%. You can withdraw money from a deposit account by giving notice to a bank. This notice is usually seven days.

A current account is a convenient and safe method of handling money. It is also called a cheque account. Your salary can go straight into your current account, and these days more and more people are paid by credit instead of in cash. Direct credit means that your employer, or anyone else who wishes to pay you money, can pay the money straight out of their account into yours.

Questions from 1 to 3 are based on the passage you have just heard.

1. Which of the following statements is NOT true about a current account?
2. What is the rate of interest for a deposit account?
3. What is direct credit?

Passage Two

One of the most important services in a modern bank is checking account. It's a safe and more convenient way for everyone to handle money. Another important service is a regular passbook saving account. You can withdraw money whenever you need it. You need only fill out a form and give it to bank clerk along with your passbook.

One more important service in a bank is traveler's cheques. They are safe and more convenient for travelers. If you lose your cheques, or someone steals them, you can get a refund. For this service, the bank asks a small fee.

The credit card is a bigger service in a bank. You need fill out a form and tell about your salary and other income. The bank issues the credit cards to the customers with good credit.

Most of these services do not provide a major source of income to the bank. The bank's largest source of income is through loans.

Questions from 1 to 3 are based on the passage you have just heard.

1. What is the checking account said to be in a modern bank?
2. What will the bank do if a customer loses his traveler's cheques?
3. To whom will the bank issue the credit cards?

Unit 2 Loans

5 *Complete sentences: In this part you will hear 6 sentences. Each sentence will be read twice. For the first time you just listen and for the second time, you'll have a break of 10 seconds following each sentence. During the break, try to complete the sentences according to what you have just heard. Please watch your spelling.*

1. *Character of the Borrower*

"Character" refers to the borrower's determination to repay the loan; it can be assessed by examining his track record. A bank can obtain information from credit card companies and other financial institutions.

2. *Capacity*

The word "capacity" indicates the person's ability, financial circumstances, and legal capacity to borrow.

3. *Collateral*

"Collateral" refers to security provided by a borrower to offset the apparent weaknesses of a loan. These weaknesses include inadequate capital, and certain risks and uncertainty arising from market conditions.

4. *Pricing of Loans*

The bank has to calculate its own costs of providing loans to customers. Most banks usually set an interest rate at some percentage which is commonly known as "margin" over the prime rate.

9 *Listen to the following sentences and choose the best answer to each of the sentence you have just heard. Each of the sentences will be only read once.*

1. Would you be kind enough to send us your debit authority next Monday?
2. The available credit line for ABC Company will be eight hundred thousand US dollars.
3. As a rule, we have to check the documents before effecting payments.
4. You have an option here to pay your bill either by cash or by credit card.
5. A security is required if you want to borrow money from bank.
6. This company is a speculative grade. You will run a greater risk to make a loan facility to it.
7. When the Fed wishes to encourage business activity, it may lower the discount rate to boost borrowing.
8. In reality, banks do face risks that non-financial firms do not.
9. Although it is a normal part of banking, excessive interest rate risk can pose a significant threat to a bank's earnings and capital base.
10. From the lender's viewpoint, moral hazard is the risk in financial markets that some borrowers may engage in activities that are undesirable or immoral.

Listen to the following conversations from a woman and a man, after each conversation there will be a question or a few questions. Find out the correct answer to the question you have heard. Each conversation will be read once.

1. W: Henry, I understand your invoice for US $1,000 is due for payment at the end of this month. Please allow me to defer payment until four weeks later.

   M: That's all right. We won't press you for immediate payment. Send us your check later on when you have money.

   Q: What does the woman ask for?

2. W: John, I regret to inform you that your account is one week overdue.

   M: Really? We were under the impression that payment of that amount would not be due until the end of this month.

W: It's overdue. Can you settle it within the next few days?

Q: When is the account due?

3. W: I saw in the estate ads you can offer a mortgage loan of 70% for 15 years. What does that mean?

   M: That means that we offer a mortgage loan of 70% of the price of the estate, say a house, to the borrower for the duration of 15 years.

   Q: What is the relationship between the two speakers?

4. M: Have you ever taken out any facilities from other banks?

   W: Yes. We did. We had a credit line of 2 million with ABC bank last year. This year we want to try your bank. We're told you offer more favorable facilities to the customers, don't you?

   Q: What does the woman want to get?

5. M: Banks face many types of risks.

   W: Can you give an example?

   M: Yes. The major type of risks is called credit risk. It means a counterpart fails to perform according to a contractual arrangement.

   Q: What are they talking about?

6. M: Banks will suffer from interest rate risk.

   W: Yes. Excessive interest rate can pose a significant threat to a bank's earning and capital base.

   Q: What does excessive interest rate risk mean to the banks?

7. M: International banking is accomplished by many different organizational types.

   W: Such as subsidiaries, branches and agencies of the parent banking firms.

   Q: Which of the following is not mentioned in the dialogue?

8. M: The Bank of England was founded in 1694.

   W: And in 1844 it was split into two parts, the Banking Department and the Issuing Department.

   Q: When was the Bank of England established?

9. M: The Bank of England also participates in the international activities of some organizations.

   W: What organizations?

   M: For example, the International Monetary Fund, the International Bank for Reconstruction and Development or the World Bank.

   Q: Which of the following is not mentioned in the dialogue?

10. M: Commercial banks in America must keep reserves on deposit at the Federal Reserve Bank or branch in their area.

    W: Why?

    M: Because they are members of the Federal Reserve System and the Federal Reserve Banks perform the functions of a central bank.

    Q: Where should the reserves be deposited?

■ *In this section, you will hear some long passages, at the end of each passage, some questions will be asked on what you've just heard. The passage and the questions will be spoken only once. After each question, there will be a pause. During the pause, you must read the four suggested answers marked A, B, C and D, and decide which is the best answer.*

Passage One

Banks act as financial intermediaries, accepting money on deposit from one group of people who may want it back on demand or at very short notice, and lending it out to other people for periods of time up to several years. The banks' function, then, is to convert short-run deposits into longer-run loans. On the one side stand people who have money which they would like to lend but who would also like to get it back whenever they wish. On the other side stand people who want to borrow but who may want to pay the money back over several years. They clearly cannot do business with one another directly. The bank acts as an intermediary, accepting deposits and paying interest on them and making loans and charging the borrowers interest at a higher rate. In doing so the bank relieves the depositor of the need to investigate whether a loan would be safe; the banks have built up considerable expertise in the granting of advances.

Questions from 1 to 3 are based on the passage you have just heard.

1. What are the depositors' wishes when they deposit money in banks?
2. What would the borrowers like to do if they borrow money from the bank?
3. What would a bank like to do when making a loan to a borrower?

Passage Two

Barclays Travelers Cheques cannot be cashed without your personal on-the-spot countersignature. Even if they are stolen or accidentally lost, your money is still safe. A special feature is that every purchaser of Barclays Travelers Cheques is provided with a booklet listing some 8,000 points around the world where refunds are obtainable. All these points are authorized to make an immediate refund for limited amounts. Any balance remaining may be speedily settled after a few necessary formalities.

The Barclays Group of Banks has the world's largest international branch network. One reason why Barclays travelers cheques are your passport to trouble-free travel. This unparalleled network ensures that the Barclays service is second to none.

Questions from 1 to 3 are based on the passage you have just heard.

1. When can you cash your Barclays travelers cheques?
2. Which of the following is NOT a feature of the Barclays Traveler's Cheques?
3. How about the service of the Barclays?

Unit 3 Foreign Exchange

6 *In this section, you'll hear a short paragraph. There are some words or phrases missing in the paragraph. It can be read three times. For the first time you just listen, and for* the second time, you'll have a break of 20 seconds. During the break, you can write down the missing words. The third time is for you to check your writing. Now let's begin.

  Companies operate and expect to be paid in the currency of the countries in which they're located. That means anyone wanting to buy from a firm in another country has to acquire some of that country's currency first. For example, if a US company that operates department stores wants to buy expensive wool sweaters from a British manufacturer, it has to pay the bill in British pounds, not US dollars. But the American firm has only dollars, not pounds. Clearly, to make the purchase, it has to exchange some dollars for pounds. We also say the firm buys pounds for dollars. The purchase is accomplished in foreign exchange market, which is organized for the purchase of exchanging currencies. The foreign exchange market operates much like other financial markets, but isn't located in a specific place like a stock exchange. Rather, it's a network of brokers and banks based in financial centers around the world. Most commercial banks are able to access the market and provide exchange services to their clients.

9 ■ *Listen to the following sentences and choose the best answer to each of the sentence you have just heard. Each of the sentences will be only read once.*

1. The Canadian dollar is the same in name as the US dollar but different in value with it.
2. The exchange rate of GBP against USD is the reciprocal of the exchange rate of USD in terms of GBP.
3. If a US company wants to purchase goods in Britain and the transaction is settled in sterling pounds, it has to exchange dollars for pounds first.
4. The foreign exchange market operates much like other financial markets, but isn't located in a specific place like a stock exchange.
5. Companies usually expect to be paid in the currency of the countries in which they're located because of the risk of exchange rates.
6. Because most countries have different currencies, payments purchased from other countries and receipts sold to other countries involve traders who use currencies other than their own.
7. A customer wants to exchange £1,000,000,000 for spot American dollars.
8. In case the traveler's cheques are lost, is it possible for me to get refunded?
9. When you travel abroad, it is always wise for you to carry your money in traveler's cheques.
10. It is always a problem to me to distinguish the buying rate and the selling rate.

■ *Listen to the following conversation from a woman and a man, after each conversation there will be a question or a few questions. Find out the correct answer to the question you have heard. Each conversation will be read once.*

Conversation 1

W: What is the rate of exchange for pound sterling into yen today?

M: For cash it is seven hundred and ninety four yen to the pound and for traveler's cheques it is eight hundred and eighteen yen to the pound.

Q: What's the exchange rate for cash?

Conversation 2

W: I'm going to Nairobi next week. That's why I want the cheque. It's better than carrying so much money with me.

M: I see. But the Swiss franc is not common currency in Kenya, you may have some trouble cashing the cheque.

Q: What kind of currency is the cheque in?

Conversation 3

Clerk: Good morning, may I help you?

Customer: Yes, I come to buy some RMB yuan for American dollars. I will stay in Shanghai for several weeks.

Clerk: You are welcome. Our bank is authorized to deal with foreign exchange and we can offer the service for customers.

Customer: I want to exchange some US dollars for RMB yuan. I've got USD 500.89.

Clerk: All right. This is an exchange memo. Please fill in your name and the amount you intend to change.

Customer: Yes. By the way, what's the rate for notes?

Clerk: Today's rate for cash purchases is RMB 8.2639/USD in notes. I can exchange the notes for you but we cannot take the coins.

Customer: Oh, really? Why not?

Clerk: We don't deal in coins, sir. Usually, we have very little request for coin exchange, and it is difficult for us to maintain the coins if they are not needed.

Customer: Oh, yes, I remember that is true in some other countries.

Clerk: So we just exchange the notes. Do you have your passport with you?

Customer: Yes, here it is.

Clerk: Well, Mr. Jackson, your five hundred dollars will be exchanged for RMB 4,131.95. Here is the money and the exchange memo. Here is your passport, please.

Customer: Thank you. Oh, need I keep the exchange memo?

Clerk: Yes, if you have leftover RMB when you leave China you may change it into foreign currency by submitting the exchange memo.

Customer: Thank you for the information. I'll keep it safe. Sorry to have bothered you.

Clerk: Not at all.

Customer: Good-bye.

Clerk: Good-bye.

Questions from 3 to 5 are based on the conversation you have just heard.

3. How much US dollars does the man want to exchange?
4. What is the exchange rate of RMB in terms of US dollar notes?
5. How much RMB Yuan has the man obtained for the US dollars?

Conversation 4

Customer: Would you please tell me where I can change the RMB Yuan back into US dollars?

Clerk A: OK, just go to the Counter No.16. They will do this for you.

Customer: Thank you.

Clerk A: You're welcome.

Clerk B: How do you do? Can I help you?

Customer: Yes, I'm leaving for America and still have some RMB with me. Can I change it back into US dollars?

Clerk B: Yes, we can convert your leftover RMB back into foreign money. How much are you going to change?

Customer: Well about 700 yuan. You see I must keep some for I may use them at the airport before I leave. It's a real problem cashing US dollars when the airport is crowded. So let me convert 650 yuan into US dollars.

Clerk B: All right. We'll do as requested. Your exchange memo and passport, please.

Customer: Here you are.

Clerk B: I'll fill in this reconversion memo for you. Just a minute, please. Well, here are the US dollars. Please check them.

Customer: Exactly.

Clerk B: This is passport and it is the reconversion memo.

Customer: Thank you very much. Oh, will you return the exchange memo to me?

Clerk B: Sorry, we must keep it on file. You see if you want to convert the leftover RMB back into foreign currencies, you should present the relevant exchange memo and the bank will keep it.

Customer: I see. Thanks a lot. Bye!

Clerk B: It's all right. Bye!

Questions from 6 to 8 are based on the conversation you have just heard.

6. Which counter can offer the service of reconversion for the customer?
7. How much RMB yuan does the customer want to exchange for US dollars?
8. Who will keep the exchange memo?

■ *In this section, you will hear a long passage, at the end of the passage, some questions will be asked on what you've just heard. The passage and the questions will be spoken only once. After each question, there will be a pause. During the pause, you must read the four suggested answers marked A, B, C and D, and decide which is the best answer.*

In the illustration, a typical foreign exchange transaction begins with a customer, which may be an individual, a company, or another bank. The customer enters the trade with the bank's dealing department. The bank's dealing department transacts the foreign exchange trade with another bank's dealing department. The bank confirms the transaction with the customer, usually by phone, and the customer approves the confirmation. A trading ticket, showing the details of the transaction—quantity of which currency at the transacted price and maturity of any forward rate agreements—is forwarded by the dealing department to the bank's operations department, the so-called back room, where appropriate accounting entries, payment instruction, and file copies are recorded.

The determinants of the size of the forward premium or discount include relative interest rates between countries. Differences in interest rates between countries move forward rates to either premium or discounts from the spot exchange rate. In addition, expected changes in macroeconomic activity, i.e. growth in gross domestic product, and expected inflation rates also will have an impact on forward exchange rates.

Forward contracts can be tailored to the needs of customers and, for example, can be contracted for maturities that range from a few days to several years. Such rates are negotiated between bank and the customer according to the market rate forward contracts can be hedgers, speculators, or arbitrageurs.

Questions 1 to 5 are based on the passage you have just heard.

1. What should a customer do if he wants to make a foreign exchange transaction?
2. How does the bank confirm the foreign exchange transaction with the customer?
3. Where will the accounting entries of the transaction be handled?
4. Which of the following will not have an impact on forward exchange rates?
5. What are the maturities of the standard forward contracts?

Unit 4 Bank Cards

5 ■ *Spot Dictation: In this section you'll hear two short paragraphs. There are some words or phrases missing in each paragraph. Each paragraph will be read three times. For the first time you just listen and for the second time, you'll have a break of 20 seconds. During the break, you can write down the missing words or phrases. The third time is for you to check your writing. Now let's begin.*

1

The U.K. Government stated in a White Paper entitled "A Post Office Giro" published in August 1965 that, in the light of those studies, the Government had concluded that a Post Office Giro, offering the usual facilities of the giro system in European countries, would be a worthwhile addition to the existing media for transmitting money. For many people with simple needs and no bank accounts, it would provide a cheap and efficient service, run by a familiar institution, for the settlement of bills, the sending of money and, if described, the receipt of their pay.

2

The banker must pay cheque drawn on him by his customer in legal form on presentation during banking hours or within a reasonable margin after the bank's advertised closing time at the branch of the bank where the account is kept, provided that (a) the customer has there sufficient funds to his credit, or the cheques are within the limits of an agreed overdraft, and (b) there are no legal bars to payment. The obligation to honor cheques is the most important of the banker's duties. The breach of this duty may involve the banker in a claim for damages.

■ *Complete sentences: In this part you will hear 6 sentences. Each sentence will be read twice. For the first time you just listen and for the second time, you'll have a break of 10 seconds following each sentence. During the break, try to complete the sentences according to what you have just heard. Please watch your spelling.*

1. A credit card is a plastic card to be used upon presentation by the cardholder to pay for goods or services.
2. Credit card customers are given a credit limit on the credit card account.
3. Banks normally set different credit lines to the different groups of cardholders.
4. Every time the cardholder uses a credit card for purchasing, he must sign a sales slip in the presence of the seller.
5. Each month the cardholder receives a statement from the bank, which lists the details of all the transactions in the month.

9 ■ *Listen to the following conversation from a woman and a man, after each conversation there will be a question. Find out the correct answer to the question you have heard. Each conversation will be read once.*

1. W: How do you pay for your purchases with a credit card?
   M: Usually I sign a sales slip in the presence of the seller, and the signature is then compared to the signature on the card.
   Q: Where should the man sign when he pay for his goods with a credit card?

2. M: What did you use to make the payment for the goods just now?
   W: A debit card.
   M: It is the same as the credit card?
   W: They are similar, but not the same.
   M: They look identical.
   Q: What does the man think of the credit card and the debit card?

3. M: I'm told that credit card customers are given a credit limit on the credit card account.
   W: You are right. The credit limit set by the issuing bank allows the cardholder to overdraw a certain amount of money if he needs.
   M: How to repay the overdraft?
   W: The bank will send a monthly statement showing the amount outstanding and time of repayment.
   Q: What are they talking about?

4. W: What do you mean by saying "outstanding balance"?

M: Well, outstanding balance refers to the amount showing on the statement the customer should repay during the time limit.

W: If the outstanding balance on my statement is $2,000, I should repay the money to the bank immediately I receive it. Am I right?

M: Take it easy. There is a grace period of 25 days for the credit card.

Q: When should the outstanding amount be repaid?

5. W: Do the banks set the same credit lines to all the customers?

M: No. Bank normally set different credit lines to different groups of cardholders.

W: How do the banks decide the credit lines of different customers?

M: Partly depending on the personal income, the occupation, and to a large extent, on the creditworthiness of the customer.

Q: What will be the credit line if a customer is a professor and has a good reputation?

6. M: I'm told that I can withdraw cash with my card under a line of credit established by the card issuer.

W: You are welcome. How much do you want to withdraw?

M: $3,460.

W: I'm sorry, you cannot withdraw so much because your balance is only $2,350.

M: Can I overdraw some more money and make it up to the amount I need?

W: No, because it is a debit card, not a credit card.

Q: How much does the man want to overdraw?

7. M: The bank seems to make no profit from the issuance of bankcards.

W: That is not true. It is a main source of income of a bank since the cardholder is charged a compound interest (say, 0.05%) on the outstanding balance if the full balance is not settled each month. Besides, the bank will charge a considerable amount of annual fee from the cardholders and the commission from the shopkeepers.

Q: What is the rate of interest on the outstanding balance?

8. W: I'd like to have a debit card as they are widely used to pay for goods and services.

M: Is it so convenience as a credit card? I heard that it couldn't be used to overdraw cash.

W: Right. That is because they are used in conjunction with a current account and the amount of the purchase is immediately debited from the account and no credit is involved.

M: So if you haven't enough money in your bank account, you cannot use your card.

Q: What is the precondition if you want to use the debit card?

9. M: Debit cards are used to activate POS terminals in supermarkets, gas stations and stores so that the cardholder can use the card to purchase goods or services, or withdraw cash through ATMs.

W: What do the terms "POS" and "ATM" stand for?

M: POS stand for "point-of-sale". A POS terminal is a computer installed in a store or s supermarket connected with a network and can send data of the transactions to the computer center immediately. ATMs stand for "Automatic Teller's Machines". They are installed in different places and provide facilities for people to deposit money or withdraw cash or transfer accounts.

Q: What is installed in the supermarket to be used to settle the transactions?

10. W: What is a smart card?

M: A smart card is a secure, portable, tamper-resistant data-storage device.

W: Is a credit card a smart card?

M: No. It is the exact size of a credit card and contains a computer with as much power as the original minicomputer. Data stored in a smart card are accessed by placing the card in or near a smart card reader and providing the specific security passwords associated with the data desired.

W: This is wonderful.

Q: What are they talking about?

■ *Listen to the short passage and choose the best answer to the question you have heard after each passage. You will hear the passage only once.*

Passage One

The use of debit and credit cards in place of many personal checks is reducing the volume of checks in the Fed's check-clearing system. Banks encourage customers to use cash machines because it enables them to reduce the volume of transactions at tellers' cages, which translates into fewer tellers employed. Debit and credit cards offer greater convenience to merchants than personal checks, because the cards permit a merchant to verify the balances in cardholders' accounts before completing a sale. Card readers instantly check your account balance through a computer connection; within seconds a balance is checked and the transaction authorized or denied.

Questions from 1 to 3 are based on the passage you have just heard.

1. What are customers encouraged to use if they need cash?
2. Which offers greater convenience to merchants?
3. What is used to check cardholder's account balance?

Passage Two

A debit card is a plastic card enabling the cardholder to purchase goods or services, or withdraw cash, the cost of which is immediately charged to his or her bank account. Debit cards are used to activate POS terminals in supermarkets, gas stations and stores. Together with credit cards, they are commonly referred to simply as bank cards.

Debit cards are widely used to pay for goods or services. They are used in conjunction with a current bank account. The amount of the purchase is immediately debited from the account and no credit is involved, hence its name.

A smart card is a secure, portable, tamper-resistant data-storage device. It is the exact size of a credit card and contains a computer with as much power aw the original minicomputer.

Questions from 1 to 3 are based on the passage you have just heard.
1. Which is not mentioned as the place where a debit card is used?
2. What kind of account is in conjunction with the debit card?
3. What is not the feature of the smart card?

Unit 5 Intermediary Services

■ *Spot Dictation: In this section you'll hear two short paragraphs. There are some words or phrases missing in each paragraph. Each paragraph will be read three times. For the first time you just listen and for the second time, you'll have a break of 20 seconds. During the break, you can write down the missing words or phrases. The third time is for you to check your writing. Now let's begin.*

1

Electronic banking has radically changed the way customers can do banking. Before-banking, checking an account balance required the customer to either go to customer service or the teller. Now, there are many methods available. For example, Internet banking which gives access to a broader range of services. These services include changing account details like address, and password, electronic funds transfer, arranging bill payments on direct debits, and performing account inquiries.

2

Agency salary and social insurance welfare business is a business whereby any subordinate institution of ICBC conducts batch inwards transfer through the advanced computer networked system, automatically transfers relevant funds into a savings account designated by a depositor, and pay his/her salary on behalf of the corporate/institutional unit or pay his/her social insurance welfares on behalf of the social insurance authorities.

■ *Complete sentences: In this part you will hear 6 sentences. Each sentence will be read twice. For the first time you just listen and for the second time, you'll have a break of 10 seconds following each sentence. During the break, try to complete the sentences according to what you have just heard. Please watch your spelling.*
1. This would reduce their financial cost and improve operational efficiency.
2. You will leap from the conventional finance management to the era of e-commerce
3. However, without the appropriate security measures, people will hesitate at paying their money on-line.
4. The agency disbursement by transfer is an efficient, safe and expedient mode.
5. That's because the ICBC has joined in the MasterCard International Organization in Feb. 1990.
6. Any depositor can pay public utilities expenses and other expenses due at any networked

savings office of ICBC

8 *Listen and complete the following conversations, each conversation will be read three times.*

1. A: Good morning, sir. What can I do for you?
   B: Good morning. I'm a customer of your bank. I've heard that your bank has opened a service called Bank-Securities Link.
   A: Oh, yes. It's a deposit account that links to your stock guarantee funds account in security companies.
   B: I see.

2. A: Let me show you around the service center of personal finance arrangement, telling you the services available to the customers now.
   B: Thank you very much.
   A: Well, here you can see, this service center has been designed for three different departments—a VIP room, a reception house and a business management office to meet the different requirements of the customers.
   B: Yes, the conditions and environment here seem to be so attractive. But what can I do when I need your service?
   A: You can have one-stop personal banking service from any one of the clerks here.

3. A: What services do you offer?
   B: You can read the balance of your account and the result of transactions, get information about interest rates, kinds of deposit, quotations of foreign exchange set by the bank, sell or buy foreign exchange or securities, etc.
   A: It sounds interesting. I may do my personal finances whenever I want.
   B: Yes, e-bank offers 24-hour service. It is very convenient for the customers.
   A: Thank you for your explanation.
   B: You are welcome.

4. B: Please fill out the application form of insurance with the amount and period on it. Write your ID card number clearly.
   A: I will... Is that so?
   B: Pass me your ID card, please. I'll check them up.
   A: Here it is.
   B: No problem. Here is your insurance document and your card. You will receive a policy from Ping An Insurance Company next month.
   A: Thank you very much.

5. A: Good morning! Can I make my mobile phone funded through your bank?
   B: Yes. Will you fund it in cash or through your savings account?
   A: I don't think I have an entrustment agreement for charge with you, and I'll pay it in cash this time.
   B: OK! May I know your mobile phone number?

A: 13951059995.

B: How much do you fund it?

A: 500 yuan. Here it is.

B: Here is the charge note for you to sign.

A: Sign it here?

B: This is the receipt of charge for you. Keep it well, please.

A: I will.

9 ■ *Listen to the following sentences and choose the best answer to each of the sentence you have just heard. Each of the sentences will be only read once.*

1. The minimum charge is $20.
2. We'll charge 5% interest on it.
3. The code number doesn't coincide with the one you give us.
4. You are requested to input your password.
5. I want to put some securities and valuables in it.
6. Besides insurance, you can also get more or less dividends.
7. It will mature two months from now.
8. It will be credited to your account automatically.
9. What's the yearly rental fee?
10. Our bank is open everyday from 8:00 a.m. to 5:00 p.m..

■ *Listen to the following conversations from a woman and a man, after each conversation there will be a question. Find out the correct answer to the question you have heard. Each conversation will be read once.*

1. W: If you have any question, please call 95588.

    M: Oh, that's very convenient.

    Q: What's the telephone number to call for the customer?

2. W: Good morning, sir. What can I do for you?

    M: Good morning. I'm a customer of your bank. I've heard recently that your bank has opened a service called Bank-Securities Link.

    Q: What is called for the service opened recently?

3. M: Well, how can I have this service then?

    W: Any customer of our bank, with a deposit not less than RMB 300, 000 yuan can win the membership.

    Q: What's a deposit for a customer to be the membership?

4. M: Could you tell me where I can buy such an insurance policy?

    W: Just at the counter of our bank.

    Q: Where can the man buy an insurance policy?

5. W: Is there any difference between dividend-participated insurance and deposit?

    M: The deposit interest is fixed, while the dividend of each policy will be transferred automatically into your account through our bank. The longer the term is, the higher the dividend.

Q: Which one is fixed?

6. W: What can I do for you?

   M: I want to pay the electricity charge. This is the Charge Card.

   Q: What does the customer want to do?

7. W: Your telephone charge is 68 yuan in total.

   M: 68 yuan. Here is 70 yuan.

   Q: How much the telephone charge is?

8. W: Well. We can arrange the phone charge deducting agency service for you to save your trips.

   M: Thank you. Let me think it over

   Q: What's service arranged by the bank for customers?

9. W: We have the advantages of computer network with 27,000 ATMs and 120,000 POS. You can enjoy pleasant and convenient services anytime and anywhere.

   M: Thank you for your information.

   Q: How many ATMS does the bank have?

10. W: Please pass me your "Current One-for-All" passbook. And input your password.

    M: All right.

    Q: What does the man input?

■ *Listen to the short passages and choose the best answer to the question you have heard after each passage. You will hear the passage only once.*

Passage One

If you want to use Internet banking services of the Bank of China, your company should open an account (basic account or settlement account) with the Bank of China. Any company wishing to take the advantage of our Internet Banking Service may request them at their local Bank of China office.

Once your request has been processed by the Bank of China, you will be asked to fill out a set of application forms and to sign an Internet Banking Service agreement with BOC or its branches. After that, you will be able to enjoy Bank of China's Internet Banking Services. Bank of China is committed to provide our clients with professional consulting, training and technical supports.

Questions from 1 to 3 are based on the passage you have just heard.

1. What should you do if you want to use Internet banking services of the Bank of China?
2. Where does a company apply for Internet banking services of the Bank of China?
3. Once your request has been processed by the Bank of China, you will be asked to fill out a set of _____.

Passage Two

Signified by the signing of the "Agency Personal Duty Refund Collection for Consumption

Abroad" agreement by ICBC Shanghai Branch, Beijing Branch and the world renowned refund agency — Global Refund Inc., ICBC took the lead in the country to offer Agency Duty Refund for Consumption Abroad.

No matter you're a domestic or foreign resident, after consuming in over 130,000 shops with Global Refund "Tax Free Shopping" mark in Austria, Belgium, Denmark, Finland, France, Germany, England, Greece, Holland, Iceland, Ireland, Italy, Luxemburg, Norway, Portugal, Spain, Sweden, Switzerland, Singapore, Argentina, Czechoslovakia, and so on, you can take your identification certificate, shopping receipts, and Global Refund's refund checks with Customs' seal acquired from these shops to ICBC to handle spot cash duty refund or collect fund from your designated account. You enjoy convenient service of consumption abroad and refund at home.

Questions from 1 to 3 are based on the passage you have just heard.
1. Which bank took the lead in China to offer Agency Duty Refund for Consumption Abroad?
2. How may shops in the world have "Tax Free Shopping" mark?
3. You enjoy convenient service of consumption abroad and _____ at home.

Unit 6 Remittance

5 *Spot Dictation: In this section you'll hear two short paragraphs. There are some words or phrases missing in each paragraph. Each paragraph will be read three times. For the first time you just listen and for the second time, you'll have a break of 20 seconds. During the break, you can write down the missing words or phrases. The third time is for you to check your writing. Now let's begin.*

1

As a general rule, a bill of exchange must be duly presented for payment, and if it is not so presented, the drawer and endorsers are discharged. This is a tally important rule. There are many cases where the holder of a bill has lost his rights completely as against the drawer and endorsers, merely because he failed to observe the very strict rules relating to presentment for payment observe the very strict rules relating to presentment for payment. The acceptor, however, remains liable on a bill accepted generally, even if it is not presented for payment.

2

A foreign exchange account is an account to receive money sent from abroad and a foreign cash account is one to deposit and withdraw cash in foreign currencies. When you send money from different types of accounts, the bank charges are different. For example, if you want to transfer some money from your foreign exchange amount, there're two kinds of fees: cable charge and processing charge. Whereas, if you use a foreign cash account, there is an extra charge for remitting cash abroad.

■ *Complete sentences: In this part you will hear 5 sentences. Each sentence will be read twice. For the first time you just listen and for the second time, you'll have a break of 10 seconds following each sentence. During the break, try to complete the sentences according to what you have just heard. Please watch your spelling.*

1. If there is no direct banking relationship between the remitting bank and the beneficiary bank, the remitting bank will have to choose an intermediary bank.
2. The beneficiary bank is entitled to credit the money wired from abroad to the client's account based only on the client's account number indicated in the payment order or wire telegraph.
3. A bank draft is a financial instrument which is issued by a bank.
4. A foreign exchange account is an account to receive money sent from abroad.
5. A bill may be drawn upon any person, whereas a check must be drawn upon a banker.

9 *Listen to the following conversations from a woman and a man, after each conversation there will be a question. Find out the correct answer to the question you have heard. Each conversation will be read once.*

1. M: May I cash these traveler's checks for $300 here?
   W: Of course. Would you please countersign them here? Also write place and date as specified.
   M: OK. Here you are.
   W: Your passport please. A moment, please. Here you are. Please check it.
   M: The amount is correct. Thank you very much.
   Q: What does the man want to do according to the conversation?

2. W: Did you hear about Mr. Williams' case last week?
   M: Yes. It's too terrible. As a matter of fact, he should not issue an open check in favor of a third party. Anyone who holds it would present it to the paying bank and obtain cash against it.
   Q: What happened to Mr. Williams?

3. M: If a customer lost his draft, what should he do?
   W: He should report it to his bank first, of course.
   M: Will the bank still pay the draft to him?
   W: The drawee bank may investigate the title of the person who holds it. If he has a good title, the draft will be paid.
   Q: What will the drawee bank do after being informed of loss of a draft?

4. W: Could you please tell me how to determine the time of payment of a bill?
   M: No problem. Where a bill is payable at a fixed period, the time of payment is determined by excluding the day from which the time is to begin to run and by including the day of payment.

Q: What is the date of payment if the bill is payable at 30 days after sight and it is accepted on July 7th?
5. M: What will happen if a draft is not presented for payment when due?
W: If this is the case, all the signatures on the bill will be discharged except the acceptor.
M: What about the check?
W: The drawer of a check is not discharged for 6 years, unless through the delay in presentation he has been injured.
Q: What are the two people mainly talking about?
6. M: Nowadays the use of traveler's check really brings great convenience to the people around the world.
W: I agree. In order to guard against fraud, the customer is generally required to write in his name on each traveler's check in the presence of the issuing bank and to countersign each instrument in the presence of the correspondent. The two signatures are then compared to make sure they are written by the same person.
Q: Which of the following is not the way to guard against fraud of a check?

Unit 7 Letter of Credit

6 ■ *Spot Dictation: In this section you'll hear two short conversations. There are some words or phrases missing in each paragraph. Each conversation will be read three times. For the first time you just listen and for the second time, you'll have a break of 20 seconds. During the break, you can write down the missing words or phrases. The third time is for you to check your writing. Now let's begin.*

Conversation 1

Clerk: Can I help you?

Wu Ming: Yes, I want to open an irrevocable L/C.

Clerk: OK. Please fill in this form first. (After a while...)

Wu Ming: It's done. Is it all right?

Clerk: Let me see, there is something you should make sure. First, you must fill in the exact L/C amount. That's the most important of all.

Wu Ming: The amount is $105,000.

Clerk: Second, you should write in details about the description, quantity and price of your goods.

Wu Ming: 10 warm air blowers, $10,500 per set.

Clerk: Last, you should specify the latest date of shipment.

Wu Ming: I'll call my manager to make it sure. Thank you very much.

Clerk: You are welcome.

Conversation 2

Cao Yang: Hello, may I speak to Brain?

Brain: This is Brain speaking.

Cao Yang: This is Cao Yang. Good afternoon, Mr. Brain.

Brain: Good afternoon.

Cao Yang: I received your L/C No.3687 yesterday. Is it a confirmed or unconfirmed L/C?

Brain: It is confirmed.

Cao Yang: But the credit is not signed " confirmed ", and I can not find the drawn clause.

Brain: Hold on, I will check it up. (After a while...) Yes, you are right. In accordance with the Sales Contract, it is a " confirmed " credit, and we forgot to notify you.

Cao Yang: So I hope you can send us an amendment as soon as possible.

Brain: Sure. I'll send it to you right now.

Cao Yang: Thank you. Good-bye!

Brain: Bye.

9 ■ *Listen to the following sentences and choose the best answer to each of the sentences you have just heard. Each of the sentences will be only read once.*

1. A draft payable within 30 days after sight is called _____.
2. ABC Company applied for a sight letter of credit for settlement instead of documentary collection.
3. If a letter of credit is issued for guarantee of performance rather than payment, such a letter of credit is called _____.
4. We'll have the L/C faxed over to you.
5. We have credited the amount under L/C 123 to your Head Office.
6. Under the documentary credit, banks are in no way concerned with the sales contract on which the credit may be based.
7. The beneficiaries have to make all the documents comply with the terms and conditions of the credit.
8. In fact, by issuing a letter of credit, a bank extends a credit facility to the importer customer.
9. If a letter of credit is issued irrevocably, it can't be canceled nor amended without permission.
10. The said letter of credit is advised to the beneficiary through you and please add your confirmation to it if required by the beneficiary.

■ *Listen to the following conversation from a woman and a man, after each conversation there will be a question or a few questions. Find out the correct answer to the question you have heard. Each conversation will be read once.*

1. W: Manager, I have to inform you that there is an error in our invoice to Mr. Smith for the shoes he ordered on May 25.

   M: OK, just change " carriage forward " to " carriage paid ". We can't lose this customer.

   Q: What did the customer order on May 25?

2. W: I'm expecting some money which was transferred to me a fortnight ago.
   M: Where's it from?
   M: London.
   W: From which bank?
   M: Barclays.
   Q: When was the transfer sent to the man?
3. M: Could you tell me what specific document you will provide?
   W: Together with the draft, we'll also send you a complete set of bills of lading, an invoice, an export license, an insurance policy, a certificate of origin, and a certificate of inspection.
   Q: What document did the woman not mention?
4. M: I'd like to know if you can look after some documents for me.
   W: Yes, sir. We have a special service, the safe department, who can answer your questions.
   Q: Who can look after the documents?
5. M: We haven't set up correspondent relations with Citibank, New York.
   W: Then we shall try to find another bank to have our letter of credit advised.
   Q: What do we learn from the conversation?
6. W: Can I help you?
   M: Would you tell me about the main contents of the documents?
   W: Name, quality, unit price and amount of goods, ports of loading and destination, price and payment terms, shipping documents, latest shipment date and validity of the L/C.
   Q: What may be the name of the document?
7. M: How can I send an L/C to my customer when I have opened it?
   W: In practice, our bank will send the L/C to one of our correspondents in the country of exporter by cable. After verifying the authenticity of the L/C, the correspondent will send the L/C to the exporter.
   Q: Who will send the L/C to the beneficiary?
8. M: I wonder if I can specify a collecting bank.
   W: Well, of course. But I suggest leaving the choice to the remitting bank.
   M: Why?
   W: Not all overseas banks can be relied upon, and it is much safer for the remitting bank to select one for you.
   Q: Who can select a collecting bank?
9. W: Mr. Green, the beneficiary has forwarded the documents to our bank. What shall we do next?
   M: We will check the documents against the terms and conditions of the L/C. If all are proper, we will settle the transaction with him. Then we forward the documents to the issuing bank.
   W: Who will reimburse us, the issuing bank or the importer?

M: The issuing bank, of course.

Q: Where does the conversation take place?

10. W: Our company will do business with ABC Wine Company in France in next two months.

M: Does the company have a good credit standing?

W: We don't have too much information about it.

M: In that case, I advise you to create a documentary credit. It will reduce the possible risk of export.

Q: Which means of settlement is the safest from the exporter's viewpoint?

■ *In this section, you will hear a long conversation, at the end of the conversation, some questions will be asked on what you've just heard. The conversation and the questions will be spoken only once. After each question, there will be a pause. During the pause, you must read the four suggested answers marked A, B, C and D, and decide which is the best answer.*

M: With the development of import and export transactions, letters of credit are playing more and more important role in foreign trade. As a bank clerk, I should know as much as possible about them. Could you give me a brief and concise introduction about them?

W: It is a pleasure, my friend. Well, you know, a letter of credit is a bank document that is established by the issuing bank to the beneficiary. The most important feature of a letter of credit is that the issuing bank undertakes to pay the beneficiary's drawings if the shipment has been made under the credit and all the documents are presented complying with the terms and conditions of the credit.

M: So a letter of credit serves as a conditional payment promise of the issuing bank,. Am I right?

W: Yes.

M: Please give me an example.

W: Suppose Dongfang is an export corporation in Beijing. Ben is an American import company with good credit standing. A sales contract has been concluded between them. The settlement of the transaction is to be made by an irrevocable letter of credit. Ben will ask its bank to issue an irrevocable letter of credit in favor of Dongfang to cover the contract. Now, we say Dongfang is the beneficiary, and Ben is the applicant of the letter of credit, and the bank that issues the letter of credit is called the issuing bank.

M: Now, Dongfang will receive the letter of credit directly?

W: No. Usually a letter of credit is advised through the issuing bank's correspondent in the place of export. So the correspondent bank is called advising bank.

M: What will the advising bank do next?

W: After it receives the credit, it will verify the authenticity of the letter of credit and see if the beneficiary can fully carry out its terms.

M: And then?

W: It will send the original letter of credit to the beneficiary and keep the copy on file.

M: So Dongfang has got the promise of payment from the importer's bank.

W: Yes. So it starts to arrange shipment of goods.

M: Will Dongfang get the payment as soon as the shipment is effected?

W: No. After the shipment, the beneficiary must present the letter of credit together with all the required documents to the advising bank in Beijing.

M: What will the advising bank do? Have a check?

W: Yes. The advising bank will check up all the documents and then negotiate them according to the terms of credit. In this case, the advising bank acts as a negotiating bank.

M: And then the issuing bank will pay the negotiating bank, right?

W: Of course. The issuing bank will reimburse the negotiating bank, that is, its correspondent bank in Beijing after it takes up the shipping documents sent by the latter.

M: The operation of a letter of credit is really complicated.

W: Exactly. We should be careful when we handle the credit business, especially we should observe the credit terms and documents strictly, or there will be a loss for both the customer and the bank.

M: Yes, indeed. And how many kinds of letters of credit are there?

W: Generally two: Personal and commercial.

M: A traveler's L/C is the personal L/C, isn't it?

W: Right.

M: What about commercial credits?

W: All of commercial credits must state whether they are irrevocable or revocable.

M: But I heard that few of them are revocable.

W: That's true. According to their nature, all may belong to the following sub-divided types.

M: What are they?

W: Documentary credits, clean credits, sight credits, acceptance credits, deferred payment credits, straight payment credits and negotiation credits, revolving credits, red clause credits, transferable credits, back-to-back credits, reciprocal credits, and standby credits, etc.

M: Today I've learned a lot. Thanks a lot. It'll be great help to my work.

W: You are welcome. See you later.

M: See you.

Questions 1 to 5 are based on the conversation you have just heard.

1. Who undertakes to pay if all the terms and conditions are complied with?
2. Who is the beneficiary according to the example mentioned in the passage?
3. What is a Traveler's Letter of Credit?
4. What is the nature of the Letter of Credit?
5. What must be stated on the commercial credits?

Unit 8 Insurance

5 ■ *Spot Dictation: In this section you'll hear two short paragraphs. There are some words or phrases missing in each paragraph. Each paragraph will be read three times. For the first time you just listen and for the second time, you'll have a break of 20 seconds. During the break, you can write down the missing words or phrases. The third time is for you to check your writing. Now let's begin.*

1

Motor vehicle refers to all kinds of two or more than two wheeled power-driven vehicles. The subject-matter of motor vehicle insurance is motor vehicle and third party liability in the main. The former belongs to property insurance category in the narrow sense while the latter falls within liability coverage. It should be stressed that the above-mentioned third party liability insurance is compulsory in most countries of the world at present so that the benefit of the victim can be ensured.

2

Application form is also known as proposal form. The following are the principle question headings common to most types of motor insurance proposal form: Applicant's name in full; Address; Occupation or trade; Date of birth; Physical disabilities and mental infirmity; Ownership; Cover required; Previous insurance history; Claim experience; Use to which the vehicle is put. Some insurers stress the application of certain questions to ensure that they obtain the premium and conditions which the risk demands and this may be particularly important where the driver of the vehicle has an unsatisfactory record of accidents or convictions.

■ *Complete sentences: In this part you will hear 6 sentences. Each sentence will be read twice. For the first time you just listen and for the second time, you'll have a break of 10 seconds following each sentence. During the break, try to complete the sentences according to what you have just heard. Please watch your spelling.*

1. You'd be eligible for a more favorable rate if you had one year's insurance experience.
2. If you insure your car against the third party liability only, the make and model of your car doesn't affect the premium..
3. The insured of the auto policy include the driver, passenger and even the pedestrian who are injured by the car.
4. We offer 20 percent discount to those with 5 years' accident free experience.
5. Coverage for the third party liability will pay for the bodily injury and property damage arising from the use or operation of your car.
6. Deductible applies if you replace your windshield.

8 *Listen and complete the following conversations, each conversation will be read three times.*

1. A: Good morning, Miss Chen. What can I do for you?
   B: Could you tell me where I can apply for personal insurance?
   A: Right here. I'll answer some questions for you.
   B: Thanks a lot.
   A: My pleasure.

2. A: Hello. This is Century Insurance Associates, Inc.
   B: What's wrong?
   A: Don't worry. There's nothing wrong. I call to see if you may have some interests in our products.
   B: What do you supply?
   A: Employee benefits, major medical / life insurance, disability income, etc.
   B: Oh, I object to discussing about death and disability in the morning.
   A: I'm deeply sorry. But....
   B: I think maybe someone else may have interest in your topic. Bye!

3. A: Hello. This is Pacific Insurance. We specialize in auto insurance. Our belief is that all drivers be accepted regardless of record.
   B: Incredible!
   A: But it is true. The motto of our company is that Pacific will when nobody will. And there is no charge for some accidents or violations.
   B: I'm impressed. Thank you. It seems that that is the very thing I'm looking for.
   A: Pacific will find the very thing to meet our customers' unique demand.
   B: I will think about it. What's your phone number?

4. A: Fire department.
   B: I'd like to speak to someone about a fire I had last night on my farm.
   A: Do you have a policy with us?
   B: I do. That's why I'm phoning you now.
   A: Alright, sir. Could you give me the number of the policy?
   B: It's FM 7680.

5. A: I'm from auto accident department. Are you Mr. Melton?
   B: Yes.
   A: I'm deeply sorry for what happened to you and your family.
   B: Thank you.
   A: How did it happen?
   B: Greg was in his car with some friends after school. The car was hit by a truck whose driver was drunk and at a high rate of speed. You see that damaged tree?
   A: I see. Let's go and have a look.
   B: Thank you. Please handle it for me.

TAPESCRIPTS

9 ■ *Listen to the following sentences and choose the best answer to each of the sentence you have just heard. Each of the sentences will be only read once.*

1. The policy number is FM 8976
2. The premium is $2,100 each year.
3. She chooses health insurance.
4. Life insurance is a means of shifting financial risks associated with death.
5. Physical examination is unnecessary for this program.
6. Are you confident to handle all these claims?
7. There is no charge for accidents.
8. This is Tony Green, sales agent of Timmerman Insurance.
9. Can you give me the number of the policy?
10. This policy doesn't cover the livestock.

■ *Listen to the following conversations from a woman and a man, after each conversation there will be a question. Find out the correct answer to the question you have heard. Each conversation will be read once.*

1. M: How much life insurance can I have?
   W: The maximum amount of life insurance you may have is $250,000.
   Q: How much life insurance can the man have?

2. W: Who can I designate to be the beneficiary?
   M: You may designate any person or legal entity as principal or contingent beneficiary.
   Q: Who can the woman designate to be the beneficiary?

3. W: Metlife is a global company?
   M: It has international insurance operations in 13 countries.
   Q: In how many countries does Metlife have international insurance operations?

4. M: How about this evening after work? I'll pick you up at 5:00 p.m..
   W: That's fine. You can come to my office. Goodbye.
   Q: What time will the man pick her up?

5. M: We have a 5-year term insurance program, which is convertible to the whole-life one when it expires.
   W: That's a good idea. I'll come to see you tomorrow if you are free.
   Q: Which insurance program can be convertible to the whole-life one?

6. W: To be honest, I don't know what deductible is. Could you tell me?
   M: Deductible is the amount you'll have to pay when you claim for a loss. The higher the deductible, the lower the premium.
   Q: Which statement is right according to the man?

7. M: As for personal property, are my autos, computers, lawn mowers covered?
   W: Your autos are not covered by the home policy but lawn mowers are.
   Q: Which personal property is not covered by the home policy?

TAPESCRIPTS **195**

8. M: Excuse me, I'd like to know the details of your child accident insurance plan. Who is eligible to participate in this insurance plan?
   W: Certainly, sir. We provide this service to all our customers with children who are unmarried full-time students aged four to twenty-four.
   Q: What qualifications are for child accident insurance plan?
9. W: Well, are there any exclusions to the plan?
   M: Exclusions include suicide within the first year of the insured period and AIDS.
   Q: What are exclusions to the plan?
10. W: Can you tell me the monthly premium?
    M: It will be 55 yuan.
    Q: How much the premium is for every month?

Listen to the short passages and choose the best answer to the question you have heard after each of the passage. You will hear the passage only once.

Passage One

Insurance companies are economic entities which are engaged in business of underwriting either life insurance or non-life insurance, and whose liabilities in relation to risks accepted are limited to their assets as declared to the authorities concerned in order to ensure a solvent standing for the benefit of the public. They enter into insurance contracts with their customers who are generally called assureds or insureds, and in consideration of a premium received therefrom, undertake to reimburse them for any loss of or damage to the insured interests during the currency of the insurance coverage.

By providing insurance protection to the public, an insurance company invariably builds up a fund of its own with the premium received from time to time for the specific purpose of paying claims filed against it for rebuilding or replacement of damaged or destroyed commodities, plants, machinery, equipment, raw material and so on.

Questions from 1 to 3 are based on the passage you have just heard.
1. Insurance companies are engaged in business of underwriting _____.
2. Insurance companies liabilities in relation to risks accepted are limited to their assets as declared to the authorities concerned in order to _____.
3. What is received from the insureds for the specific purpose of paying claims filed?

Passage Two

An insurance interest involves a relationship between the person applying for the insurance and the subject matter of the insurance. The doctrine of insurable interest was developed as a means of ensuring that the insurance contract would not be used for wagering purposes and also to mitigate the moral hazard. In the absence of the doctrine of insurable interest, an insurance policy might be used as gambling contract and could be an inducement to commit arson.

Insurable interest in property and liability insurance is established by means of a pecuniary relationship between the insured and the subject matter of the insurance.

This relationship requires a pecuniary interest, and insurable interest is limited to the extent of that pecuniary interest. Perhaps the most obvious of these relationships is ownership.

Questions from 1 to 3 are based on the passage you have just heard.

1. The doctrine of insurable interest is necessary _____.
2. Which of the following statements is not true?
3. In the absence of the doctrine of insurable interest, an insurance policy might be used _____.

Unit 9 Securities

9 *You will listen to a telephone conversation. The conversation will be read only once. Listen carefully and decide whether the following statements are true or false. Mark T for true and F for false in the brackets in front of each statement.*

Peter: Hello?

Joe: Hi, Peter. It is Joe Kerry.

Peter: Morning, Joe. It's nice to hear you. Anything I can help?

Joe: Yeah. I've just got my first paycheck and I want to buy some shares. But I don't know much about the stock market. Since you work for a bank, I guess you can teach me something about it.

Peter: My pleasure. Before you start investing in the stock market, you have to get certain basics in place.

Joe: Like what?

Peter: Well, people like you and me cannot just go to a stock exchange and buy and sell shares. Only the members of the stock exchange can. These members are called brokers and they buy and sell shares on our behalf. If you want to start investing in shares, you need to get a broker first.

Joe: It sounds complicated. How can I find a broker?

Peter: The Stock Exchange directory or the National Stock Exchange Website will give you a list of brokers. Most of them entertain retail clients.

Joe: Then what?

Peter: To buy stock you must open an account with a stock broker. The requirements for opening an account vary. You will have to fill out an application, and will probably be asked to deposit a cash balance in your brokerage account.

Joe: After that, I could buy and sell stocks?

Peter: Yeah. You can simply place a buying or selling order either by going to the trading floor, or over the phone or internet. When you put in an order to buy or sell shares, your broker will place your order on the market. The buying and selling orders are queued and traded depending on price and time. The better-priced bids will have priority. If there are several bids at one price, then the one placed first will have priority.

Joe: What else should I know?

Peter: In order to select shares, you need to understand some terms used in the stock market, such as IPO, Stock Ticker symbol, Final Prospectus...

Joe: Oh, Oh, please slow down. It's too much for me at one time. I guess I'll go and open the account first. Thank you so much.

Peter: You are welcome.

Unit 10 Banking Business Letters

5 ■ *Spot Dictation: In this section you'll hear two short paragraphs. There are some words or phrases missing in each paragraph. Each paragraph will be read three times. For the first time you just listen and for the second time, you'll have a break of 20 seconds. During the break, you can write down the missing words or phrases. The third time is for you to check your writing. Now let's begin.*

1

A letter is really a substitute for a personally delivered message. Your letter is your representative to the person you can't talk to face to face. The tone of your writing shows your attitude. You will want the tone and style of your letter to create a friendly respondence on the part of the receiver. Do not write when you are angry. If you do write, tear up and start over when you have recovered "cool".

2

In any office there is much discussion and not always unanimous agreement on the format to be used in typing letters. To begin with, your company letterhead should give the necessary information about your company. The letter should not be difficult to read. Most business letters should be less than one page in length. Your readers expect to find a clear statement of your purpose for writing, all the necessary information for them to act and a specific action to do.

■ *Complete sentences: In this part you will hear 5 sentences. Each sentence will be read twice. For the first time you just listen and for the second time, you'll have a break of 10 seconds following each sentence. During the break, try to complete the sentences according to what you have just heard. Please watch your spelling.*

1. A letter expressing appreciation should be genuine and rather informal.
2. When you send out a letter inviting someone to attend a meeting, be sure to give all the facts.
3. A letter of congratulations, which should be enthusiastic and brief, is always appreciated

by the recipient.
4. A letter of recommendation should indicate the person's experience and his value as a worker in whatever situation.
5. A successful letter of application requires you to submit the facts about your skills and abilities.

Keys

Unit 1 Deposits

1 Step 1: Fill in a deposit slip;
Step 2: Choose the method of withdraw by the password or by the passbook;
Step 3: Put in the password if you choose the former.

2 1. C 2. A 3. B 4. A 5. A 6. A 7. A

3
1. the time deposits
2. the demand deposits
3. the passbook
4. the bank card
5. The deposit slip
6. loss reporting
7. the single interest
8. the compound interest
9. check the balance
10. foreign currency account

4
balance — sum paid into an account
deposit — a deposit account
fixed account — the fixed time deposit becomes due
current account — checking account
saving account — bank account from which money can be drawn without previous notice
mature — any type of account that earns interest

(Also: difference between two columns of an account; any type of bank account that earns more than a deposit account)

5 1. (1) earn (2) in principle (3) withdrawn (4) depositor (5) group
(6) instant (7) limited (8) without any notice being formally required
2. (1) insure (2) case (3) the requirements to open a bank are very difficult
(4) enter (5) tend (6) exists (7) assessments
(8) especially if a large bank were to fail

1. simple interest is calculated and is usually stated in years
2. particularly when a high value of transactions is involved

3. the amount of money in the relevant deposit account
4. repayable on demand   he has the right to draw cheques
5. sight deposits   time deposits   certificates of deposit
6. usually over £100,000   cannot be withdrawn until an agreed maturity date

6 Step 1: Fill in the application for loss reporting;
Step 2: Present his or her credentials;
Step 3: Apply for a new certificate of deposit.

7 1. The teller tried to handle cash for the depositors.
2. A depositor wanted to open a checking account.
3. A depositor forgot to endorse his paycheck.
4. The bank wanted to store the customer's check on microfilm.
5. A depositor wanted to write a check.

8 1. (1) Can I help you?
   (2) I can open
   (3) handle it
   (4) You're welcome.
2. (1) Is there anything I can do for you?
   (2) How much cash do you want to deposit in your account?
   (3) the deposit slip
3. (1) Certainly
   (2) demand account
   (3) current account
   (4) withdraw my money
4. (1) withdraw some money
   (2) Your certificate is not due yet.
   (3) go through formalities as quickly as possible
   (4) think much of the customers
5. (1) deposit some money
   (2) have an account
   (3) time deposit
   (4) the application form
6. (1) What kind of currency is it
   (2) What term would you like, demand or fixed
   (3) withdraw money before the due time
   (4) the current deposit rate

9 1. B 2. B 3. A 4. D 5. A 6. B 7. D 8. D 9. B 10. B
   1. D 2. D 3. A 4. D 5. B 6. D 7. C 8. B 9. C 10. B
Passage One 1. B 2. D 3. D
Passage Two 1. B 2. A 3. D

Unit 2 Loans

1 1. B   2. D

2 1. long-term loan   2. terms
       3. loan application   4. credit standing
       5. repayment   6. operational state
       7. interest rate   8. guarantor
       9. floating rate loan 10. regulations

4 1. service   2. principal   3. source of income   4. cash-flow   5. submit
       6. capability 7. repay   8. business   9. real   10. repayment capability

   1. repayment   2. financial   3. sure   4. capital,
   5. competition 6. loan   7. strong   8. commitment.

5 (1) determination   (2) assessed   (3) financial circumstances   (4) security
       (5) offset   (6) inadequate capital   (7) uncertainty   (8) calculate
       (9) percentage   (10) margin

7 1. A   2. C   3. B   4. B   5. D

8 1. (1) How much do you want to loan
       (2) OK. What about the interest rate
       (3) Do you mean I need to repay the loan including the interest each month
   2. (1) What can I do for you
      (2) check your credit
      (3) check your documents
   3. (1) What can I do for you
      (2) What currency of loan do you want
      (3) What about the interest rate
      (4) How much do you want to loan
      (5) We'll have to check your documents

9 1. A   2. C   3. D   4. C   5. C   6. C   7. B   8. A   9. A   10. A
       1. B   2. B   3. C   4. B   5. D   6. C   7. A   8. C   9. A   10. D

Passage One   1. C   2. A   3. B
Passage Two   1. A   2. C   3. B

Unit 3 Foreign Exchange

1 Function 1: make temporary payment
       Function 2: regulate the customer's foreign exchange on hand
       Function 3: instrument for foreign exchange speculation

2 1. bank note rate   2. spot rate   3. foreign exchange   4. short rate
5. single rate   6. note   7. cash   8. identification
9. sign   10. discount

4 1. 根据我们的外汇管理条例,超过 20,000 元以上的人民币是被禁止携带出出境的。
2. 请到 6 号柜台办理。
3. 我想兑换一些钱来支付我在这里的花费。
4. 不过一周内假期一开始我将回美国去。
5. 目前我的工资还剩 2,000 元人民币。
6. 根据我国目前的外汇管理规定……
7. 好的,可是签在什么地方。
8. 在印有"当付款代理人(或出纳人员)面前复签"字样的地方。

5
Note of small denomination	会签小额钞票
Counter signature	复签
Foreign exchange certificate	外汇券
quotation	报价单, 行情表
floating rate	浮动汇率
Official exchange rate	法定汇率
withdrawal slip	取款单

6 (1) located   (2) buy   (3) country   (4) expensive
(5) manufacturer   (6) British Pounds   (7) exchange some dollars for pounds
(8) foreign exchange   (9) financial markets   (10) a stock exchange

7 1. exchange   2. reference   3. notes   4. frequently   5. fluctuate
6. favorable   7. commission   8. unused   9. convert   10. souvenir

8 1. (1) May I help you
(2) arrived
(3) change
(4) for
(5) would you like to change
(6) 2,000
(7) exchange rate
(8) rate
(9) can check it
(10) I will come

2. (1) How much do you wish to change
(2) Have you got any identity card
(3) exchange amount
(4) full name

(5) address

(6) nationality

(7) passport number

3. (1) What can I do for you

(2) How much do you want to change

(3) In what denominations do you want this money

9 1. B 2. A 3. A 4. B 5. A 6. B 7. B 8. C 9. B 10. A

1. B 2. D 3. C 4. A 5. B 6. D 7. C 8. C

1. D 2. A 3. B 4. D 5. A

Unit 4 Bank Cards

1 1. Handle withdrawals and transfer on an ATM, shopping, handle salary payment service, apply for telephone banking service, make an automatic banking, etc.

2. A debit card may be issued to you at the same time at any savings office after you transact the deposits and deposit a certain amount of cash (RMB 1 yuan at least) at the card issuing institution.

2 1. Debit card 2. Credit card

3. credibility/creditworthiness 4. authorization

5. overdraft 6. sponsor

7. exchange slip 8. grace period

3 1. T 2. F 3. T 4. F

4 1. You need to fill out an application form for credit card as well as provide the following documents.

2. The bank will decide your credit lines according to the amount of initial deposit you make.

3. The ratio of the amount of deposit to the credit lines is 10:1.

4. You can enjoy 20—50 days of interest-free period for your consumption.

5. Overdraft interest will be charged at the rate of 0.05% per day.

6. 3% service charge will be deducted automatically from your card.

7. I need to get the authorization, please wait a moment.

8. The POS machine showed that there were some communication problems in your card.

9. Our bank didn't receive the authorization number from your bank due to communication failure between the two banks.

10. My card is stuck in the ATM.

5 1. (1) entitled   (2) in the light of

(3) offering the usual facilities of the giro system in European countries

(4) worthwhile　　(5) money　　(6) needs

(7) it would provide a cheap and efficient service　　(8) settlement　　(9) receipt

2. (1) drawn　　(2) banking hours　　(3) margin　　(4) account

(5) funds　　(6) or the cheques are within the limits of an agreed overdraft

(7) obligation　　(8) involve　　(9) damages

1. pay for goods or services
2. a credit limit on the credit card account
3. to the different groups of cardholders
4. he must sign a sales slip in the presence of the seller
5. which lists the details of all the transactions in the month

6

Credit card — card that allows its holder to buy goods and services on credit

cipher — secret writing in which a set of letters or symbols is used to represent others

credit rating — assessment of how reliable sb is in paying for goods bought on credit

overdraft — amount of money by which a bank account is overdrawn

credit-worthy — accepted as safe to give credit to, because reliable in making repayment

7
1. 银行每月都会提供对账单以方便您理财。
2. 我行借记卡可开立各种储蓄账户，为您提供存取款便利，避免携带多种存折之烦恼。
3. 我行各种信用卡均达到国际标准，并可集人民币和美元两种货币于一卡，在全世界均可使用。
4. 申请表在我行各分行均可提供，也可在我行网页下载。

8
1. (1) change　　(2) credit card　　(3) advance　　(4) against　　(5) draw
   (6) draw　　(7) done　　(8) handle　　(9) exchange
2. (1) cash　　(2) cash　　(3) authorized　　(4) authorize　　(5) slip
3. (1) the line of credit　　(2) charges　　(3) commission　　(4) a annual
4. (1) available　　(2) How much　　(3) Five hundred　　(4) Authorization
   (5) exceed　　(6) cashed　　(7) exchange　　(8) passport
   (9) passport　　(10) way　　(11) passport

9 1. C　2. B　3. A　4. C　5. B　6. D　7. D　8. A　9. A　10. D

Passage One　1. A　2. B　3. A
Passage Two　1. D　2. A　3. D

Unit 5　Intermediary Services

1 Point 1: Safe deposit box is a kind of service rendered by the bank.

KEYS 205

Point 2: The bank keeps valuables for the renter in the form of renting a safe deposit box. Usually safe deposit boxes are metal compartments stored within the bank vault.
Point 3: Safe deposit box gives the customer both control over access to the stored valuables and privacy.

2 1. D 2. C 3. A 4. A 5. D 6. A

3
1. intermediary service
2. agency service
3. consignment service
4. commission insurance
5. phone-bank
6. mobile phone bank
7. e-bank
8. bank-securities link
9. payroll account
10. wage passbook

4
commission — a fee or percentage allowed to a sales representative or an agent for services rendered
discount — to deduct or subtract from a cost or prices
dividend — a part of a company's profit that is divided among the people who have shares in the company
premium — the amount paid or payable, for an insurance policy
fee banking — banking transaction that income is gained by providing services
fiduciary — a person who is trusted to manage trustor's property

5
1. (1) Electronic banking (2) account balance
   (3) teller (4) Internet
   (5) password (6) electronic funds transfer
   (7) bill payments (8) account inquiries
2. (1) Agency salary (2) subordinate
   (3) inwards transfer (4) funds
   (5) savings (6) depositor
   (7) corporate (8) authorities

1. financial cost   2. e-commerce   3. on-line
4. disbursement   5. Master Card   6. utilities expenses

6 Type 1: Toll station
It provides payment agent services for mobile phone fee, local telephone fee, Internet fee, tuition etc., and all-roundly meets various payment needs of the clients. The clients at different regions can also enjoy the payment services with different local features.
Type 2: Personal financing
To meet the needs of the clients for sustaining property appreciation and enable the clients to control their own properties at any time or place, "Personal Financing" provides various financing services with unique features for you, i.e. designing financing plans, applying for financing services, entering into various financing agreements, tailor-making financial information, pre-engaging services, etc.

7

	A	B	C
1.	(1)	(3)	(1)
2.	(3)	(1)	(2)
3.	(2)	(2)	(3)
4.	(1)	(4)	(4)
5.	(2)	(2)	(5)

8 1. (1) What can I do for you
   (2) Bank-Securities Link
   (3) your stock guarantee funds account in security companies
2. (1) personal finance arrangement
   (2) a VIP room
   (3) so attractive
   (4) one-stop personal banking service
3. (1) quotations
   (2) securities
   (3) e-bank offers 24-hour service
4. (1) application form of insurance
   (2) check them up
   (3) next month
5. (1) entrustment agreement
   (2) 13951059995
   (3) charge note

9 1. A 2. A 3. D 4. B 5. A 6. B 7. A 8. A 9. D 10. A
   1. C 2. D 3. A 4. A 5. D 6. D 7. B 8. B 9. B 10. C

Passage One 1. A 2. D 3. B
Passage Two 1. A 2. B 3. A

Unit 6 Remittance

1 1. 4 parts: remitter, beneficiary, remitting bank and paying bank.
2. T/T, M/T and D/D. T/T

2 1. T/T, Telegraphic transfer   2. M/T, Mail transfer   3. D/D, Demand draft
4. remittance slip   5. paying bank   6. remitter
7. beneficiary   8. collection   9. cash
10. term draft   11. discount   12. acceptance
13. dishonor   14. reimbursement

3

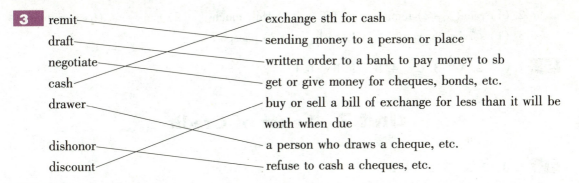

remit — sending money to a person or place
draft — written order to a bank to pay money to sb
negotiate — buy or sell a bill of exchange for less than it will be worth when due
cash — exchange sth for cash
drawer — a person who draws a cheque, etc.
dishonor — refuse to cash a cheques, etc.
discount — get or give money for cheques, bonds, etc.

4
1. I want to remit US $5,000 to my friend in New York.
2. You need to fill in a remittance slip.
3. I want to check if the remittance has arrived.
4. Could you show me your passport please?
5. Which is the quickest way of remittance?
6. How long will it take to remit money to Tokyo in the quickest way?
7. Can you help me cash this check?
8. How long will it take to collect this draft?
9. What is the charge for remitting US $5,000 to Frankfurt?
10. T/T is the quickest way of remittance.

5
1. (1) duly (2) drawer (3) tally important (4) holder (5) against
   (6) failed to observe the very strict rules relating to presentment for payment
   (7) however
2. (1) receive (2) cash (3) foreign currencies (4) charges
   (5) transfer (6) cable charge (7) processing charge (8) remitting

1. will have to choose an intermediary bank.
2. the client's account number indicated in the payment order or wire telegraph.
3. is a financial instrument
4. an account to receive money sent from abroad.
5. be drawn upon a banker.

6
1. international practice, valid passport; 2. countersigned, presence;
3. foreign, abroad; 4. save, cable charges.

7
1. 电汇作为一种最快的结算工具有助于出口商加快现金流动。
2. 与信用证和托收相比,汇付具有手续简单、费用低廉的特点。
3. 由国外向国内汇款是金融结算的一种方式,利用该方式国外汇款人可通过一家银行将外币款项支付给国内收款人。
4. 兑换汇票时,汇票持有人需在汇票背面背书盖章或签名。

8
1. (1) Could (2) remittance (3) has arrived (4) check
   (5) name (6) passport (7) handle it for you

2. (1) remit (2) remit (3) T/T (4) How much (5) money (6) remittance
3. (1) service for you (2) cash (3) passport

9 1. C 2. A 3. C 4. B 5. B 6. C

Unit 7 Letter of Credit

1 1. B 2. A 3. D 4. B

2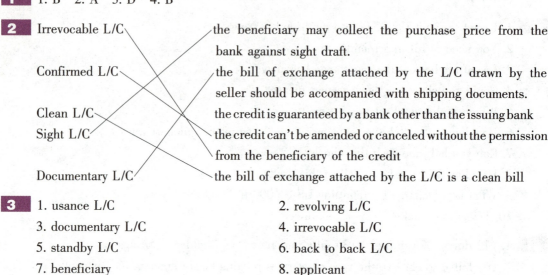

Irrevocable L/C — the beneficiary may collect the purchase price from the bank against sight draft.

Confirmed L/C — the bill of exchange attached by the L/C drawn by the seller should be accompanied with shipping documents.

Clean L/C — the credit is guaranteed by a bank other than the issuing bank

Sight L/C — the credit can't be amended or canceled without the permission from the beneficiary of the credit

Documentary L/C — the bill of exchange attached by the L/C is a clean bill

3
1. usance L/C
2. revolving L/C
3. documentary L/C
4. irrevocable L/C
5. standby L/C
6. back to back L/C
7. beneficiary
8. applicant
9. principal
10. original

4 (1) L/C (2) interest (3) deal (4) sight draft
(5) tie-up (6) concession (7) 6,000 (8) down

5
1. 开证行
2. 代收行
3. 保险单
4. 销货合同
5. 客户
6. 付款行
7. 承兑
8. 卸货港
9. 装运港
10. 国际惯例
11. 发票
12. 运费条款
13. 转运
14. 展期
15. 偿付

6 Conversation 1
(1) open an irrevocable L/C (2) fill in (3) exact L/C amount
(4) description (5) price (6) latest date of shipment

Conversation 2
(1) confirmed (2) unconfirmed (3) drawn clause
(4) Sales Contract (5) notify (6) amendment

8 (1) Yes, please.
(2) Good morning, Mr. Zhou.
(3) due to some reasons of our sales department
(4) we must acknowledge the beneficiary's consent
(5) If the beneficiaries agree,
(6) if they don't

9 1. B 2. B 3. D 4. C 5. D 6. B 7. C 8. B 9. D 10. A
1. B 2. C 3. B 4. D 5. D 6. C 7. C 8. D 9. A 10. A
1. D 2. A 3. B 4. B 5. A

Unit 8 Insurance

1 Principle 1: Principle of indemnity is one of the most important precepts for many types of insurance, particularly for property insurance. According to this principle, the insured may not collect more than the actual loss in the event of damage caused by an insured peril. This principle serves to control moral hazards that might otherwise exist.

Principle 2: Principle of insurable interest holds that an insured must demonstrate a personal loss or else be unable to collect amount due when a loss caused by an insured peril occurs.

Principle 3: Principle of subrogation grows out of the principle of indemnity. Under the principle of subrogation one who has indemnified another's loss is entitled to recovery from any liable third parties who are responsible.

Principle 4: Principle of utmost good faith requires a higher standard of honesty is imposed on parties to an insurance agreement than is imposed through ordinary commercial contracts. The principle of utmost good faith has greatly affected insurance practices.

2 1. A 2. C 3. B 4. A 5. A

3 1. insurance agent 2. insurance amount 3. insurance rate 4. auto accident
5. bodily injury 6. deductible 7. auto policy 8. collision
9. upset 10. claim

4
- insurance policy — a written agreement between an insurance company and a policyholder
- premium — a payment for insurance protection
- the insured — a person who purchases insurance
- claim — a request for payment
- the law of large numbers — probability calculation of the likelihood of the occurrence of perils on which premiums are based
- insurer — a person who sells insurance

5 1. (1) motor vehicle (2) subject-matter
   (3) third party liability (4) property insurance
   (5) liability coverage (6) insurance
   (7) compulsory (8) ensured
2. (1) proposal form (2) applicant's
   (3) occupation or trade (4) mental infirmity
   (5) cover required (6) claim experience
   (7) premium (8) accidents or convictions

1. favorable rate 2. the make and model
3. the pedestrian 4. discount
5. coverage 6. deductible

6 Type 1: Life Insurance: The chief difference between life and other forms of insurance is that in the latter, the contingency insured against may or may not happen. While in life insurance , the event against death protection is unavoidable sooner or later. On the whole, the prevailing life insurance contracts in the world today are chiefly term insurance, whole-life insurance, endowment insurance and annuity insurance.

Type 2: Health Insurance: Individual health insurance can be classified into two major categories, namely, disability income insurance and medical expense insurance. The former provides periodic payments when the insured is unable to work as a result of illness, disease, or injury. The basic benefit provided is a substitute income to replace at least a portion of the insured's earned income. Medical expense insurance supplies benefits for medical care.

Type 3: Accident Insurance: Personal accident insurance refers to insurance for fixed benefits in the event of death or loss of limbs or sight by accident and / or disablement by accident. The so-called accident must be accidental, unexpected and unintentional.

7
	A	B	C
1.	(1)	(3)	(5)
2.	(2)	(4)	(2)
3.	(3)	(2)	(1)
4.	(4)	(1)	(3)
5.	(5)	(5)	(4)

8 1. (1) What can I do for you
   (2) I can apply for personal insurance
   (3) answer some questions
   (4) My pleasure
2. (1) What do you supply
   (2) insurance
   (3) I'm deeply sorry. But...

3. (1) auto insurance
   (2) Incredible
   (3) charge
   (4) I'm impressed
   (5) meet
4. (1) Do you have a policy with us
   (2) Could you give me the number of the policy
5. (1) accident
   (2) what happened to you and your family
   (3) How did it happen
   (4) Let's go and have a look

9 1. A 2. C 3. C 4. A 5. B 6. A 7. D 8. D 9. B 10. A
   1. C 2. A 3. A 4. A 5. B 6. D 7. D 8. A 9. C 10. B
Passage One 1. A 2. D 3. C
Passage Two 1. D 2. B 3. D

Unit 9 Securities

1 1. F 2. F 3. T 4. F 5. T

2 1. B 2. A 3. C 4. A 5. B 6. B

3 1. stock 2. fund 3. trust 4. dividends 5. earnings 6. broker
   7. primary market 8. secondary market 9. stock exchanges 10. OTC exchanges
   11. bullish 12. bearish

4 1. 今天上午,深市开盘为1605.08点,与昨天收盘的综合指数相比上升了21点。
   2. 在行情上涨的情况下,汽车板块的多数股票有所好转。
   3. 有时很难确定股票达到波峰和波谷的时间。
   4. 绩优股的价格有望上涨。
   5. 股票价格很快回升。
   6. The stock exchange is one of the places where the public can invest their money.
   7. High-tech stocks have suffered a sudden drop in market share.
   8. The wild fluctuation in share values was because of the price war.
   9. Shanghai Securities Exchange ended higher, up 20 p.
   10. Wal-Mart showed a slight fall in share price last week.

5 Ownership: stocks represent ownership while bonds don't.
   Return: return on bonds is fixed while the return on stocks is variable.
   Priority: bondholders enjoy a higher priority in claiming repayment than stockholders.
   Maturity: bonds have fixed maturities while there is no maturity on stocks.

Voting: common stocks represent voting rights while preferred stocks don't.

Dividend: dividends on common stocks are variable while dividends on preferred stocks are fixed.

Priority: preferred stockholders are paid off before the common stockholder in the event of liquidation.

6 1. D 2. A 3. D 4. C 5. B 6. B 7. A 8. C

7 1. A 2. D 3. B 4. B 5. D

8 1. Issuing Treasury securities is a means for government to regulate the money supply.
2. Interest on this bond is exempt from local taxes.
3. Besides corporate bonds, the clients can buy government bonds.
4. Inflation is another risk to the investment in bonds.
5. Many people don't hold bonds until they mature.
6. 债券的利息收入水平与债券的信用等级成反比。
7. 发行债券是公司为某些大型项目筹集资金的重要渠道。
8. 同时也买些绩效较好、较稳定的债券来降低风险,是个好办法。

9 1. F 2. F 3. T 4. T 5. F

Unit 10   Banking Business Letters

1 1. The letter head, the date, the inside name and address, the salutation, the body, the complimentary closure, the signature.
2. The order of year, month and day is different. British English: day, month, year; American English: month, day, year.
3. The subject heading summarize the theme of the letter and helps to ensure that the letter is passed without delay to the right person or department.
4. These headings are used when it is desired to address a letter to a particular member of an organization.

2 1. T 2. F 3. F 4. F 5. T 6. T

3

Column A	Column B	Column A	Column B
transfer	余额	remittance	担保
statement	订单	proceeds	修改通知书
balance	偿付	security	货款
order	对账单	countersign	汇款
reimbursement	转账	amendment	会签

4 1. 承兑交单   Documents against acceptance   D/A
2. 付款交单   Documents against payment   D/P

3. 信汇	Mail transfer	M/T
4. 电汇	Telegraphic transfer	T/T
5. 票汇	Demand draft	D/D
6. 信用证	Letter of credit	L/C
7. 海运提单	Bill of lading	B/L

5 1. (1) substitute (2) message (3) representative (4) attitude
   (5) respondence (6) angry (7) have recovered
2. (1) format (2) letterhead (3) necessary information (4) in length
   (5) statement (6) purpose for writing (7) specific action

1. be genuine and rather informal
2. be sure to give all the facts
3. which should be enthusiastic and brief
4. the person's experience and his value as a worker in whatever situation
5. to submit the facts about your skills and abilities

6 1. Thank you for your invitation letter of December 12, 2005.
2. Once the credit is put into use, our bank will debit your account according to the drawn amount.
3. We feel very pleased that we have reached agreement with you on the cargo under the subject.
4. We suggest to make payment by T/T when the goods are prepared for shipment.
5. As to payment, our bank will open a letter of credit in favor of your bank, the amount of which is the whole value of the goods.

7 1. C 2. A 3. B 4. D 5. D

8 1. You have $4,000 of loans outstanding.
2. We hope you will be able to close your loan accounts before December 31.
3. You may simply neglected the loan, instead of violating our credit provisions intentionally.
4. We are enclosing a report on the said company for your use in private and reference.
5. The above information should be treated as strictly in confidence. There is no responsibility for the unreality on our part.
6. Please propose the discrepancies after checking the bill of November, 2007.
7. The due date of this payment is October 15, 2007.
8. For the fixed-rate loan with mortgages, the bank will charge interest at the same rate in the whole valid period.
9. We are authorizing you to draw on ourselves a sight draft amounting to $10,000, enclosing the following documents.
10. The usance draft under this L/C will be negotiated as a sight draft, discounted by our bank. The discount fees or interest and acceptance fees should be borne by the importer.

9 兹回复编号为 FA1234 的销售合同,2000 箱经由东风号轮船装运的牛肉罐头已于 9 月 18 日抵达青岛。我方提货后发现有 125 箱货物短装。船公司告知我们只有 1875 箱被装上船。因该损失不容忽视,故请求你方在提交最后三种货物时将短装的 125 箱补足。请在装运港核实并确定 2000 箱货物是否被全部装上船。盼电复。

10 Dear Sirs,

We confirm having received the copy of the said L/C. We are informing you that we have not received the original L/C after carefully checking the records.

We have advised the beneficiary based on the copy of the said L/C, according to which we shall make negotiation, providing that the original L/C can't reach in time.

Anticipating your early reply.

Appendix

International Currency Code

亚洲	货币名称		货币符号		辅币进位制
	中文	英文	原有旧符号	标准符号	
中国香港	港元	HongKong Dollars	HK $	HKD	1HKD=100 cents（分）
中国澳门	澳门元	Macao Pataca	PAT.；P.	MOP	1MOP=100 avos（分）
中国	人民币元	Renminbi Yuan	RMB ¥	CNY	1CNY=10 jao（角） 1 jao=10 fen（分）
朝鲜	圆	Korean Won		KPW	1KPW=100（分）
越南	越南盾	Vietnamese Dong	D.	VND	1VND=10（角）=100（分）
日本	日圆	Japanese Yen	¥；J.¥	JPY	1JPY=100 sen（钱）
老挝	基普	Laotian Kip	K.	LAK	1LAK=100 ats（阿特）
柬埔寨	瑞尔	Cambodian Riel	CR.；J Ri.	KHR	1KHR=100 sen（仙）
菲律宾	菲律宾比索	Philippine Peso	Ph. Pes.；Phil. P.	PHP	1PHP=100 centavos（分）
马来西亚	马元	Malaysian Dollar	M. $；Mal. $	MYR	1MYR=100 cents（分）
新加坡	新加坡元	Singapore Dollar	S. $	SGD	1SGD=100 cents（分）
泰国	泰铢	Thai Baht（Thai Tical）	BT.；Tc.	THP	1THP=100 satang（萨当）
缅甸	缅元	Burmese Kyat	K.	BUK	1BUK=100 pyas（分）
斯里兰卡	斯里兰卡卢比	Sri Lanka Rupee	S. Re. 复数：S. Rs.	LKR	1LKR=100 cents（分）
马尔代夫	马尔代夫卢比	Maldives Rupee	M. R. R；MAL. Rs.	MVR	1MVR=100 larees（拉雷）
印度尼西亚	盾	Indonesian Rupiah	Rps.	IDR	1IDR=100 cents（分）
巴基斯坦	巴基斯坦卢比	Pakistan Pupee	Pak. Re.；P. Re. 复数：P. Rs.	PRK	1PRK=100 paisa（派萨）

续表

亚洲	货币名称		货币符号		辅币进位制
	中文	英文	原有旧符号	标准符号	
印度	卢比	Indian Rupee	Re. 复数：Rs.	INR	1INR＝100 paise（派士）（单数：paisa）
尼泊尔	尼泊尔卢比	Nepalese Rupee	N. Re. 复数：N. Rs.	NPR	1NPR＝100 paise（派士）
阿富汗	阿富汗尼	Afghani	Af.	AFA	1AFA＝100 puls（普尔）
伊朗	伊朗里亚尔	Iranian Rial	RI.	IRR	1IRR＝100 dinars（第纳尔）
伊拉克	伊拉克第纳尔	Iraqi Dinar	ID	IQD	1IQD＝1000 fils（费尔）
叙利亚	叙利亚镑	Syrian Pound	£. Syr. ; £. S.	SYP	1SYP＝100 piastres（皮阿斯特）
黎巴嫩	黎巴嫩镑	Lebanese Pound	£L.	LBP	1LBP＝100 piastres（皮阿斯特）
约旦	约旦第纳尔	Jordanian Dinar	J. D. ; J. Dr.	JOD	1JOD＝1,000 fils（费尔）
沙特阿拉伯	亚尔	Saudi Arabian Riyal	S. A. Rls. ; S. R.	SAR	1SAR＝100 qurush（库尔什）1qurush＝5 halals（哈拉)沙特里
科威特	科威特第纳尔	Kuwaiti Dinar	K. D.	KWD	1KWD＝1,000 fils（费尔）
巴林	巴林第纳尔	Bahrain Dinar	BD.	BHD	1BHD＝1,000 fils（费尔）

大洋洲	货币名称		货币符号		辅币进位制
	中文	英文	原有旧符号	标准符号	
澳大利亚	澳大利亚元	Australian Dollar	$ A.	AUD	1AUD＝100 cents（分）
新西兰	新西兰元	New Zealand Dollar	$ NZ.	NZD	1NZD＝100 cents（分）
斐济	斐济元	Fiji Dollar	F. $	FJD	1FJD＝100 cents（分）
所罗门群岛	所罗门元	Solomon Dollar	SL. $	SBD	1SBD＝100 cents（分）

欧洲	货币名称		货币符号		辅币进位制
	中文	英文	原有旧符号	标准符号	
欧洲货币联盟	欧元	Euro	EUR	EUR	1EUR＝100 euro cents（生丁）
冰岛	冰岛克朗	Icelandic Krona（复数：Kronur）	I. Kr.	ISK	1ISK＝100 aurar（奥拉）

续表

欧洲	货币名称		货币符号		辅币进位制
	中文	英文	原有旧符号	标准符号	
丹麦	丹麦克朗	Danish Krona（复数：Kronur）	D. Kr.	DKK	1DKK＝100 ore（欧尔）
挪威	挪威克朗	Norwegian Krona（复数：Kronur）	N. Kr.	NOK	1NOK＝100 ore（欧尔）
瑞典	瑞典克朗	Swedish Krona（复数：Kronur）	S. Kr.	SEK	1SEK＝100 ore（欧尔）
俄罗斯	卢布	Russian Ruble (or Rouble)	Rbs. Rbl.	SUR	1SUR＝100 kopee（戈比）
波兰	兹罗提	Polish Zloty	ZL.	PLZ	1PLZ＝100 groszy（格罗希）
捷克	捷克克朗	Czechish Koruna	Kcs.；Cz. Kr.	CSK	1CSK＝100 Hellers（赫勒）
斯洛伐克	斯洛伐克克朗	Slovak Koruna	Kcs.；Cz. Kr.	SKK	1SKK＝100 Hellers（赫勒）
匈牙利	福林	Hungarian Forint	FT.	HUF	1HUF＝100 filler（菲勒）
瑞士	瑞士法郎	Swiss Franc	SF.；SFR.	CHF	1CHF＝100 centimes（分）
英国	英镑	Pound, Sterling	£；£Stg.	GBP	1GBP＝100 new pence（新便士）
罗马尼亚	列伊	Rumanian Leu（复数：Leva）	L.	ROL	1ROL＝100 bani（巴尼）
保加利亚	列弗	Bulgarian Lev（复数：Lei）	Lev.	BGL	1BGL＝100 stotinki（斯托丁基）
阿尔巴尼亚	列克	Albanian Lek	Af.	ALL	1All＝100 quintars（昆塔）

美洲	货币名称		货币符号		辅币进位制
	中文	英文	原有旧符号	标准符号	
加拿大	加元	Canadian Dollar	Can. $	CAD	1CAD＝100 cents（分）
美国	美元	US Dollar	US $	USD	1USD＝100 cents（分）
墨西哥	墨西哥比索	Mexican Peso	Mex. $	MXP	1MXP＝100 centavos（分）
危地马拉	格查尔	Quatemalan Quetzal	Q	GTQ	1GTQ＝100 centavos（分）

续表

美洲	货币名称		货币符号		辅币进位制
	中文	英文	原有旧符号	标准符号	
萨尔瓦多	萨尔瓦多科朗	Salvadoran Colon	₡	SVC	1SVC=100 centavos（分）
洪都拉斯	伦皮拉	Honduran Lempira	L.	HNL	1HNL=100 centavos（分）
尼加拉瓜	科多巴	Nicaraguan Cordoba	CS	NIC	1NIC=100 centavos（分）
哥斯达黎加	哥斯达黎加科朗	Costa Rican Colon	₡	CRC	1CRC=100 centavos（分）
巴拿马	巴拿马巴波亚	Panamanian Balboa	B.	PAB	1PAB=100 centesimos（分）
古巴	古巴比索	Cuban Peso	Cu. Pes.	CUP	1CUP=100 centavos（分）
巴哈马联邦	巴哈马元	Bahaman Dollar	B. $	BSD	1BSD=100 cents（分）
牙买加	牙买加元	Jamaican Dollars	$.J.	JMD	1JMD=100 cents（分）
海地	古德	Haitian Gourde	G. ;Gds.	HTG	1HTG=100 centimes（分）
多米尼加	多米尼加比索	Dominican Peso	R. D. $	DOP	1DOP=100 centavos（分）
特立尼达和多巴哥	特立尼达多巴哥元	Trinidad and Tobago Dollar	T. T. $	TTD	1TTD=100 cents（分）
巴巴多斯	巴巴多斯元	Barbados Dollar	BDS. $	BBD	1BBD=100 cents（分）
哥伦比亚	哥伦比亚比索	Colombian Peso	Col $	COP	1COP=100 centavos（分）
委内瑞拉	博利瓦	Venezuelan Bolivar	B	VEB	1VEB=100 centimos（分）
圭亚那	圭亚那元	Guyanan Dollar	G. $	GYD	1GYD=100 cents（分）
苏里南	苏里南盾	Surinam Florin	S. Fl.	SRG	1SRG=100 cents（分）
秘鲁	新索尔	Peruvian Sol	S/.	PES	1PES=100 centavos（分）
厄瓜多尔	苏克雷	Ecuadoran Sucre	S/.	ECS	1ECS=100 centavos（分）
巴西	新克鲁赛罗	Brazilian New Cruzeiro G	Gr. $	BRC	1BRC=100 centavos（分）
玻利维亚	玻利维亚比索	Bolivian Peso	Bol. P.	BOP	1BOP=100 centavos（分）

续表

非洲	货币名称		货币符号		辅币进位制
	中文	英文	原有旧符号	标准符号	
智利	智利比索	Chilean Peso	P.	CLP	1CLP＝100 centesimos（分）
阿根廷	阿根廷比索	Argentine Peso	Arg. P.	ARP	1ARP＝100 centavos（分）
巴拉圭	巴拉圭瓜拉尼	Paraguayan Guarani	Guars.	PYG	1PYG＝100 centimes（分）
乌拉圭	乌拉圭新比索	New Uruguayan Peso	N. $	UYP	1UYP＝100 centesimos（分）
埃及	埃及镑	Egyptian Pound	£E.；LF.	EGP	1EGP＝100 piastres（皮阿斯特）＝1,000 milliemes（米利姆）
利比亚	利比亚第纳尔	Libyan Dinar	LD.	LYD	1LYD＝100 piastres（皮阿斯特）＝1,000 milliemes（米利姆）
苏丹	苏丹镑	Sudanese Pound	£S.	SDP	1SDP＝100 piastres（皮阿斯特）＝1,000 milliemes（米利姆）
突尼斯	突尼斯第纳尔	Tunisian Dinar	TD.	TND	1TND＝1,000 milliemes（米利姆）
阿尔及利亚	阿尔及利亚第纳尔	Algerian Dinar	AD.	DZD	1DZ＝100 centimes（分）
摩洛哥	摩洛哥迪拉姆	Moroccan Dirham	DH.	MAD	1MAD＝100 centimes（分）
毛里塔尼亚	乌吉亚	Mauritania Ouguiya	UM	MRO	1MRO＝5 khoums（库姆斯）
塞内加尔	非共体法郎	African Financial Community Franc	C. F. A. F.	XOF	1XOF＝100 centimes（分）
上沃尔特	非共体法郎	African Financial Community Franc	C. F. A. F.	XOF	1XOF＝100 centimes（分）
科特迪瓦	非共体法郎	African Financial Community Franc	C. F. A. F.	XOF	1XOF＝100 centimes（分）
多哥	非共体法郎	African Financial Community Franc	C. F. A. F.	XOF	1XOF＝100 centimes（分）
贝宁	非共体法郎	African Financial Community Franc	C. F. A. F.	XOF	1XOF＝100 centimes（分）
尼泊尔	非共体法郎	African Financial Community Franc	C. F. A. F.	XOF	1XOF＝100 centimes（分）
冈比亚	法拉西	Gambian Dalasi	D. G.	GMD	1GMD＝100 bututses（分）
几内亚比绍	几内亚比索	Guine-Bissau peso	PG.	GWP	1GWP＝100 centavos（分）

续表

非洲	货币名称		货币符号		辅币进位制
	中文	英文	原有旧符号	标准符号	
几内亚	几内亚西里	Guinean Syli	GS.	GNS	辅币为科里 cauri，但 50 科里以下舍掉不表示；50 科里以上进为一西里。
塞拉里昂	利昂	Sierra Leone Leone	Le.	SLL	1SLL＝100 cents（分）
利比里亚	利比里亚元	Liberian Dollar	L. $ £; Lib. $	LRD	1LRD＝100 cents（分）
加纳	塞地	Ghanaian Cedi	₡	GHC	1GHC＝100 pesewas（比塞瓦）
尼日利亚	奈拉	Nigerian Naira	N	NGN	1NGN＝100 kobo（考包）
喀麦隆	中非金融合作法郎	Central African Finan-Coop Franc	CFAF	XAF	1XAF＝100 centimes（分）
乍得	中非金融合作法郎	Central African Finan-Coop Franc	CFAF	XAF	1XAF＝100 centimes（分）
刚果	中非金融合作法郎	Central African Finan-Coop Franc	CFAF	XAF	1XAF＝100 centimes（分）
加蓬	中非金融合作法郎	Central African Finan-Coop Franc	CFAF	XAF	1XAF＝100 centimes（分）
中非	中非金融合作法郎	Central African Finan-Coop Franc	CFAF	XAF	1XAF＝100 centimes（分）
赤道几内亚	赤道几内亚埃奎勒	Equatorial Guinea Ekuele	EK.	GQE	1GQE＝100 centimes（分）
南非	兰特	South African Rand	R.	ZAR	1ZAR＝100 cents（分）
吉布提	吉布提法郎	Djibouti Franc	DJ. FS; DF	DJF	1DJF＝100 centimes（分）
索马里	索马里先令	Somali Shilling	Sh. So.	SOS	1SOS＝100 cents（分）
肯尼亚	肯尼亚先令	Kenya Shilling	K. Sh	KES	1KES＝100 cents（分）
乌干达	乌干达先令	Uganda Shilling	U. Sh.	UGS	1UGS＝100 cents（分）
坦桑尼亚	坦桑尼亚先令	Tanzania Shilling	T. Sh.	TZS	1TZS＝100 cents（分）
卢旺达	卢旺达法郎	Rwanda Franc	RF.	RWF	1RWF＝100 cents（分）
布隆迪	布隆迪法郎	Burundi Franc	F. Bu	BIF	1BIF＝100 cents（分）
扎伊尔	扎伊尔	Zaire Rp Zaire	Z.	ZRZ	1ZRZ＝100 makuta（马库塔）

续表

非 洲	货币名称		货币符号		辅币进位制
	中 文	英 文	原有旧符号	标准符号	
赞比亚	赞比亚克瓦查	Zambian Kwacha	KW.；K.	ZMK	1ZMK＝100 ngwee（恩韦）
马达加斯加	马达加斯加法郎	Franc de Madagascar	F. Mg.	MCF	1MCF＝100 cents（分）
塞舌尔	塞舌尔卢比	Seychelles Rupee	S. RP(S)	SCR	1SCR＝100 cents（分）
毛里求斯	毛里求斯卢比	Mauritius Rupee	Maur. Rp.	MUR	1MUR＝100 centimes（分）
津巴布韦	津巴布韦元	Zimbabwe Dollar	ZIM. $	ZWD	1ZWD＝100 cents（分）
科摩罗	科摩罗法郎	Comoros Franc	Com. F.	KMF	1KMF＝100 tambala（坦巴拉）

The Primary Domestic and Foreign Banking Institutions

国　　内	
国家开发银行	China Development Bank
中国农业发展银行	Agricultural Development Bank of China
中国进出口银行	The Export-Import Bank of China/ China Exim Bank
中国银行	Bank of China
中国工商银行	Industrial and Commercial Bank of China
中国建设银行	Construction Bank of China
中国农业银行	Agricultural Bank of China
交通银行	Bank of Communications
中国民生银行	China Minsheng Banking Corp., Ltd
招商银行	China Merchants Bank
中信银行	China Citic Bank
华夏银行	Huaxia Bank
中国光大银行	China Everbright Bank
兴业银行	Industrial Bank Co., Ltd
广东发展银行	Guangdong Development Bank
深圳发展银行	Shenzhen Development Bank
上海浦东发展银行	Shanghai Pudong Development Bank
厦门国际银行	Xiamen International Bank
浙商银行	China Zheshang Bank
徽商银行	Huishang Bank
渤海银行	Bohai Bank

续表

国　外	
世界银行	World Bank
国际清算银行	Bank of International Settlement
亚洲开发银行	Asian Development Bank
东亚银行(中国香港)	The Bank of East Asia
恒生银行(中国香港)	Hang Seng Bank Limited
淡马锡控股(新加坡)	Temasek Holdings
英格兰银行(英国)	Bank of England
苏格兰皇家银行(英国)	Royal Bank of Scotland
渣打银行(英国)	Standard Charted Bank
汇丰控股(英国)	HSBC Holdings
巴克莱银行(英国)	The Barclays Bank, PLC
欧洲中央银行(欧盟)	European Central Bank
德意志银行(德国)	Deutsche Bank AG
瑞士联合银行(瑞士)	The United Bank of Switzerland
美联储(美国)	The Federal Reserve
花旗银行(美国)	Citibank
摩根大通银行(美国)	JP Morgan Chase Bank
美洲银行(美国)	Bank of America
美联银行(美国)	Wachovia Bank
三菱东京日联银行(日本)	Bank of Tokyo-Mitsubishi UFJ, Ltd
瑞穗银行(日本)	Mizuho Bank

The Central Banks

国家名称	中文名称	英文名称
阿根廷	阿根廷共和国中央银行	Central Bank of the Republic of Argentina
亚美尼亚	亚美尼亚中央银行	Central Bank of Armenia
阿鲁巴	阿鲁巴中央银行	Central Bank of Aruba
澳大利亚	澳大利亚储备银行	Reserve Bank of Australia
奥地利	奥地利国民银行	Oesterreichische Nationalbank
巴林	巴林货币署	Bahrain Monetary Agency
比利时	比利时国民银行	National Bank of Belgium
贝宁	西非国家银行	Central Bank of West African States
玻利维亚	玻利维亚中央银行	Central Bank of Bolivia
波斯尼亚	波斯尼亚和黑塞哥维那中央银行	Central Bank of Bosnia and Herzegovina
巴西	巴西中央银行	Central Bank of Brasil
保加利亚	保加利亚国民银行	Bulgarian National Bank
布基纳法索	西非国家银行	Central Bank of West African States
加拿大	加拿大银行	Bank of Canada
智利	智利中央银行	Central Bank of Chile
中国	中国银行	Bank of China
哥伦比亚	哥伦比亚共和国银行	Bank of the Republica of Colombia
哥斯达黎加	哥斯达黎加中央银行	Central Bank of Costa Rica
科特迪瓦	西非国家银行	Central Bank of West African States
克罗地亚	克罗地亚国民银行	Croatian National Bank

续表

国家名称	中文名称	英文名称
塞浦路斯	塞浦路斯中央银行	Central Bank of Cyprus
捷克	捷克国民银行	Czech National Bank
丹麦	丹麦国民银行	Danmarks Nationalbank
东加勒比海	东加勒比海中央银行	The East Caribbean Central Bank
厄瓜多尔	厄瓜多尔中央银行	Central Bank of Ecuador
萨尔瓦多	萨尔瓦多中央储备银行	The Central Reserve Bank of El Salvador
爱沙尼亚	爱沙尼亚银行	Eestonian Bank
欧盟	欧洲中央银行	European Central Bank
芬兰	芬兰银行	Bank of Finland
法国	法兰西银行	Bank of France
德国	德意志联邦银行	Deutsche Bundesbank
希腊	希腊银行	Bank of Greece
危地马拉	危地马拉银行	Bank of Guatemala
几内亚（比绍）	西非国家银行	Central Bank of West African States
匈牙利	匈牙利国民银行	National Bank of Hungary
冰岛	冰岛中央银行	Central Bank of Iceland
印度	印度储备银行	Reserve Bank of India
印度尼西亚	印度尼西亚银行	Bank of Indonesia
爱尔兰	爱尔兰中央银行	Central Bank of Ireland

续表

国家名称	中文名称	英文名称
以色列	以色列银行	Bank of Israel
意大利	意大利银行	Bank of Italy
牙买加	牙买加银行	Bank of Jamaica
日本	日本银行	Bank of Japan
约旦	约旦中央银行	Central Bank of Jordan
肯尼亚	肯尼亚中央银行	Central Bank of Kenya
韩国	韩国银行	Bank of Korea
科威特	科威特中央银行	Central Bank of Kuwait
拉脱维亚	拉脱维亚银行	Bank of Latvia
黎巴嫩	黎巴嫩银行	Bank of Lebanon
立陶宛	立陶宛银行	Lietuvos Bankas
卢森堡	卢森堡中央银行	Central Bank of Luxemburg
马其顿	马其顿共和国国民银行	National Bank of the Republic of Macedonia
马里	西非国家银行	Central Bank of West African States
马尔他	马尔他中央银行	Central Bank of Malta
毛里塔尼亚	毛里塔尼亚银行	Bank of Mauritius
墨西哥	墨西哥银行	Bank of Mexico
摩尔多瓦	摩尔多瓦国民银行	The National Bank of Moldova
莫桑比克	莫桑比克银行	Bank of Mozambique
荷兰	荷兰银行	ABN AMRO Bank

续表

国家名称	中文名称	英文名称
荷兰安的列斯群岛	荷兰安的列斯群岛银行	Bank van de Nederlandse Antillen
新西兰	新西兰储备银行	Reserve Bank of New Zealand
尼日尔	西非国家银行	Central Bank of West African States
挪威	挪威中央银行	Norges Bank
秘鲁	秘鲁中央银行	Central Reserve Bank of Peru
波兰	波兰国民银行	National Bank of Poland
葡萄牙	葡萄牙银行	Bank of Portugal
卡塔尔	卡塔尔中央银行	Qatar Central Bank
俄罗斯	俄罗斯中央银行	Central Bank of Russia
塞内加尔	西非国家银行	Central Bank of West African States
新加坡	新加坡金管局	Monetary Authority of Singapore
斯洛伐克	斯洛伐克国民银行	National Bank of Slovakia
斯洛文尼亚	斯洛文尼亚银行	Bank of Slovenia
南非	南非储备银行	The South African Reserve Bank
西班牙	西班牙银行	Bank of Spain
斯里兰卡	斯里兰卡中央银行	Central Bank of Sri Lanka
瑞典	瑞典银行	Sveriges Riksbank
瑞士	瑞士国民银行	The Swiss National Bank
坦桑尼亚	坦桑尼亚银行	Bank of Tanzania
泰国	泰国银行	Bank of Thailand

续表

国家名称	中文名称	英文名称
多哥	西非国家银行	Central Bank of West African States
突尼斯	突尼斯中央银行	Central Bank of Tunisia
土耳其	土耳其共和国中央银行	Central Bank of the Republic of Turkey
乌克兰	乌克兰国民银行	National Bank of Ukraine
英格兰	英格兰银行	Bank of England
美国	美国联邦储备委员会	Board of Governors of the Federal Reserve System
赞比亚	赞比亚银行	Bank of Zambia
津巴布韦	津巴布韦储备银行	Reserve bank of Zimbabwe

International Financial Institutions

中文名称	英文名称	简称
美国证券投资者保护基金	Securities Investor Protection Corporation	SIPC
美国商品与期货交易委员会	Commodities Futures Trading Commission	CFTC
美国国家期货协会	National Futures Association	NFA
澳大利亚证券和投资委员会	Australian Securities and Investment Commission	ASIC
英国金融服务管理局	Financial Services Authority	FSA
期货经纪商	Futures Commission Merchant	FCM
美国证券交易监督委员会	Securities and Exchange Commission	SEC
国家证券经纪商协会	National Association of Securities Dealers	NASD
芝加哥期权交易所	Chicago Board Options Exchange	CBOE
美国国际证券交易所	International Securities Exchange	ISE
纽约商业期货交易所	New York Mercantile Exchange	NYMEX
纽约商品交易所有限公司	Commodity Exchange Inc.	COMEX
石油输出国组织	Organization of the Petroleum Exporting Countries	OPEC
伦敦洲际交易所	Intercontinental Exchange	ICE
芝加哥商业交易所	Chicago Mercantile Exchange	CME

References

1. 郝绍伦. 金融英语导航. 合肥：中国科学技术大学出版社, 2002
2. 赵明. 现代商业银行实用英语. 成都：西南财经大学出版社, 2000
3. 郝绍伦. 金融英语. 合肥：中国科学技术大学出版社, 2006
4. 李景, 刘江, 杨存真. 银行服务英语 100 句. 北京：北京语言大学出版社, 2004
5. 宋建亭. 敢说商贸金融英语. 北京：机械工业出版社, 2006
6. 钟乐平, 韩江红. 敢说银行服务英语. 北京：机械工业出版社, 2006
7. 陈庆柏, 王景仙. 金融英语信函与对话. 北京：世界图书出版公司北京公司, 2001
8. 黄玉真. 银行实用英语. 北京：外文出版社, 2002
9. 英语服务中心, 沈瑞年. 银行商务英语. 北京：世界图书出版公司北京公司, 1997
10. 陈建辉, 关兴华, 杜艳萍. 实用金融英语听与说. 武昌：武汉大学出版社, 2006
11. 沈素萍, 张红. 金融专业英语函电写作. 北京：对外经济贸易大学出版社, 2006
12. 李丽, 马跃. 金融英语. 北京：对外经济贸易大学出版社, 2007
13. 闫屹, 王艳坚. 金融英语. 南京：东南大学出版社, 2005
14. 王正元, 钟玲. 金融保险行话连篇. 大连：大连理工大学出版社, 2002
15. 高波, 杜晓进. 银行服务实用英语口语. 北京：中国金融出版社, 1999
16. 赵世刚. 银行英语. 北京：北京大学出版社, 2007